IN A TIME
OF WAR

JAMES DURNEY

IN A TIME
OF WAR

KILDARE 1914-1918

MERRION

First published in 2014 by Merrion
an imprint of Irish Academic Press
8 Chapel Lane
Sallins
Co. Kildare

British Library Cataloguing in Publication Data
An entry can be found on request

978-1-908928-85-6 (paper)
978-1-908928-86-3 (cloth)
978-1-908928-87-0 (PDF)

Library of Congress Cataloging in Publication Data
An entry can be found on request

Designed and typeset by www.sinedesign.net

Printed in Ireland by SPRINT-print Ltd

Dedicated to my great-grandfather,
James Durney,
and his two brothers,
Patrick and Matthew Durney, veterans of WWI

'I am tired and sick of war. Its glory is all moonshine. It is only those who have neither fired a shot not heard the shrieks and groans of the wounded who cry aloud for blood, for vengeance, for desolation. War is hell.'

–Gen. William Tecumseh Sherman, 1879

Contents

Acknowledgements

In writing this book – and compiling information over many years – I have been helped by dozens of people who just wanted to tell the forgotten, or unknown, story of their relatives' part in WWI. I would like to thank the many who provided information, support, photographs, etc., for this book and so made it a much better production: Mario Corrigan, Kildare Collections and Research Services, Newbridge Library, Newbridge, Co. Kildare; Karel Kiely, Genealogy Department, Newbridge Library, Newbridge, Co. Kildare; Peter Connell; Clem Roche; Ger McCarthy; Liam Kenny; Timmy Conway; Mick Mulvey; Noel Delaney; Frank O'Brien; Mary Rose Everan; Deirdre Twomey; Tom Reddy; John Garry; Aidan Byrne; Paddy Newman; Veronica Heavey; Andrew Brown; Liam Kenny; Fearghal McClellan; Julie O' Donoghue; Chris Holzgräwe; Kathleen Brophy; Sean Sourke; Ciaran Hickey; Co. Kildare Archaeological Society for permission to use photographs and contributions to the book. I would also like to thank Conor Graham, Lisa Hyde, and the team at Irish Academic Press. Also my son, Brian, who designed the maps for the book. Last, but not least, I would like to thank my wife, Caroline, for her patience and support.

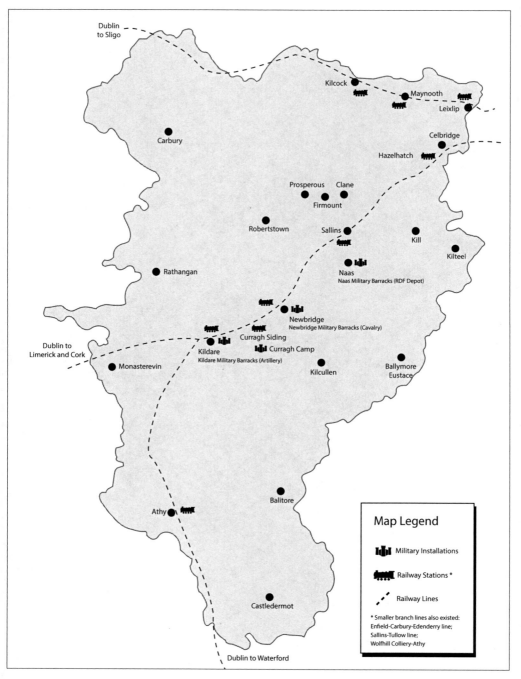

Co. Kildare, c.1914

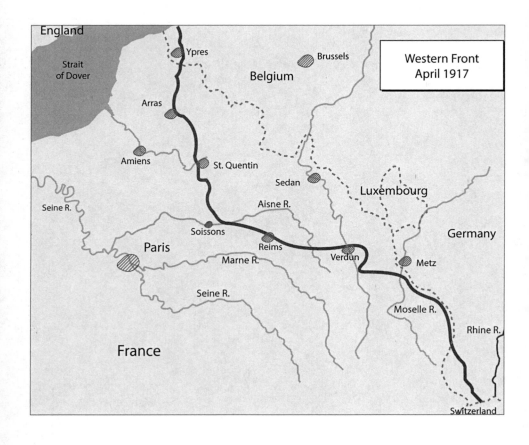

INTRODUCTION

The Reading Room, Sandes Soldiers' Home, Curragh Camp, July 1916.
Photo: Kildare Collections and Research Services.

WHEN IN AUGUST 1914 the German Kaiser demanded freedom of movement through Belgium for his army to invade France, King Albert flatly refused. Britain, Belgium's guarantor and France's ally, rushed to the defensive. The French thought they could count on British help, while the Germans were sure Britain would remain neutral. British policy was so muddled that it could be interpreted more or less according to taste. The British Empire feared a united Europe under a strong leader – Germany – so it went to war under a pretext of saving 'little Belgium', but in reality to stop a military defeat of France. Britain's intervention turned a continental conflict into a world war.

The war which ensued was widely expected to last for three or four months. Like many wars, before and since, it was going to be over by Christmas. Conventional wisdom assumed that modern warfare would be more intense than in the past, but more decisive. Whichever side could gain the upper hand in the early stages would have the means for swift victory. In the end, the fighting lasted not for four months but for more than four years. The Great War, or World War I, was the bloodiest, most widespread conflict the world had known up to that time; resulting in over thirty million casualties, it left much of Europe in ruin, and revolutionised modern warfare.

In 1914 Home Rule for Ireland looked like a certainty, but the outbreak of war in Europe delayed this and, instead of it being put on the statute books unconditionally, the implementation of home rule was used as a playing card by British officials to encourage, at first, Irish recruitment, and then conscription. On a military level the Irish Volunteers were committed to supporting the implementation of home rule, while the Ulster Volunteer Force were formed to resist it. However, both paramilitary forces were ideal recruiting pools for the British army and many members eagerly joined the fight 'for the freedom of small nations'. Nationalists thought if Ireland demonstrated its loyalty in Britain's hour of need then they would be rewarded with self-government, while unionists expected a 'special relationship' if they showed their loyalty. The British government were happy playing each side to get what they wanted – Ireland's manpower.

County Kildare, due to the presence of the Curragh Camp and multiple barracks at Naas, Newbridge and Kildare, and the confirmed loyalty of the local gentry and professional class, was always a good recruiting ground for the British army. Between 1914 and 1918 Kildare contributed well above the average quota of recruits. Nevertheless, while the majority of people supported the war effort, there was a reactionary element which would have no time for it. By the time the war ended a new political party had swept the polls and a military campaign for Irish independence was fermenting. When the soldiers returned it was to a changed environment and a widely-held belief that they had fought in the wrong war. What happened in County Kildare, and Ireland, between August 1914 and December 1918? What created the initial enthusiasm for the war and what caused its decline? How did the populace progress from being loyal subjects of the crown to become rebels?

1 PLAN OF WAR

Tented camp for the Essex Regiment, Curragh Camp. Photo: Kildare Collections and Research Services.

THE OUTBREAK OF the Great War has been justly described as the most complex series of happenings in recent history. When a Serbian nationalist shot dead the Austrian Archduke Franz Ferdinand in Sarajevo on 28 June 1914 it set in motion a chain of events that resulted in a calamitous war. At the time all the great powers of Europe were engaged in an interlocking pattern of alliances: Austria-Hungary with Germany; Serbia with Russia and Britain and France with Belgium. On 23 July Austria-Hungary sent Serbia an ultimatum, pressing demands for the suppression of nationalist groups in Serbia, which threatened to incite rebellion within Austria-Hungary. Serbia acceded to some demands, but rejected others and began mobilising its army. Subsequently, Austria-Hungary broke off relations with Serbia and mobilised its own forces. Russia, Serbia's ally, unsuccessfully attempted to persuade Austria-Hungary to modify the terms of its ultimatum and thereby avoid war. The German Kaiser, William II, promised Austria-Hungary Germany's support in any actions taken against Serbia. Meanwhile, Russia made initial preparations to mobilise its forces in

1

the event of a war. Britain attempted to set up a negotiated settlement, but the plan was rejected by Germany.

On 28 July Austria-Hungary declared war on Serbia. In response Russia ordered a partial mobilisation against Austria-Hungary. Germany, promising modification of the ultimatum to Serbia, warned Russia against continuing mobilisation. The Russian tsar, Nicholas II, hesitated, then ordered full mobilisation. On 1 August Germany declared war on Russia. France had already committed support to Russia and began mobilising its forces. The following day, when German troops marched into Luxembourg to begin the implementation of the Schlieffen Plan, France declared a state of emergency. The Schlieffen Plan, drawn up by the chief of staff, Alfred Graf von Schlieffen, in 1905, called for a quick elimination of France from the war to allow concentration of German forces against Russia before it could fully mobilise. The plan required for France to be attacked from the north (through the Low Countries) and by a second (left) flank farther south aiming to encircle Paris and attack the French army in the rear. Under a false pretext that French aeroplanes had bombed Nuremberg, Germany declared war on France. The Kaiser demanded that the Belgian government permit the free passage of his army across Belgium into northern France. When Belgium refused the right of transit and said it would resist, the German army invaded Belgium.[1]

Germany assumed that Britain would remain neutral, but to its dismay Britain, guarantor of Belgian neutrality under an 1839 European treaty, demanded the withdrawal of German troops from Belgian soil by midnight on 4 August, and ordered a mobilisation of its troops on Sunday, 2 August.[2] All over Britain and Ireland military establishments received orders to mobilise. General mobilisation followed, with a takeover of the railways for military transport. At this time many of the battalions of the regular British army were on training exercises, while others were in barracks, but all responded with quiet elation when orders were received. For many it was the culmination of a lifetime's preparation. The mobilisation of the British army worked smoothly. Test mobilisations on divisional level over the years prior to 1914 had proved how efficient the arrangements could be. Regular Army reservists, alerted by telegram and public notice, reported to their regimental depots, and within twenty-four hours were kitted and despatched in drafts to the Home Service battalions. The military establishment in Ireland was immediately directed towards preparation for combat.[3] The following notice appeared in all Irish national and provincial newspapers:

> Ex-soldiers of the regular army of special reserve, from 19–42 years of age, can enlist for one year or during the war. Other men 19–30 years of age, can enlist for three years or period of the war.[4]

In a lecture on the war delivered in Naas Town Hall Col. de Burgh, D.L. said Britain was fighting this war to prevent 'one man and one nation from tossing the world and depriving small nations of their independence'. Yet Britain had denied Ireland freedom for several hundred years, so it seemed hypocritical that she should risk a major confrontation over Belgium's sovereignty. There was arguably another important reason why Britain went to war in Europe. Throughout the days of 31 July–3 August one thing above all maintained Cabinet unity – the fear of letting in the Conservative and Unionist opposition. Prime Minister Herbert Asquith depended on the votes of the Irish Parliamentary Party to sustain his Liberal Party in Government. Two previous attempts to bring in Home Rule in the 1880s and 1890s had failed to get through parliament, but Asquith, under political pressure to pass a Home Rule Bill, saw an opportunity to settle the Irish question once and for all. The Liberals' decision to try to enact Home Rule inflamed Unionist sentiment, with Protestants arming themselves to prevent its imposition. The possibility of civil war was real and leading Tories and senior army officers were not unsympathetic to the Protestant cause. The sudden onset of the European diplomatic crisis served, as Asquith remarked, to pour oil on the stormy Irish waters.[5] In the House of Commons, on 3 August, John Redmond, M.P., declared:

> ...Today there are in Ireland two large bodies of Volunteers, one of which has sprung into existence in the North and another in

the South.

I say to the Government that they may to-morrow withdraw every one of their troops from Ireland. Ireland will be defended by her armed sons from foreign invasion, and for that purpose the armed Catholics in the South will be only too glad to join arms with the armed Protestant Ulstermen.

Is it too much to hope that out of this situation a result may spring which will be good, not merely for the Empire, but for the future welfare and integrity of the Irish nation? Whilst Irishmen are in favour of peace, and would desire to save democracy of this country from all the horrors of war, whilst we will make any possible sacrifice for that purpose, still if the necessity is forced upon this country we offer this to the Government of the day.

They may take their troops away, and if it is allowed to us, in comradeship with our brothers in the North, we will ourselves defend the coasts of Ireland.[6]

Redmond's conciliatory gesture was met with deafening applause, but with this speech 'he forfeited his status as the standard bearer of Irish nationalism' and sounded the death knell of his political career.[7] Militant nationalists were momentarily thrown off balance, while the press, both nationalist and unionist alike, were fulsome in their praise of Redmond's speech. The *Kildare Observer* editorial, of 8 August 1914, followed Redmond's lead:

No Irishman – no man of Irish blood in any part of the world – will read Mr John Redmond's speech in the House of Commons on Monday without a thrill of pride. The speech embodies a very hopeful and splendid fact. Following Sir Edward Carson's recent statement to a correspondent that Ireland confronted with the danger of foreign aggression, has achieved, with the object of repelling that aggression, the national unity for which so many of her statesmen and poets have sighed in vain. 'Take away your troops,' [s]aid Redmond to the Government, 'and in comradeship with our brethren in the North, we will ourselves defend the coast of Ireland.' In this competition of patriotism, in this great political amnesty, no Irish Unionist will lag behind any Irish Nationalist. If England is so hard pressed that her forces in Ireland are needed elsewhere, she may withdraw them with an easy mind. As Saxe said at Fontenoy, 'the Irish still remain'. We have two national armies, numbering 200,000 men. Most of these are armed; many of them are highly drilled and disciplined; they all belong to one of the finest fighting races in the world. With these two armies, acting in unison, and inspired by a common love of country, we shall see Ireland through the troubles of this terrible crisis, and shall protect her shores. Who could do the work better? Who has a better right to do it?

At a meeting of Athy Urban District Council (UDC) on 6 August 1914, Mr Michael Malone proposed, seconded by Mr James Deegan and supported by Messrs Joseph Whelan and Thomas Plewman:

That this Council heartily approved of Mr Redmond's policy in offering to protect this country with the Irish National Volunteers in Irish comradeship with the Ulster Volunteers during the present war and we earnestly hope his statesmanlike action may have the effect of healing the wound which so long was open between England and Ireland and of uniting all sections of the Irish people for the common good of our fatherland.[8]

Educated at Clongowes Wood College, near Clane, Co. Kildare, John Redmond was the leader of the Irish Parliamentary Party. He believed that Irish loyalty to England during its difficulty in Europe would be noted and rewarded. However, in time only 'Ulster's' loyalty was remembered and Southern Ireland's conveniently forgotten.

Many of the more professional men of the Irish Volunteers were former soldiers of the British army, most of them still liable as reservists for military service. With the declaration of war the Volunteer reservists, over 7,000 men, were called back to the colours. The Irish Volunteers when first formed in November 1913 had been quite independent of the Irish Party and John Redmond had only secured control of the movement in June 1914.[9]

On 4 August, the day after Redmond's speech, Britain, protesting the German army's violation of Belgian neutrality, declared war on Germany.[10] Because of the political situation in Ireland the declaration of war was met with a short-lived sense of relief. War in Europe meant peace in Ireland. For several months previously the Ulster Volunteer Force (UVF) had been preparing to resist the implementation of Home Rule, while the Irish Volunteers (IV) had been formed 'to secure the rights and liberties common to all the people of Ireland'. Armed conflict seemed inevitable and the possibility of civil war was quite real.[11] British leaders expressed gratitude that war in Europe had reprieved the country from a bloody showdown in Ireland. Foreign Secretary Sir Edward Grey said in the House of Commons: 'One thing I would say: the one bright spot in the very dreadful situation is Ireland.' Sir William Birdwood, secretary to the government of India, wrote: 'What a real piece of luck this war has been as regards Ireland – just averted a civil war and when it is over we may be all tired of fighting.'[12]

Many people on the ground welcomed the declaration of war, too. The changed political mood was reflected in the local press. The *Kildare Observer* of 8 August 1914 reported that: 'The result of the English ultimatum to Germany was awaited by many at the Post Office in Naas on Tuesday midnight.'

Only a week before Naas had witnessed a large demonstration of protest against the shooting dead of three people and the wounding of eighty-five more in Dublin by the British army on 26 July. A consignment of rifles and ammunition had been landed at Howth harbour for the Irish Volunteers. A small force of police and soldiers, from the King's Own Scottish Borderers, intercepted the Irish Volunteers as they marched back with their ordnance to Dublin. After a brief and violent confrontation the police and troops withdrew. Crowds of civilians jeered and physically attacked the Scottish troops at several points, but at Batchelor's Walk they turned on their tormentors and opened fire. Among the three fatalities was Mary Duffy, a widow who had a son in the Royal Dublin Fusiliers. On the following Wednesday hundreds of Irish Volunteers, including a 100-strong cycle detachment from Kilcullen, marched to the scene of the Naas meeting and drew up in military order around the platform erected in the Square. Rev. M. Norris, the parish priest (P.P.) of Naas, chaired the meeting. Speeches made by Fr Norris, Fr Hipwell and local councillors, D. J. Purcell, M. Fitzsimmons and J. E. Butterfield, condemned the heavy handed approach to the arming of the Irish Volunteers compared to the blind eye turned to the activities and arming of the UVF in the north of the country. (The day before the Batchelor's Walk incident 5,000 Ulster Volunteers had marched through Belfast fully armed and with four machine guns.) The demonstration at Naas ended with a demand for the return of 'ten rifles seized illegally by the military'. Fr Hipwell said they would not be thwarted or impeded by any section of their countrymen in their demand for Home Rule. At the Curragh Camp the proposed arrival of the King's Own Scottish Borderers was not welcomed by the other troops, whose relationships with the local population was good. There were many Irish troops on the Curragh, too, and the subsequent diversion of the Scots elsewhere was welcomed by everyone.[13]

On receiving the mobilisation order military stations in Co. Kildare became a hive of activity. The ordnance, cavalry and infantry staff at the Curragh Camp were busily engaged on Sunday and Monday (2 and 3 August) working from early Monday morning to late at night. The necessary stores, which were attached to each and every unit, were augmented to make up the requisite stock. Armourers shops were busy preparing arms, while the cavalry were engaged, among other things, in sharpening their swords. Some 2,000 men, including the 27th Brigade Royal Field Artillery (RFA) and the 2nd and 3rd Batteries Royal Horse Artillery (RHA) from Newbridge were reviewed by Maj. Gen. Sir Charles Ferguson. General G. H. Gough left the Curragh for Aldershot where he was to assume command of a cavalry corps. From an early hour on Monday morning wagon loads of arms and ammunition were conveyed from the Curragh magazine to Newbridge railway station and forwarded to supplement the stores of the Dublin garrisons. However, because of John Redmond's pledge to assist the government security, on arms convoys was at a low level, thus enabling troops in barracks to continue preparing for a move to Europe. The military authorities took over Sheridan's Concert Hall in Newbridge and the Stand House in the Curragh for the purpose of occupying them with troops during the mobilisation.[14]

The *Leinster Leader* reported that there were 'remarkable scenes in Naas'. The most regular destination for Co. Kildare reservists were the two battalions of the Royal Dublin Fusiliers. About 280 men of the Special Reserve who had been called up for service arrived at the Depot of the Royal Dublin Fusiliers, at Naas Military Barracks. Special arrangements were made to have them conveyed to Dublin by train en route to Gravesend, England, where the regiment was stationed. When the hour of departure came the gate of the barracks was surrounded by a large crowd of relatives and friends. The band of the local unit of the Irish Volunteers arrived with their banner, which was inscribed 'Nás na Riogh' (The meeting place of the Kings) and 'Nás Abu'. The gates were opened and the Volunteer band passed in as the guard stood to attention. The men of the Dublin Fusiliers were already drawn up on the barrack square with the Pipers Band of the regiment and with the Volunteer band at its head they marched out. Passing through the gates and the surrounding crowd the Volunteer Band played a lively quickstep, followed by nationalist airs like 'A nation once again', 'Who fears to speak of '98', and 'The wearing of the green'. Large crowds thronged the sidewalks as the column marched down the Main Street to the railway station.[15] The platform and bridges of the station were densely crowded with spectators. The *Kildare Observer* said

> ... as the train steamed out, amid the strains of 'Auld Lang Syne,' played by the Volunteer Band and the explosion of fog signals, there was a remarkable demonstration on the part of the spectators who cheered the men vociferously, hats, handkerchiefs and umbrellas being wildly waved. The cheers, needless to say, were heartily returned by the departing soldiers,

who, in a few minutes were beyond earshot, and on their way to their destination.[16]

In Athy the Post Office was open all night on Tuesday for the transmission of messages from the army authorities to the men of the reserve in the district. Affecting scenes were also witnessed at Athy railway station on 5 August when the first batch of the reserve departed by the mid-day train. Their families and friends accompanied the reservists to the station. Sir Anthony Weldon, of Kilmoroney and John Duncan, a local shopkeeper and a member of Athy UDC, were at the station to see off the men. The reservists went to various destinations to join their respective regiments. In addition to the reserve, Athy also sent men to join the South Irish Horse at Limerick, the officer's cadet corps attached to the universities and the medical and veterinary branches of the army.[17]

For two days in Kildare Town the Royal Field Artillery were unloading arms and taking them to the barracks of the 46th and 47th regiments in the town. The men in the barracks were said to be 'ready for the front at any moment', and soldiers on leave were called back to their barracks. Members of the Royal Irish Constabulary (RIC) were on duty at the bridges over the river Liffey and on railway bridges near Newbridge and the Curragh. Military Intelligence had taken over control of Kildare railway station, where thousands of reservists and recruits were arriving daily, and from which fully equipped units were departing.[18] Troops leaving the Curragh were addressed by Fr Murphy and told that this was 'not a war of aggression, nor which there was any lust for conquest or oppression or aggrandisement. It was a strife of national existence, and had been forced on them'. Putting it simply, Britain had gone to war for a just cause.[19]

The economic impact of the war was felt immediately. As in Britain, banks were closed until 7 August and food prices rose within days. Although there was no valid reason for raising food prices the *Kildare Observer* reported that some shopkeepers in Athy demanded increased prices for many articles. The *Observer* called for an explanation for the increase saying that if this happened in Europe the shopkeepers would quickly find themselves in trouble with the authorities.

> So far there seems no necessity for the extraordinary rise that has taken place, as plenty of food stuffs are available, and the harvest, which promises to be a bountiful one, will be coming in at an early date. No famine need be feared, and any attempt to create panics or runs on banks should be strongly opposed.

Retailers blamed the wholesalers, who in turn blamed the creameries, the farmers and cross-channel suppliers. The latter had suspended credit facilities and demanded cash with every order. The prices of most of the necessities of life were also raised in Naas on 5 August and to a considerable extent, especially sugar, which made 4½ d. per lb. Flour was up 2s. 6d. per cwt. The best grade coal was quoted at 30s. and 32s. 6d. per ton.[20]

Once mobilisation orders were dispatched most horse owners in Co. Kildare received government notices of the War Office's intentions to commandeer animals. The Army Remount Department was very busy around the county. The Headquarters Depot for Irish remounts was established at the offices of the Stand House as hundreds of horses arrived daily from the region for cavalry, artillery and transport units. Private owners also had their horses requisitioned. The Kildare Hunt stables at Jigginstown was visited by military officers and all the horses taken for service, together with mounts from locals, including Mr Young and Mr Thomas Berney, a saddler specialising in military saddles. Even the Jarveys' horses, and other steeds met on the street, were held for examination. Numerous horses were purchased around the county for good prices and practically all the hunters and many farmers' heavy horses were also called in. Horses were ruthlessly commandeered, though on a generous scale of compensation – £40 for a troop horse and £60 for an officer's charger, which enabled some owners to recycle indifferent hunters. One man boasted that a broken-down animal had fetched him £45.[21]

Frederick V. Devere, Secretary of the North Kildare Farming Society, received a letter from the Remount Department on 18 December 1914, asking farmers in the county to take in mares in foal. The mares could do light work, for which no charge would be issued, as it assisted the state, and also benefited the county and the local farmers. It was stressed that no farmer could have more than two mares. The farmer would look after the mare and send the foal to the Remount Department when it was born.[22]

As a result of the urgent need for recruits Parliament consented to an increase of half a million men for the regular army on 6 August 1914. On 11 August a general proclamation called for another 100,000 men to volunteer for three years, or the duration of the war. This new force, or K1 (Kitchener's First) as it was known, became First New Army. Later, on 13 September, a further 100,000 were called for. This was K2, which formed Second New Army.

Within a few weeks of the outbreak of war no less than three Irish divisions – the 10th (Irish), 16th (Irish) and 36th (Ulster) – were formed from Irishmen who responded to Lord Kitchener's call to arms.[23] As Secretary of State for War, he was responsible for all aspects of military organisation in Ireland. Kitchener began to totally reorganise the British army, raising 1,700,000 men in service battalions by May 1915, creating an army of volunteers to reinforce the depleted regular army in Belgium and France.[24]

Born in Co. Kerry in 1850, Horatio Herbert Kitchener was Britain's foremost soldier. An arch-conservative Kitchener epitomised the anti-Irish bias of the British military establishment. He facilitated the reorganisation of the UVF as the 36th (Ulster) Division, but blocked plans by John Redmond for the formation of a southern Irish division from members of the National Volunteers. Kitchener seemed to have no plans to set up the Volunteers as a defence force and considered drafting the Territorial Army into Ireland. He was totally opposed to home rule for Ireland and did not like or trust his fellow countrymen and initially proposed dispersing Irish recruits through the numerous regiments in the army.[25] Kitchener snubbed the Irish war effort many times; he even returned proposed colours for a suggested Irish brigade produced by Lady Mayo's Royal Irish School of Art Needlework.[26]

Nevertheless, many believed that England would still show kindness for Irish loyalty. At a meeting of Kildare County Council on 17 August 1914, the following resolution was proposed by Mr Charles Bergin and seconded by Mr Patrick Phelan. It resolved:

> That in view of the present grave crisis, whereby our country is threatened with calamity, we, the Kildare Co. Council, endorse the action of Mr John Redmond, pledging the support of the National Volunteers to defend our shores against invasion, and hereby undertake in the event of our office staff taking up arms to keep their respective offices open until their return, and our secretary is hereby directed to make the necessary arrangements for the purpose of carrying out this resolution into effect.[27]

With these loyal sentiments echoing from the chambers of the local council Kildaremen once again took up arms to defend Britain. Those of the Ascendancy class not already in the army or navy lost no time in joining up, while the labouring classes flocked to the two great centres for recruitment in Co. Kildare – the towns of Naas and Athy.

During the war more than 2,000 men from Athy and district joined the British army. Many were former soldiers, while others joined to escape the poverty of Irish life, or were caught up in the excitement of the time. Athy had a long tradition of service in the British army and the life of the town and its people was, by history, and latterly by economic necessity, closely linked to service in the Crown forces. Both the Leinster Regiment, based in Birr, Co. Offaly, and the Dublin Fusiliers, based in Naas, drew many recruits from the South Kildare area. In the first week of August 1914 a full-time recruitment office was opened in Leinster Street, Athy. Initially recruiting was very heavy and while it eased off considerably in 1915, the *Leinster Leader* of 3 June 1915 reported that: 'the last official figures obtainable about recruiting in Athy showed that 1,600 men from it and its environs had joined the colours.' Athy responded better than any other town outside of Ulster to Britain's call. A nun from the local Convent of Mercy had noted that: 'All the men of our town who belonged to the militia or reserved forces were summoned to the Front.

Every other day they came to the convent to beg for Sacred Heart scapulars, Agnus Deis, etc., to take away with them. Few of these poor fellows ever saw their homes again.'

Naas had various British regiments stationed in the town barracks through the years. Many local men joined these regiments and served in various parts of the world prior to 1914. The regular unit stationed in Naas (the barracks was completed in 1813) was the 3rd Battalion of the Royal Dublin Fusiliers. Prior to, and especially during 1914–18, this regiment enlisted many men from Naas and the surrounding area. Most of those who enlisted came from the poorest streets of the town at the time such as Loch Búi, Back Lane and the Rathasker Road cottages. It was not unusual, and was even encouraged, for all of the men in a household – perhaps a father and son, or three or four brothers – to join up. A major reason for enlistment was the high level of unemployment among the labouring class, who provided a traditional source of recruitment for the British army.[28]

On 18 September 1914 the royal assent was given to the Third Home Rule Bill, but with two provisions: (i) that the bill should not come into operation until the end of the war, (ii) that it would not come into operation until parliament had time to make special amending legislation for Ulster. At Woodenbridge, in his own constituency of Co. Wicklow, John Redmond made another serious error of judgement by calling on the Irish Volunteers to offer their services 'not only in Ireland itself, but wherever the firing line extends in defence of right, of freedom and religion in this war'.[29]

This speech at Woodenbridge went much further than Redmond's 3 August House of Commons intrusion, when he committed the Irish Volunteers to home defence only. With no preliminary debate or consultation with his supporters Redmond committed nationalist Ireland to support the war. Almost immediately, the Volunteer movement split. On 25 September, a statement signed by Eoin MacNeill and nineteen others of the twenty-seven members of the original provisional committee of the Volunteers declared Redmond's twenty-five nominees expelled from the committee, declaring that Redmond had no right to offer the services of the Volunteers to a foreign government.[30]

Decisive meetings of Volunteers companies took place all over Ireland, the overwhelming majority passed resolutions supporting Redmond's stance and repudiated that of MacNeill and the Provisional Committee. Redmond's prestige was such that he brought the vast majority of the Volunteers with him. At a meeting of the Naas Volunteer Committee it was resolved:

> That we, the members of Naas Volunteer Corps, at this juncture in the affairs of the movement, desire to place on record our unswerving loyalty to the policy enunciated by Mr John Redmond, and pledge our support in any action he may take in the interests of Ireland for the future organisation of the movement.

A following Co. Committee of the Kildare National Volunteers, held in the Town Hall, Naas, reported that Ballymore-Eustace Volunteers had decided to follow the leadership of Redmond; Maynooth decided to follow Redmond by forty-two votes to fourteen; Celbridge had split, but a majority were for Redmond. Athy, Castledermot, Allen, Carbury, Ballysax, Newbridge, Kilcullen and Monasterevan representatives had also declared for Redmond. The following resolutions were passed by the Co. Kildare Volunteer Corps:

1. That we congratulate Mr Redmond on his success in having the Home Rule Bill placed on the statute Book;

2. That we condemn the action of the original Provisional Committee in expelling Mr Redmond's nominees from their committee without first seeking the sanction of the Irish Volunteer Corps throughout Ireland.[31]

By late October it was estimated that a total of 158,360 volunteers (henceforth to be called the National Volunteers) supported Redmond as against 12,306 of the more extreme and active members who broke away to form their own force, retaining the name of Irish Volunteers.[32] Although this number was small, the split would have serious consequence. A revolutionary conspiracy began to take shape for which the whole concept of Home Rule was irrelevant.[33] In Co. Kildare, as in the rest of Ireland, a substantial majority remained with Redmond and the National Volunteers. They would provide a considerable recruitment pool for the British army.

2 A GARRISON COUNTY

Cavalry Barracks, Curragh Camp, c. 1910. Photo: Kildare Collections and Research Services.

THERE HAD BEEN a foreign military presence in Kildare since the arrival of the Normans in 1170. The Norman lord, William Marshall, built the first stone castle in the town of Kildare and this was followed by more permanent military fortifications throughout the county over the following centuries.[1] British troops were billeted in many of the urban centres during periods of unrest and some barracks were built in towns like Naas and Athy. However, it was the outbreak of the 1798 Rebellion which led to the building of more permanent structures. The rebellion, instigated by the United Irishmen, began just after dawn on 24 May. Fighting quickly spread throughout Leinster, with the heaviest combat taking place in County Kildare where, despite crown forces successfully beating off almost every rebel attack, the insurgents gained control of much of the county. Military forces in Kildare were ordered to withdraw to Naas for fear of their isolation and destruction as had happened at the barrack in the village of Prosperous. One of the causes of the outbreak in Co. Kildare was the policy of 'free quarters' whereby troops were forcibly billeted upon the populace in an effort to quiet the country and recover arms. The rebellion lasted three months, but ended in defeat for the United Irishmen. Unrest continued until early 1804, with another failed rebellion a year earlier by Robert Emmett, which again involved many Kildare insurgents.[2]

After nearly two decades of unrest it was clear Britain's means of control needed to remain tangibly visible. The solution was to build permanent military barracks throughout the country. There were over 60,000 British troops in Ireland and the commander of the forces expressed his views on the necessity for the maintenance of a large force in the country with a view to its defence, general discipline and comfort of the army. He maintained permanent barracks should be erected as the temporary quarters troops found themselves in were not good for the health and the well-being of the men. The Duke of Wellington described the attitude of the landowners to the building of barracks:

> At all times the Irish gentlemen have been anxious to have barracks for troops established, each in his own neighbourhood, and they would sell land for the accommodation of government for that object. The establishment of a barrack affords a prospect of security, requires the outlay of a large sum of money immediately, and if occupied by troops, the outlay in the neighbourhood of their subsistence, maintenance, etc.[3]

It was, of course, true. Landowners welcomed the proposals to build barracks in their midst as it offered a prospect of selling land and, if occupied by troops, the prospect of further money generated by the military inhabitants.

In 1801 a barracks was commenced in Cork city. Six years later General the Earl of Harrington, Commander of the Forces in Ireland, proposed that new barracks be built countrywide and as many of the temporary barracks vacated. Over the following two decades the programme of building continued. The first new barracks to be built in County Kildare was that at Naas, which replaced an old base on the South Moat. The construction of the infantry barracks, on the Limerick road, commenced in August 1810. It was built to accommodate eighteen officers and 300 men, or double that number in time of war. The regular troops stationed in the barracks were generally popular in the town, but militia units were not always liked locally. While Naas became an important military centre, the town was also the main urban focal point in the county and did not become as dependent on the army as other centres. Trade in the town no doubt benefited from the military presence, but in return the townspeople had to tolerate the rough habits of some of the troops stationed there. In 1873 the barracks became the depot of the Royal Dublin Fusiliers and drew recruits from the sub-district of Dublin, Kildare, Carlow and Wicklow, beginning nearly forty years of association between the Dublin Fusiliers and Naas.[4] During the First World War the Barracks was a great centre for recruitment and by June 1917 a total of 26,611 men had joined up in Naas, including over 250 men from the town. During the war the Dublin Fusiliers Regiment increased to eleven battalions. However, most of them could not be handled at Naas and nine battalions trained in Dublin, the Curragh and other locations.[5]

Recruits were accommodated in the barracks until they were uniformed and were then sent to the Curragh for training. Men came from as far away as England and Scotland to join the renowned Dublin Fusiliers. A Frenchman from Paris even arrived at the barracks and said he was attracted by the 'fame of the Dublins' and wished to join them. A reporter from the *Leinster Leader* visited Naas barracks and recorded what he saw:

> Groups of these poor fellows, most of them presenting a fine manly and respectable appearance, could be seen on any day during the week walking aimlessly up and down the Main Street of Naas and out along the country roads … Squatting about in all directions, the future defenders of the British Empire, waiting to go through the ordeal of fitting khaki uniforms. The congestion is so great that many things appertaining to the comfort of the recruits have to remain unattended to but the poor fellows grin and bear it. You would pity one poor Irish lad as he lay stretched out on the grass humming to himself a few

lines of Kickham's ballad, The Irish Youth: 'Dear countryman, take heed of what I say. If you ever join the British ranks, you'll surely rue the day.'[6]

Naas UDC offered the use of the Town Hall to the military as recruits continued to arrive in the town and men of the Royal Dublin Fusiliers arrived back from the Front. To ease the overcrowding in the barracks it was intended to set up an auxiliary training camp for recruits in a field opposite the barracks, and huts were to be erected to accommodate 500 men. Up to 700 would be accommodated in the barracks itself. Rumours of bad conditions persisted. Apart from the barracks being overcrowded, with adequate sleeping accommodation impossible to fulfil, it was believed by the *Leader* journalist that a health inspection should be made of the base. The rations were so inadequate that a house-to-house collection was made in Naas town on behalf of the men during the first week of September. The number of recruits sent from Dublin and other centres to the Naas Depot caused the shortfall in food. Recruits were provided with vouchers to enable them to obtain food on their arrival, but as the barrack authorities did not know how many would arrive it was not easy to provide food for an indefinite number of men. The serving of notices to quit married quarters on the wives and families of men at the Front caused further concern. Another rumour circulating in the town was that the old jail – abandoned since 1890 – had been cleaned out and was to be taken over by the military, either for recruits or to contain German prisoners.

In an attempt to alleviate one of the problems in the barracks a request was made to Naas Workhouse that cases of infectious diseases should be taken into the union hospital, as the fever hospital in the Curragh had been converted for the use of the wounded. It was decided that fifteen men should be received at Naas, with room for five or six smallpox cases. The average cost of maintenance of three patients per day was £1. Out of 800 reservists examined at Naas depot for field service with the Royal Dublin Fusiliers only one was found to be permanently unfit.[7]

The second new barracks to be built in the county was the large cavalry barracks at Newbridge, on a site of thirty-nine Irish acres, purchased from local landlords: Eyre Powell, who owned the entire townland of Greatconnell; the Hon. Ponsonby Moore, of Moorefield; and the Hannon family, of Kilbelin. Contracts were signed in 1812 and work on the barracks began in 1813 and its construction took several years. The resulting demand for labour brought many workers to the area, inflating the population. Eyre Powell also owned the land opposite the barrack site and, realising the enormous potential for trade with the coming of the military, divided the land into plots and built a row of houses, which became shops with living accommodation. This was the foundation of the town and Newbridge grew rapidly. Accommodation in the barracks was provided for a cavalry force of fifty-eight officers, 810 men and 980 horses, and for two infantry officers and 105 men. The availability of water, forage and provisions locally was the main reason why the site was chosen and the closeness of the Curragh for exercise purposes was also seen as an advantage.[8]

However, it was in March 1855 that the biggest phase of barrack construction began when work commenced on the Curragh for a permanent encampment to eventually accommodate 10,000 men. The *Leinster Express* of 5 May 1855 said:

> The camp at the Curragh has been devised as a means whereby our young soldiers may be trained up in all the varied duties of strict field services, and be made somewhat accustomed to the labours which the soldier is called on to perform even whilst exposed to the deadly fire of the enemy, so that the troops will be found of real efficiency when, amidst the trenches or on the battlefield, they will be brought in contact with war in all its stern reality.

Hundreds of men were employed in removing furze bushes, clearing the ground and making mortar. Two firms employed 1,100 men to build huts, stables, quarters, offices and so on, while several contractors brought 70,000 gallons of water each day from the river Liffey. Others were busy supplying forage and provisions. One firm, Messrs Holmes, had 500 men employed at the camp, and 500 more at their factory in Liverpool, employed in preparing the materials for the houses in timber and iron works. The section of the contract taken by Messrs Holmes included the erection of the quarters for the officers, with messrooms and offices. The *Leinster Express* remarked on the amount of food needed for the 2,000 strong workforce, as well as their followers. Pubs in the area did a roaring trade. The building of the encampment required such a large work force that soon farmers in the county were complaining of a shortage of labourers.[9]

Within four months accommodation for 5,000 men was ready for occupation. Explaining the advantage of the new camp at the Curragh, assistant adjutant general of the Royal Engineers, Lt. Col. Henry Lugard, noted that it would provide a 'means of accommodating a large force of Infantry for the purpose of being trained and manoeuvred in conjunction with Cavalry and Artillery ... For such a purpose it is admirably suited, having the extensive Cavalry barracks of Newbridge contiguous and 5,000 acres of Curragh as a drill ground'.[10]

The Curragh Camp was to evolve into the largest military station in Ireland and continued to be an important training centre for the British army until 1922. It was one of the few examples of the complete permanent military town; entirely self-contained and designed to accommodate a military and civilian population of 10,000. When it was finished many civilians found employment in barrack workshops, canteens and general maintenance. The camp was also to provide economic benefit to the tradesmen, farmers, labourers and small holders, as well as the business and professional people of the district and the adjacent counties and was regarded as part and parcel of local society and economy.[11]

An artillery barracks was built in Kildare Town around 1901 with accommodation for 1,000 men. Kildare soon became a garrison county tied to the British military presence, economically through its trade, and loyally through the integration of the military with the civilian population. While Kildare was a reasonably prosperous county in times of economic hardship, and particularly around its urban centres, the county became a major recruiting area for the British army. Naas Military Barracks became the depot of the Royal Dublin Fusiliers; Newbridge, a cavalry barracks; Kildare, an artillery barracks; and the Curragh the headquarters of the British army in Ireland. Many of the soldiers stationed in the county had families with them and they provided a sizeable source of revenue in the mid-Kildare area. Such a large military presence had obvious beneficial effects on the economy of the county. Employment was provided for many local men as civilian labourers in the various military barracks. Horses were bred locally and sold to the army. Local contracts for the soldiers' foodstuffs and forage for the horses also made the fortune of many people in the area.[12]

Newbridge, in particular, benefited from the military presence. James and Frances Price, both natives of Leitrim, came to Newbridge from Dublin in 1895, and bought a large retail premises with living accommodation above and a stores yard. They had ten children. Bill, born in Newbridge in 1904, recalled:

> Newbridge was a grand busy little town when the British Army was here. One lived off the army; no matter what one had to sell the army bought it – from a horse to a chicken. One could poach a couple of salmon or shoot pheasant, anything, the army would buy it – hay, straw, logs. There was no fear in the town or never any violence, except an occasional brawl from over-drinking. But there was no sectarianism; they were part of society and they were welcome.[13]

British soldiers also felt at home in the barracks and towns of Co. Kildare. English soldier W. H. Scott, stationed in Newbridge with the 4th Queen's Own Hussars, had many happy recollections and pleasing incidents of his time there. From August 1916 to January 1917, Scott was the soldier violinist who played in the little orchestra at the Newbridge cinema, which was then situated over a large wood and saw-mill yard. He contacted the *Leinster Leader* fifty years later to say 'I still have in my possession a long poster advertisement printed at the offices of the *Kildare Observer*, Naas, dated the 1st October '16, with my name as violinist playing solos each Sunday evening at the Cinema.'

Scott was looking for information on some of the proceedings he played at.

> The happy event I wish to recall took place about September, October or November '16. It was a grand ball and dance the Cinema pianist and I were asked to play for after the cinema was over. The dancing commenced about 11.15 p.m. in a large upstairs room or hall decorated with flags and bunting to commemorate Easter '16. What an evening we all had, I, in particular, eating, drinking and playing for the dancing among my many friends. At early morning (5.30 a.m.) I had to leave the dancing and make for the Barracks. It is the exact date of the dance I wish to know if possible so I may celebrate the 50th anniversary of my happy sojourn in Newbridge. I am sure there must be many people still living in Newbridge who can remember and recall that delightful evening.[14]

Lt. Col. Charles O. Head was posted to a new artillery brigade forming in Newbridge in autumn 1914. When he arrived he found the barracks packed with 'men in civilian dress', new recruits for Kitchener's New Army. At Kildare a good store of uniforms was found and were issued to 'the unkempt, variegated crowd which had trudged from Newbridge to Kildare', making them, according to Lt. Col. Head, unrecognisable in their new attire. Near the end of September the brigade was moved to a tented camp on the Curragh, near Donnelly's Hollow. The weather was damp and miserable and many of the new recruits suffered severely from bronchial catarrh. The shortage of materials made training difficult and boring, but when some horses and guns were procured things picked up.[15]

In Newbridge the townspeople had grown accustomed to the bustle of preparation for overseas duty, as a brigade of the RHA and RFA had already departed for Europe. The good conduct of the troops was admired by the local reporter for the *Leinster Leader* who wrote:

> Passing along Newbridge at night you find a few thousand men
> quiet, orderly, but cheerful. There has not been the slightest
> necessity, in connection with the large body of men who are
> constantly about the town when the work of the day is over, for
> the interference of the constabulary or military police. There
> has not been a complaint of an individual soldier out of the
> thousands which have arrived or passed through for the past
> week to the Curragh Camp. In Newbridge barracks alone there
> are some 2,000 men, in addition to the necessarily reduced staff
> of the artillery.[16]

The siting of the artillery barracks in Kildare brought about the first increase
in the town's population since the Famine, but Kildare, like Naas, did not
develop great dependence on the military population either, due to its role
as a market town and commercial centre for the expanding horse industry in
the area.[17] The construction of the barracks provided a period of prosperity
because of the workers employed in the barracks building programme. The
population grew further with the stationing of over 800 men. A considerable
number of horses were also accommodated. This brought a boom for local
businesses, property owners and traders. Rented property was in short supply
and the military authorities built houses within the confines of the barracks
to accommodate military families, increasing the barrack population to 1,020
in 1911.[18]

Because of the military presence, and also its proximity to Dublin, Kildare
became one of Ireland's most strongly Protestant counties, with thirty-five
established churches and four 'other places of protestant worship'.[19] The
population of County Kildare in 1911 was 66,627 and the census recorded
54,684 Catholics and 11,943 Protestants in the county. Of the Protestant
population the census recorded there were 10,498 Church of Ireland or
Anglican, 611 Presbyterians and 834 others in the county. Kildare's Protestant
population, at 15.76 per cent, was above the national average of 13.3 per
cent, and this fact boded well for high recruitment numbers in the county.
Kildare possessed many large and influential landowning families such as

the FitzGeralds and the Earl of Mayo, at Palmerstown. These loyal families employed butlers, gardeners and staff who were all pro-British. The Protestant population of Kildare contributed a large proportion of their numbers to the armed services. This was seen as an assertion of that section of Irish society's loyalty to the government. As the war progressed Catholic support waned, but the Protestant recruitment numbers joining remained relatively steady.[20]

While there were some negative aspects of having so many troops stationed in Co. Kildare, there was also the positive economic and social aspect of the presence of the military, their families and the many civilians employed by them. The financial benefits generated by the military brought much-needed revenue to all classes of Kildare people. The country gentry welcomed the officers to the seasonal balls, hunting fields, racecourses, polo grounds, cricket pitches and shooting parties throughout the county. Non-commissioned officers and men brought spending power to the shops and hostelries of the neighbouring towns. Economic and social bonds were cemented between the military and civilian population. The military was, therefore, not a colonial army of strangers – many were married locally – and their presence provided much of the county with its livelihood.

As well as the society weddings of the officers and gentry of the county there were regular unions between the other ranks and local women. Con Costello found that in a survey of 7,103 marriages between 1802 and 1899 in five Church of Ireland and four Roman Catholic churches in the Curragh area there were 965 military weddings. The majority of the ceremonies took place in the Protestant church at Newbridge, and the women were mainly from the town or from the Curragh camp and locality. A total of 225 military weddings took place in the Catholic churches in Kildare, Kilcullen and Newbridge, with 145 in the latter town. In the Curragh garrison church (named St Brigid's from 1893) there were 273 marriage ceremonies between 1855 and 1896. Of the ninety-eight women whose addresses were recorded, forty-eight were from Co. Kildare, forty-eight from different parts of the country, and two were from England.

In an analysis of the 965 military marriages it was found that 387 of the brides could be regarded as 'local'. However, the exact number of Kildare-born women was impossible to clarify as the registers do not give place of birth, and women who had followed their men to the county may have given their address of residence there. The church registers also indicate that of the 2,739 births registered in the Catholic garrison church from 1855–99 between 3 and 4 per cent indicated that the father was Protestant. This would imply that there were frequent marriages between local women and soldiers and that the children of such unions, if the mother was Catholic, were baptised in that faith.[21]

There was a great deal of social interaction between the military and the civilian population. Shops and pubs did well, as men had to eat and most soldiers liked to drink. A major source of entertainment for the civilians of all classes were the military revues, field days, manoeuvres or ceremonial celebrations. For the officers of the British army one of the great attractions of service in Kildare was the prospect of hunting with the county and the neighbouring packs of hounds, and of participating in, or attending, the race meetings on the Curragh and at Punchestown, as well as the regimental and other point-to-point fixtures. The Kildare Hunt Club was the principal sporting outlet for the officers from the Curragh, Newbridge, Kildare and Naas barracks. Membership of the hunt included regular officers living in rented houses locally, who might have individual membership, or gentlemen who hunted on mess subscription from their regiment. The general officer commanding in Ireland, and the general officers from the Curragh or Newbridge were usually members.[22]

Garrison life in Co. Kildare was quite idyllic. The officer class fitted in well with their social peers and many of them settled locally. Commander-in-Chief Ireland (1908–12), General Sir Neville Lyttleton, described army life in Ireland as a 'haven of rest'. He said: 'We did all we could to keep up the tradition of hospitality at the Royal Hospital, many balls, dinners, and parties for Punchestown Races, and the yearly Horse Shows. We, in turn, were most hospitably entertained at many country houses, and in Dublin itself.'[23]

The culture of the British army in Ireland was that officers were largely of Protestant and unionist origin while Catholics made up the masses of the rank and file. Urban areas, too, had large numbers of ex-servicemen who were also loyal to the government. The friendly intercourse that was carried on between the military and the civilian population in general was of great benefit to both the army and the county. The most significant gain was a financial one. As with the social benefits, all classes prospered on the flow of money from the War Department and the regiments. This continued throughout the war years.

By October 1914 there were some 14,000 men stationed at the Curragh Camp, in addition to those in Naas, Newbridge and Kildare.[24] As the number of recruits increased daily the training areas became inadequate, and in the autumn of 1914 the construction of new shooting ranges became necessary. The Secretary of State for War had the powers to enable a range to be opened at the Little Curragh, towards Friarstown and Rathbride. As it required the closing of a road when firing was in progress persons who might find themselves injured because of this could make redress to the War Department. Another range was constructed at Castledillon, near Straffan, which created employment to over eighty men. The range was used by troops from Dublin, whose presence in the area created a 'boon to local shopkeepers'.[25]

Troops stationed in Ireland were among the first wave of British forces arriving in France. Many of the officers and men who fell at the Marne, the Aisne, and Ypres during autumn 1914 had left the barracks of the Curragh, Kildare, Newbridge and Naas. Within a few weeks the British army lost four times as many soldiers as during the three years of the Boer War. The British army in 1914 was a small professional force of 247,432 men, of which half was dispersed across the Empire. Britain, alone among the European belligerents, had no system of universal military service, and unlike the European powers, which mustered millions of trained conscripts, summoned into uniform only a further 145,347 reservists – ex-soldiers contractually liable to recall – and 268,777 men of the part-time Territorial Force. Although the process went relatively smoothly, some men wrenched from civilian life responded with reluctance and even truculence.[26]

Men from as far away as the British Dominions of Canada, Australia and New Zealand joined up. (Eight Kildare-born soldiers were killed serving with the Australian army; three with the New Zealanders and one with the Canadians.[27]) George Hicks, son of ex-RIC man, George Frederick Hicks, Bert, Athy, was wounded in the leg and shoulder, serving with the 24th

Victoria Rifles. He was involved with the campaign of recruitment in Canada, to replace men for the Irish Rangers regiment lost at the Front.[28] Naas native Arthur John Dowling was a tobacconist in Northwood, a suburb of Sydney, when he enlisted in the Australian army on 9 September 1915. A veteran of South Africa, where he had served twelve months with the Army Service Corps, Dowling was too old for active service and thus, survived the war.[29]

Maurice Alwyn Adams enlisted at Tokomaru Bay, Wellington in the New Zealand Field Artillery. He was born in Kill, the son of Rev. James Adams, Rector of Kill, and Frances Maud Johnston, and emigrated to New Zealand sometime after 1907. On 13 November 1915 the 8th Reinforcements, New Zealand Field Artillery, sailed for the European and Middle East war zones, on board two transports, the *Willochra* and *Tofua*. Among the men, horses and equipment was Maurice Alwyn Adams. The first stop was at Suez, Egypt, on 18 December 1915. After a period of training and assignation to units the reinforcements continued on to England and then the Western Front. The New Zealand Division settled in on the stalemated Western Front as part of the Second Army in 1916. In the spring of 1917 the Second Army began preparations for a major attack on Messines Ridge. Wire-cutting and artillery bombardments began on 21 May as troops, tanks and artillery massed for the main attack to begin on 4 June. Maurice Alwyn Adams never saw the major offensive. He was killed on 28 May 1917, probably by German counter battery fire on the New Zealand positions. He left a wife, Mrs Lily Adams, of 34 Adelaide Road, Wellington. Three years later, on 17 May 1920, a service conducted by his father, the Ven. Archdeacon Adams, was held at St John's Church, Kill, for the purpose of unveiling a memorial tablet, placed in the Church by the parishioners, in memory of those who died during the Great War.[30]

When war was declared Britain was fully committed to sending a major expeditionary force to Europe. Implementing this commitment would call for unprecedented efforts and sacrifices. In Ireland active public support was wide, but not universal. Because of the quantity of military institutions in the county Kildare was seen as an excellent source of recruitment from the very beginning of the war. However, public sentiment among the labouring classes was not that much in favour of the war. The response to the initial call to arms came from the unionist community, Catholic professionals, the upper classes and nationalists who identified strongly with the promised Home Rule dispensation. Subsequent working-class recruitment was very much on economic grounds. The printing of long lists of casualties in the newspapers and the horror stories of men back from the Front was hardly an incentive to would-be recruits, or their families. There was a good deal of apathy and while hundreds of Kildaremen quickly offered themselves to the army, many more potential recruits decided to stay at home.

3 THE WAR·FRONT

Company D, 1st Battalion, Irish Guards, March 1915. Joseph Keating (Usk, Kilcullen) middle row, extreme left. Photo: Julie O'Donoghue.

WHEN WAR WAS declared in early August some regular Irish soldiers quickly found themselves in France, destined for combat. The 2nd Royal Irish Rifles were swiftly transported from Tidworth barracks in England to France, while the 1st Royal Irish Rifles, stationed in Aden, was shipped back to Britain to prepare for battle. The 1st Royal Dublin Fusiliers had further to travel, being stationed in Madras, south-west India, while the 1st Royal Munster Fusiliers made the longest voyage of all, coming from Rangoon, in south-east India. Men in the reserve reached the Front quicker, joining their units almost immediately.[1]

Command of the British Expeditionary Force (BEF) to France was given to Sir John French, a sixty-one-year old cavalryman of Irish lineage who had resigned as Chief of the Imperial Staff during the 'Curragh Mutiny' a few months earlier.[2] In March 1914 fifty-eight cavalry officers at the Curragh Camp threatened to resign their commissions rather than obey commands, which they believed would involve coercing Ulster into accepting Home Rule, or prevent the possibility of armed UVF action. It was feared that army and police barracks in the north of Ireland would be raided by the UVF in a bid to procure arms.[3]

From 7 August the BEF began landing at Le Havre. As they marched along the roads of northern France that glorious summer they sang the most popular song of the war, 'It's a long way to Tipperary.' Nearly half of the men of the BEF were recalled reservists and some units were made up of two-thirds reservists. Some had been out of uniform for seven years and most were physically unfit. In the rushed mobilisation and departure for the Front, there had been no time for training. Unaccustomed to route marches, many suffered foot blisters and shoulder sores from carrying equipment. Some were carrying weapons for the first time in years. But there were worse shocks in store. The opening days of the conflict brought scenes of carnage, which had never been witnessed before.[4]

European nations had made plans for a continental war for some time and by 1910 it seemed almost inevitable. All the prospective belligerents proposed to attack. The Germans had planned for the capture of Paris since 1906. The Schlieffen Plan, named after former chief of staff, Alfred Graf von Schlieffen, called for a massive sweep into northern France through Belgium and Luxembourg and the annihilation of the French army in a rapid knock-out blow. Then the German army would turn on Russia. Britain had long considered Germany as the most possible and dangerous of potential adversaries and had entered the Triple Entente (1907) with France and Russia. The Schlieffen Plan involved the invasion of Belgium, thus providing Britain with an opportunity for entering the war, to which she had long been effectively committed.[5]

The conflict began with free manoeuvre in Belgium and northern France, in which casualties reached epic proportions. The French clashed with the Germans in the forests of the Ardennes and were soundly defeated with tremendous losses. In one day alone, 27,000 men in the French army were killed – a much larger loss than the British suffered on 1 July 1916, the first day of the Battle of the Somme, which is regularly, and wrongly, cited as the First World War's bloodiest day. A full retreat by the Belgian army left the French no choice but to do likewise, which in turn left the British right flank open to attack. As the French fell back the major weight of the wheeling German army fell on the BEF at Mons and another French force at Charleroi.[6]

The first British shots of the war were fired early on the morning of 22 August by cavalry from the 4th Royal Irish Dragoon Guards, north of the Mons-Condé Canal. Whereas at the beginning of the war the German and French armies numbered well over a million men each, divided into eight and five field armies respectively, the BEF initially numbered only about 80,000 soldiers divided into two corps. Unlike the largely conscript armies of Germany and France, however, the BEF was an entirely professional force made up of long-service volunteer soldiers and was, on balance, probably the best trained and most experienced of the European armies of 1914. In particular, pre-war British army training emphasised rapid marksmanship, meaning that the average 'Tommy' was able to hit a man-sized target fifteen times per minute at a range of 300 yards with his Lee-Enfield rifle. On 23 August masses of German infantry hit the British line and the young conscripts paid a heavy price as the 'mad minute' of at least fifteen aimed rounds took a heavy toll.

The Germans received a setback, but they had superior numbers and were able to outflank the British position. The Allied forces in Belgium fell into retreat. Luckily for the Allies the Germans weakened their right flank on 25 August by sending troops to fight the Russian army on the Eastern Front – a strong right flank was a crucial element of the Schlieffen Plan. By the first week of September the French capital was facing disaster. At the very last moment, General J. Joffre impressed 600 Renault taxis to ferry all available French reserves to the line of the Marne. The German centre had too little momentum; the German right was too far away, so the line fell back. The Allied retreat did not end until 5 September at the Marne river, the last major water obstacle on the route to Paris. Here, the Allies counterattacked, pushing the Germans back to the Aisne river. The campaign involved a million men on both sides. Casualties were horrendous: Allied 263,000; German 250,000.[7]

The press in Co. Kildare reported on war events. Men who had enlisted received commissions or had rejoined the army. The newspapers also reported on local casualties. The harsh reality of war reached dozens of Kildare homes as news of the dead and wounded was relayed. By the end of August eight men born in Co. Kildare had been killed in action in France and Belgium. The first fatalities were Lt. Harold Martin Soames and Major Charles Stewart Holland, killed in action on 23 August, while four more officers born in Kildare were killed in the fighting on 26 August. Although these men were born in Co. Kildare they were all of English parentage. The first Kildare resident to die was Private William Whelan, 2nd Royal Dublin Fusiliers, who was killed in action, in Belgium, on 27 August. Born in Castledermot, he was the son of Patrick and Mary Whelan and husband of Bridget Whelan, Carlowgate, Castledermot.[8]

The first Kildare officer killed was Major Hubert Crichton, 1st Irish Guards, who was killed in the retreat from Mons on 1 September. Born in 1885, at Mullaboden, Ballymore-Eustace, the son of Lt. Col. The Hon. Charles and Lady Madeline Crichton, Hubert joined the British army in 1896 when he was twenty-one. He was with the Nile Expedition of 1898 and at the subsequent battle of Khartoum, receiving the Egyptian Medal with Clasp (each battle, or action covered by the medal is represented with a clasp) and received the Queen's Medal with Clasp in the South African War.[9]

Among the dead on the first casualty list was Lance Corporal William Corcoran (Athy) 1st Irish Guards, who was also killed in action on 1 September and Private Patrick Joseph Heydon, 1st Irish Guards, who died on 4 September. Patrick Joseph Heydon was born in Athy, the son of Patrick and Mary Heydon, of Churchtown House, Churchtown, Athy. Also killed were two well-known officers linked to Co. Kildare: Lieutenant Thomas de Burgh, Oldtown, Naas and Captain C. F. Blacker, of Johnstown, Naas. Lieutenant Thomas de Burgh, the youngest son of Colonel de Burgh, of Oldtown, Naas, was reported missing on 16 September, after a reconnaissance at Conde Bridge on the Aisne river. He was believed to have being killed by a shell explosion, although his body was never recovered. Born in 1888, he was educated at Wellington College and Sandhurst, and received his commission in 1910. Lt. de Burgh was described as a fine horseman and an all-round sportsman. He was one of four brothers on active service and was serving with the 31st Lancers, Indian Army, who were attached, at the outbreak of war, to the 5th

Royal Irish Lancers. Lt. de Burgh was officially reported as killed in action a year later. [10]

Captain Cecil F. Blacker, 2nd Connaught Rangers, was wounded in the leg and body at the battle of Mons, but died several days later of pneumonia at Netley Hospital, England. His remains were brought back to Ireland and his funeral took place at Maudlins Cemetery, Naas. On arrival at Sallins railway station the coffin was conveyed to an impromptu wagon drawn by one horse and covered with a Union Jack and a collection of wreaths. The *Kildare Observer* reported that there was no military element about it, which was to be regretted, but the exigencies of the time made a military funeral impossible. A large number of recruits who had arrived on the same train, who were destined for Naas barracks, formed up and marched in the sad procession, which was headed by the young officer's father – Major Frederick Blacker – and his mother and sister. The grave at Maudlins Cemetery was lined with moss and evergreens, intersected with bunches of sweet pea, stocks, asters and other flowers. Sergeant Finnegan, 2nd Connaught Rangers, was on the same train. He was going home on sick furlough to Dunlavin, Co. Wicklow. Sgt. Finnegan had accompanied Major Blacker on the greater part of the journey back to England, but had been sent to a hospital in Brighton, and did not hear of his officer's death until he reached Sallins. Despite his injuries Sgt. Finnegan accompanied the remains to their final resting place and laid a regimental badge on the coffin. [11]

British reinforcements landed at Ostend in late September and together with the BEF transferred to the Allied left flank, began to push forward. Prevented from going through to Paris, the Germans sought an opening further north, and each side now began trying to turn its enemy's western flank, with the object of winning the war rapidly and economically. The ensuing manoeuvres, during late October and early November, as the two sides tried to outflank one another, are known as the 'race to the sea' – that is, to the Belgian seaports. For the Germans, seizure of the Channel ports would create an overwhelmingly powerful strategic position from which to negotiate a peace. After a series of encounters the two forces clashed again at the Belgian city of Ypres (the British pronounced it 'Wipers'). In two battles around this city the Germans lost 135,000 men dead and wounded, while these exertions had all but wiped out the original British army. Out of 163,000 men engaged the British suffered 55,000 casualties. Except for the divisions formed from the returned overseas garrisons, the old army was destroyed. In the years ahead more than 200,000 British soldiers would die in what became known as the 'Ypres salient'.[12]

In October and November the Front stabilised along the whole length of a double trench-line running from Nieuport on the Belgian coast, all the way to the Swiss border. For the next three years the line hardly moved until, in March 1917, the Germans voluntarily surrendered the central Somme sector and retired to stronger, previously prepared lines twenty miles to the rear.[13] All up and down the Western Front the trench system was transformed, out of necessity, into a permanent labyrinth as the Allies and the Germans settled into a stalemate which neither side could break. This was to be home for many men from the short grass county for the next three–four years. The days passed with regular monotony punctuated by violent bursts of combat, patrolling, raids, artillery barrages and full-scale attacks. In ninety miles of trenches, even in the quietest times, hundreds of British officers and men were killed and wounded daily, just as a matter of course. The staff officers called it 'wastage'.[14] Routine patrols in No Man's Land, and the practice of raiding the enemy trenches for intelligence gathering or 'blooding' new units, pushed up casualties.

Conditions at the Front were wretched. The front line was smelt long before it was reached. The stench of rotting flesh was everywhere, barely repressed by the chloride of lime sprinkled on particularly offensive sites. Dead men, mules and horses were sometimes not buried for months and became part of the landscape. Lingering pockets of poison gas added to the unappetising atmosphere. The front lines consisted of three parallel trenches – a front line trench, a centre line trench and a reserve trench – all linked by communications trenches. The front line trench was from fifty yards to a mile from its enemy's counterpart. The ground between rival trenches was known as 'no man's land' and was littered with shell-holes and, after a time, the rotting bodies of the unclaimed dead. Several hundred yards behind the front line trench was the support trench line; several hundred yards behind that was the reserve line. The reserve trench was usually out of enemy range. There were three kinds of trenches: firing trenches; communications trenches, running roughly perpendicular to the line and connecting the three lines; and 'saps', shallower trenches thrust out into 'no man's land', providing access to forward observation posts, listening posts, grenade-throwing posts, and machine gun positions. The end of a sap was usually not manned all the time. Coming up from the rear, one reached the trenches by following a communication trench sometimes a mile or more long. It often began in a town and gradually deepened. By the time the troops reached the reserve line they were well below ground level.

A firing trench was supposed to be six to eight feet deep and four or five feet wide. On the enemy side a parapet of earth or sandbags rose about two or three feet above the ground. A corresponding 'parados' a foot or so high was often found on top of the friendly side. One- or two-man holes, known as 'funk-holes', were dug into the sides of trenches, and there were deeper dugouts, reached by a dirt stairs, for use as command posts and officers' quarters. On the front of a trench was a fire-step two feet high on which the defenders stood, firing and throwing grenades, when repelling attacks. A well-built trench did not run straight for any distance but was 'traversed' to prevent enfilade and shell fire having much effect. In other words every few yards a good trench zig-zagged, with frequent traverses designed to contain damage within a limited space. Moving along a trench thus involved a great deal of turning and weaving. The floor of a proper trench was covered with wooden 'duckboards', beneath which were sumps a few feet deep to collect water. The walls, perpetually crumbling, were supported by sandbags, corrugated iron, or bundles of sticks or rushes. Except at night and in half-light, soldiers only looked over the top through periscopes. The few snipers on duty during the day observed No Man's Land through loopholes cut in sheets of armour plate. The entanglements of barbed wire had to be positioned far enough out in front of the trench to keep the enemy from sneaking up to grenade-throwing distance.[15]

The British trenches were wet, cold, smelly, thoroughly squalid and not as efficient as the German works. They were decidedly amateur, vague, unplanned and temporary. The French works were much the same, while the German trenches were deep, elaborate, clean and permanent. To make matters worse the British section of the Front was at Flanders and Picardy – areas notorious for dampness. The British trenches were dug where the water-table was the highest and the annual rainfall the most abundant. Their trenches were always wet and often flooded several feet deep. Thigh boots and waders were issued as standard articles of uniform. The men developed 'trench foot' and 'trench fever' from constantly standing in wet and muddy trenches.[16]

Sgt. Robert Doherty on a visit to his brother W. J. Doherty, of Main Street, Naas, said the intense coldness of the nights in the trenches around Ypres taxed the endurance of the troops, but none more terribly than those fresh from the Indian climate. A regular soldier with the Royal Irish Fusiliers, Doherty complained that the Irish regiments got very little mention or credit for their fighting abilities and that the only ones to get any were the 'Irish Rifles. They are nearly all Belfast fellows'.[17]

Lice, mites, flies and rats continually irritated the men. The troops were accompanied everywhere by lice, which the professional delousers in rest positions behind the lines, with their steam vats for clothes and hot baths for troops, could do little to eliminate. Rats gave constant trouble. They were big and black, with wet, muddy hair. They fed largely on the flesh of dead men and horses. The men shot them, or beat them to death with pick-handles.[17] While in action, men also suffered intense fatigue. Many suffered from 'shell-shock', and developed stammers and uncontrollable nervous reactions, or went mad. These men were often harshly treated, accused of cowardice and sent back into the line. There was very little sympathy from the top brass for the troops in the front lines.

The food was monotonous, particularly at the Front – a diet of bread, biscuits and tinned corned beef called 'bully beef'. Yet men ate three times a day. The men who did best were the poor – a full stomach, meat every day. They came back from the Front fitter, broader and stronger. George Adam, the British propagandist, declared that the troops were 'better fed than they are at home'. And he was right. Each man's daily ration amounted to: 1¼ pounds of fresh meat (or 1 pound of preserved meat); 1¼ pounds of bread; 4 ounces of bacon; 3 ounces of cheese and ½ pound of fresh vegetables (or 2 ounces dried) together with small amounts of tea, sugar and jam. In the trenches fresh meat was rare. Instead there was bully beef or 'Maconochie', a tinned pork-and-vegetable stew named after its Aberdeen-based manufacturer. While they did tend to grow tedious in the long run, both products were surprisingly good, with the men favouring Maconochie. 'Pearl biscuits' substituted for fresh bread while in the trenches; they reminded the men of dog biscuits.[18]

In actual combat troops hardly had time to eat. A letter from Captain Poole H. Hickman, commander of D Company, 7th Dublins, printed in the *Kildare Observer* recalled the landings at Suvla Bay in August 1915 and his scant time to have a meal of sorts. 'We left Mitylene at 3 p.m., Friday, August 6th, and arrived here at 4 a.m. on Saturday morning. We carried our rations with us – a sandwich for the voyage and two days' iron rations, consisting (each day's ration) of a tin of bully beef, tea, sugar, biscuits and Oxo tablets.' D Company suffered twenty-two casualties in the day's fighting. After a bayonet charge they established themselves in the Turkish trenches. Capt. Hickman said '… and on Sunday morning at 1.30 I ate a biscuit, which was my first food since breakfast the previous morning.' Capt. Hickman was killed in action on 15 August 1915.[19]

Food was not always plentiful, however. Bill Dunne (Colbinstown) served on the Western Front with the 1st Battalion, Irish Guards. He was wounded by a shell splinter in February 1916 and, at the battle of Passchendaele Ridge in October 1917, a German bullet hit his nose and left him with a long scar. In the battle he and thirty-four other British soldiers were captured and placed in a cage of wire mesh, but they managed to escape and make their way back to the British lines. During his time in the trenches Bill learned what it meant to be short of food on several occasions. At Laventie their supplies of food ran short, and Saxon-Bavarian troops in the enemy trenches 150 yards away taunted him and his comrades by displaying empty bully-beef tins on the points of their bayonets. 'They even filled the tins with clay and fired them into our trenches with catapults,' Bill Dunne recalled. The Germans were more fond of bully beef than the British and it was a sought-after item on enemy trench raids.[20]

For the men in the trenches rations were of the utmost importance and some were willing to risk life and limb to keep the front-line soldiers supplied. Bertram de Weldon (Kilmoroney, Athy), serving with the 10th Lancashire Regiment wrote to his brother, Tony, on 3 August 1915:

> Our lads have taken to bad conditions in their usual solid and stated way. The great difficulty is the mutual soldiers carelessness – especially when [enemies] are about. Here is an episode today. Two men went out in the dark to bring up the meals found the tray heavy and went to sleep under a hedge. At 5 o'clock in the afternoon they felt hungry, and decided to chance it. Carrying the meals they strolled across the open in broad daylight o the trenches. I hear it was very exciting watching there and that pretty nearly the whole line tunnel came round to see them safe through. But what asses![21]

When a company was out of the line, it fared better. It was then serviced by its company cookers – stoves on wheels – and often got something approaching the official quota, as it might in a particularly somnolent part of the line, when hot food at times came up at night in the large covered containers known as 'Dixies'.[2] The men were paid in local currency and were able to buy additional food when not in action – an option not available to many of those at home in Kildare or Ireland, who simply went hungry. Potentially, it meant soldiers ate an estimated 4,600 calories a day, compared with a workingman's 3,400 a day at home. (It is now 3,530 on average in Ireland, though the recommended intake is 2,400–2,800.)[23]

In fact, the food offered by the army was far superior to what many were used to at home. The average daily consumption of potatoes in Ireland had fallen from 184 ounces in 1839 to 28 ounces in 1904, in rural areas, and 17 ounces in urban areas. Consumption of food and drink such as eggs, butter, tea and sugar accounted for 10.6 ounces of an average male labourers' daily consumption by 1904. Shop-bought food, like biscuits, bread, sugar, tea and other 'delicacies', supplemented the diet of all classes. Bread, potatoes and porridge still formed the staple diet of the poor, but there was a greatly increased consumption of dairy products and meats. More affluent people took to having bacon and eggs at breakfast time. The main meal was taken in the middle of the day and invariably comprised of meat, potatoes and vegetables, usually cabbage, carrots, turnips, parsnips or peas. Other foodstuffs eaten were boiled eggs, bread mixed with boiled milk, and sometimes cheese. The less affluent lived on a relatively poor diet, both heavy on meat and potatoes, or on tea and bread and little else. While poor labourers had greater access to new types of food such as beef, pork, bacon and fish they tended to eat them sparingly, and it tended to be the poorer cuts of meat that the labouring classes dined on. There was much more bacon consumed amongst the lower classes, with fatty American bacon being cheaper and thus more easily accessible. Even poorer families tasted meat once a month or on special occasions. In 1904 meat consumption in rural areas was 0.3 ounces daily; in urban areas, it was 1.12 ounces. Bacon consumption was slightly higher: rural areas, 1.7 ounces daily; urban areas, 1.16 ounces.[24]

A myth of the First World War is that troops spent all their time in the trenches. Normally the British troops rotated trench duty on a sixteen-day timetable. Troops usually spent three to eight days in the front-line trenches followed by a similar length of time in the support trench, and four days in the reserve trenches. Then it was time for four days of rest, in a camp situated a few miles away from the fighting. A unit would move back up again – at night – to relieve an element in the front-line trench. However, when the British army was short of men, troops could spend up to thirty days in the trenches. All in all infantrymen spent 45 per cent of their time out of the trenches.[25]

Living conditions in the front line were atrocious. Officers in forward trenches would sleep in shifts within muddy little rooms called 'dugouts' while the rank and file would have to cope with evermore inferior dugouts – misleadingly dubbed 'shelters', they were simply rectangular caves carved into the walls of the trench. The shelter was built one foot above the floor level of the trench and was usually able to accommodate two men lying down with enough room to sit up straight.[26] Most men slept where they could – sitting down, even standing up. Living conditions in Ireland at the time were quite basic, so men were used to hardship, but nothing prepared them for life in the trenches. Many of the men from Kildare had lived in second- and third-class houses – poorly-built single-storey cottages – with no running water or toilets. Some families lived in fourth-class houses and one-room dwellings – many of them deemed unfit for human habitation by medical authorities. It would be absurd to say that the conditions in the trenches were not worse: houses were bad, but they were not made of mud. The officer class perhaps suffered more. They were used to much more comfort in their first-class dwellings with running water and reasonable toilet facilities, servants, good clothes and decent diet.

Captain Charles Weld was born at Downings, Prosperous. He was educated in England from a young age, so was accustomed to being away from his family. As a 'gentleman' Capt. Weld was entitled to have a private soldier assigned to take care of his needs, known as a 'batman', though the official term was 'soldier servant'. A batman was usually chosen by the officer himself, and Capt. Weld's servant was a man from his own locality, Hugh Reilly. The job was usually seen as a desirable position as the soldier was exempted from more onerous duties and often got better rations and personal favours from his officer. In his diary Capt. Weld gave minimal information and rarely complained of the terrible conditions in the trenches. He did with frequency, however, mention what the weather was like:

> Rain for the last few days. Trenches knee deep in mud and
> water. Everyone drenched.
> Weather fine.
> Rain again.
> Rain continues.
> Day fine and warm.[27]

The army was ill-equipped for the front-line conditions. More casualties resulted from illness than enemy action. Men trudged knee-deep through wet and muddy trenches. Feet too swollen to wear shoes were wrapped in straw. Trench foot (a medical condition caused by prolonged exposure of the feet to damp, unsanitary and cold conditions) and other diseases ate at their morale. As early as November 1914 J. Whiteside Dean, of Naas, forwarded a letter from Col. Arthur Loveband, 1st Royal Dublin Fusiliers, to the editor of the *Kildare Observer*, appealing for woolly vests and drawers at once for his men. The popular Col. Loveband said that 'General Winter' was on its way and described the soldiers lot in the trenches as a 'severe one'.[28] Col. Loveband was shot dead during a gas attack on 'Mouse Trap Farm' on 24 May 1915. The Dublins had just finished stand-to at 4.00 pm and rum was being issued, a tablespoonful to a man, when a bombardment began and a wall of gas rolled down each side of their position. So close were the German and Dublin trenches at this point that there was little time to put on gas masks. The German assault infantry followed close behind their gas and were able to gain entry into the trenches. Col. Loveband was shot in the face and died instantly. (He left a wife, Mabel, and daughter, Lettice.) His second-in-command, Major Mangan, died from gas poisoning. The farm was taken and retaken in a day of heavy fighting.[29]

The day at the Front began about an hour before first light, about 4.30 a.m. Since dawn was the favourite time for launching attacks at the order to 'stand-to' everyone, officers and men, mounted the fire-step, weapon ready, and peered toward the German line. When it was almost full light and clear the Germans were not going to attack that morning, everyone 'stood down' and began preparing breakfast in small groups. The rations of tea, bread and bacon, brought up in sandbags during the night, were broken out. The bacon was fried in mess-tin lids over small smokeless fires. The rum issue was doled out from a jar with the traditional iron spoon, each man receiving about two tablespoonfuls. Some put it into their tea, but most swallowed it straight. It was a most precious commodity, and serving it out was almost like a religious ceremony.

During the day the men cleaned weapons and repaired those parts of the trench which had been damaged during the night. They wrote letters, deloused themselves, or slept. Entertainment in the trenches consisted of the usual soldiers' pastimes of playing cards, storytelling and reading. Men went to and fro on sentry duty or working parties. The officers strolled about, conducting inspections, trying to look nonchalant to inspirit the men.[30] Despite the class difference officers were close to 'their' men. Junior officers and NCOs were the backbone of the army. They acted as managers, teachers, coaches and father figures. Without their officers and NCOs the men were lost. In the battle for the village of St Julien in April 1915 one company of Dublins, having lost its officers and NCOs, fell back. Others followed, and as they did so they were confronted by a single slight figure. Dressed in an ancient 'British warm' and armed only with a blackthorn stick, he was instantly recognisable to the men – Lt. Col. Loveband, the commanding officer. As he walked towards his men he made the lie-down signal with his hand and stick. They obeyed and dug in. Then they were shelled and gassed. Col. Loveband's presence was a morale booster for the retreating men. Undismayed by their repulse and heavy losses, but delighted in finding the 'old man', the Dublins dug in and held on.[31]

Good relations between officers and men were vital in maintaining morale. Officers read and censored the men's letters, which brought them close to their charges, and wrote letters to their families and to the relatives of soldiers killed and wounded in action. Private Andrew Farrell, of Fair Green Lane, Naas, was killed in action on the Somme on 23 July 1916. He was an apprentice printer with the *Kildare Observer*, but had left to work in a munitions factory in Falkirk, Scotland. Andrew Farrell enlisted on 19 September 1915 and left for the Front on 30 May 1916 with the Machine Gun Corps. His mother, Mrs Eliza Farrell, received the following letter on 27 July 1916:

> B.E. Forces, France
> 23 July 1916
> Dear Madam – It is with the most sincere regret that I have to write and tell you that your son, No. 28996, Private A. Farrell, of my Company, has been killed in action, about 5.30 pm on 23 July 1916. My officers and men, one and all, join me in my desire to convey to you the great loss your son is to not only his parents and relatives, but his King and Country, and also

to my Company. He was quite one of the best soldiers I had in my Company – brave, steady, always reliable, smart, and in every way a credit to the corps. I am arranging that his body be brought back from the trenches and that he will be interred in the cemetery by a Catholic Priest with full military honours. He will be greatly missed by both officers and men, but it is gratifying to know that he died the death of a soldier, fighting for a great cause and no man can do more than give his life for his King and Country. I may state that he was instantly killed by shell fire and it will be something to know that the end was sudden and painless. Please accept the most sincere sympathies of officers and men of this Company in your great bereavement. Yours sincerely,

P. Mathisen (Captain)

O.C. 121 MG Company, France, 23 July 1916.

Mrs Farrell also received letters of sympathy from Fr Kerr, Irish chaplain to the forces, and Lt. Thomas, 121 MG Company.[32] The postal connection between home and the trenches was rapid and efficient. Letters and parcels normally took about four days, sometimes only two. Exotic foodstuffs could easily be sent across, not just standard non-perishables like tinned kippers and oysters, tinned butter and fowl, pate and chocolate, cheese and cherry brandy and wine, but perishables like gingerbread, cakes and tarts; fresh fruit and butter and eggs; and fresh flowers for the officers 'table'. The efficiency of the postal arrangements meant that there was parcel traffic in both directions and souvenirs could be dispatched readily with the result that many a Kildare home had a memento from the Front.[33]

The men's affection for their officers was often reciprocated. When Major Lord Desmond FitzGerald, brother of the Duke of Leinster, was killed by a bomb explosion at a base camp, the whole battalion lined the road to his grave in Calais Cemetery. The popular officer was adjutant of the 1st Irish Guards since the beginning of the war, had been wounded twice, awarded the Military Cross and his name at the time had been put forward for the Distinguished

Service Order. His obituary said he was a capable officer 'most popular with his men, in whose welfare he took the most lively and kindly interest'.[34]

For much of the war the average British soldier got only ten days leave for every fifteen months of service. The difficulty experienced in obtaining leave was a recurring theme of letters from men at the Front. Many soldiers discovered that their first visit 'home' was a trip to a hospital in Britain to be treated for serious injury, or trench fever. This counted as 'leave', and they would have to join the bottom of the queue for leave when they returned to the Front.[35] The Western Front was close enough for men to go home on leave, while soldiers serving in other theatres, like the Middle East, could not travel home. Captain James P. Roche, returned to Monasterevan on 'leave' in October 1916. He was a trench mortar officer with the 16th Irish Division for the previous twelve months, but only received 'leave' when he contracted trench fever and was sent home for treatment and rest.[36] Another aspect of returning home on leave was that some men did not want to return to the horrors of active duty.

After evening stand-to, the real work began. Wiring parties repaired the wire in front of the position. Digging parties extended saps toward the enemy. Carrying parties brought up rations, ammunition, mail and heavy engineering materials needed for the constant repair and improvement of the trenches. Night patrols and raiding parties headed out into No Man's Land. As morning approached all work ceased and by the time of stand-to nothing human was visible above ground.[37]

Capt. Weld probably spoke for many when he described the continuous work in his diary entry for 29 December 1915:

> We went on night fatigue and are all fed up with this continual night work. We have to march 5 miles then work six hours arriving back about 4 a.m. feeling worn out and generally drenched to the skin. Yet I suppose it must be done.[38]

Another gentleman soldier, former Clongowes Wood student, Lt. Thomas J. Kelly, Royal Army Medical Corps, drew a vivid description of the front-line trenches after a German attack in an extract from his diary dated 25 September 1914:

> 2.30 p.m. – The shelling re-commenced, and I had to go to the trenches, as the Royal Irish were suffering heavily and had sent down for a medical officer, their own one having been killed. I took 40 bearers and 10 stretchers and off we went round the corner to the road that leads to the trenches. It is a road of rapid motion. The showers of shrapnel and the constant whistling and buzzing of bullets do not tempt anyone to linger… At last we got to the trenches and to the wounded who were lying around outside them. Many slightly wounded were able to look after themselves when bleeding was stopped. The severely wounded cases were difficult to get away, but by putting them on to the stretchers along the ground, we at last succeeded with comparatively slight loss. When all the wounded were gone I was able to satisfy my curiosity and have a peep through a loop-hole at the enemy trenches. They were less than 200 yards away just here, and through glasses I could make out every detail. Just in front of our trenches were entanglements, and here and there, caught in the wire, in some cases still erect were dead Germans, the dead faces wearing the fierce expression of their last moment. In one case an arm was raised aloft and the hand clutched a grenade; the man had evidently been hit while in the act of throwing it. Between our wire and the enemy entanglements the ground was covered with prostrate forms, British and German lying side by side. We knew that some were still alive, but wounded and helpless. When we sent out our R.A.M.C. men the Bosches fired, and after several being hit we got orders not to try anymore. It was indeed a 'no man's land' where the wounded died and the dead were unburied. While the light lasted we could not recover them, and then there is no night here. When the sun goes down the searchlight comes

up. Immediately in front of the enemy field works were piles of dead, a long line of still, grey forms, the result of several attacks in close formation; and behind that you could see the daylight through the loopholes in the parapets of the trenches. We generally covered our loopholes with a curtain of sackcloth, as then the Germans could not see the light coming through and sight rifles on them... At 5 p.m. I left the trenches and had tea with the officers of the regiment in a 'dug-out'. When I returned to the dressing station I heard that a shell got one of my stretcher parties on its way back. Result – four bearers wounded and the man on the stretcher killed.[39]

Thomas J. Kelly left Clongowes Wood College in 1908. Commissioned as a lieutenant into the Royal Army Medical Corps he was awarded the Military Cross, was 'Mentioned in Despatches' and ended the war as a major, having being wounded in action.[40]

By the end of 1914 sixty-five Kildaremen had lost their lives in the conflict. While some were the sons of British soldiers born in Kildare, the majority of them were born and reared in the county. If 1914 had been a bad year, worse was to come – approximately 220 Kildaremen would be killed in 1915.[41]

4 RECRUITMENT IN COUNTY KILDARE

The Seventh Earl of Mayo, Dermot Bourke, of Palmerstown House, Naas, was one of the leading unionists in southern Ireland. Photo: Co. Kildare Archaeological Society.

BY 1900 THE British army no longer contained the huge proportion of Irishmen that it did in the 1830s when 40 per cent of its men were from Ireland. However, when war broke out in August 1914 close to 20,000 Irishmen were in the regular forces, while another 30,000 were reservists.[1] The proportion of Irish in the army (9.1 per cent) was close to that of the Irish element in the population of the British Isles (9.7 per cent). The 1911 Census found there was a total of 33,717 'Persons engaged in defence of Country', with the figure for Co. Kildare alone as 6,264. This figure was almost 10 per cent of the county population of 66,627.[2] (Many of these persons, however, were not Irish, but rather British-born.) From the beginning of the war Kildare's numbers were well above average. The presence of the Curragh Camp of course increased figures beyond most other counties. The location of the Royal Dublin Fusiliers, in Naas, meant that those in the surrounding areas would have the added inducement of joining a regiment close to home.

At the outbreak of the war five sons of Christopher and Margaret Connell, from Celbridge, were already serving members of the British army.

Christopher, Patrick, Richard, Robert and Thomas Connell – who ranged in age from 18–24 – were all serving in the 1st and 2nd Battalions of the Royal Irish Rifles with the BEF. Although a Belfast-based regiment, in 1914 33 per cent of the 'regulars' were from outside Ulster. The casualty list of 15 October 1914 contained the names of two of the brothers – Patrick and Thomas – who were wounded and in a Paris hospital, but it was later clarified that Patrick was actually a POW in Limburg Camp in Germany. All five brothers survived the conflict. Altogether nine members of the same family served with the colours.[3]

The initial expeditionary force numbered approximately 70,000 infantrymen and with the inclusion of the Artillery, Engineers, Medical and Logistic Services, the Irish contingent numbered no less than 15,000 officers and men. More followed as the regulars forming the overseas garrisons were relieved by Territorial Force units and came home to form five new regular divisions. The Territorial Force was a volunteer active-duty reservist force formed in 1908 by the amalgamation of the previously civilian-administered Volunteer Force, with the Yeomanry. At the outbreak of the war the special reserve battalions of the Irish regiments were called up. All their officers and men were sent to France in drafts as replacements for the enormous casualties suffered by the regular battalions, demands for which could not be met by regular army reservists alone. To meet the manpower demands of the regular battalions on active service, the twenty reserve and special reserve militia battalions of Irish regiments were retained in Ireland to provide training and reinforcement holding units.[4]

In response to calls from all quarters thousands of men and boys made their way to recruiting centres throughout the county. The *Kildare Observer* gave great support to the recruitment campaign and from 15 August 1914 onwards printed an advertisement looking for recruits to the Royal Dublin Fusiliers.[5] Both the conservative *Kildare Observer* and the nationalist *Leinster Leader* frequently published recruitment posters in their papers. Over 42,000 men joined the army in the first five wartime months of the war, but after the initial flurry in August and September 1914 recruiting subsided.[6] At the beginning of the war, a volunteer had to stand 173cm to get into the army. By

11 October 1914 the need for men was such that the standard was lowered to 165cm, but after the British army sustained 30,000 casualties in October a man only had to be 162cm to get in.[7]

Despite the initial surge of recruits it soon became clear that regular and reserve soldiers would not be enough to defeat the might of Germany. In the seven-month period from the beginning of the war in early August 1914 to the end of February 1915, 50,017 men volunteered for military service in Ireland. The recruiting campaign soon ran out of steam. In the next twelve months only 45,036 stepped forward.[8] In many ways this was a natural shortfall, the result, mainly, of not having a conscription bill in place. It could only be expected that the initial excitement of war and the first surge of those joining the forces would peter out. Additional motivation, in the form of allowances and local recruitment meetings, was required. To stem the shortfall various rallies and recruitment meetings were organised throughout the country and Kildare was no exception.

At Naas Quarter Sessions, Judge Brereton Barry, K.C., addressed the Grand Jury appealing to the jurors to 'do something more – something more outside the Grand Jury box, and that is, as representative men of this county, to use your influence as far as you possibly can to endeavour to get your fellow countrymen – the young men of this county – to join in averting the terrible danger which is now hanging over us by this dreadful war.' Later the following resolution was adopted by the Grand Jury:

> That we, the Grand Jurors of the Co. of Kildare, call upon our fellow-countrymen to come forward in the present crisis and join the army in defence of our country, recognising, as we do, the grave peril which threatens not alone this nation, but all civilised humanity from the hordes of German marauders and barbarians, who are endeavouring to overrun Europe, and are committing outrages on the defenceless town and cities of the countries they are fighting against, and against non-combatants on the high seas.

Judge Barry said the resolution was a highly proper one and he was very gratified that they had taken that view of it.[9]

The Central Council for the Organisation of Recruiting in Ireland (CCORI) was formally established on 23 April 1915 in an effort to extend the recruiting campaign and to tap areas in the country that had previously provided few recruits.[10] Recruiting figures began to rise partly in response to vigorous marketing, posters, pamphlets and public meetings. In June 1915 Sir Anthony Weldon, Lord Lieutenant for Kildare, requested the people of the county to form a recruitment committee, as various other counties seemed to be setting up similar bodies. Weldon's request for a recruitment committee was responded to and the County Kildare Recruiting Committee was formed with Mr M. J. Minch as Chairman and Mr T. Langan, Honorary Secretary. Initially a series of lectures on the War were held around the county. The *Observer* pointed out, in an editorial on 28 August 1915, that the county had done well in the matter of recruiting, but that Kildare and every other county in England and Ireland could do much better.[11]

Apart from Dublin and the north-east, the counties with heaviest recruitment were clustered in the midland belt stretching from Longford southwards to Tipperary and Carlow. Few recruits came from the Atlantic seaboard (except Sligo), with particularly low ratios for Kerry, Mayo and Donegal. Despite Ulster's dramatic support for enlistment, only about 43 per cent of recruits were Protestant. As in Britain the spring surge of enlistments gave way to a lull in the summer and autumn, followed in winter by a brief recovery attributable to more effective cooperation between the Irish Party, the Irish Executive and the new Department of Recruitment for Ireland, formed in October 1915 under Lord Wimborne, the Irish Lord Lieutenant, which took over the work of the CCORI.[12] In July 1915 a strenuous recruiter for the British army, The O'Mahony, issued a plea for more men. At this time no firm figures were available to the public but The O'Mahony felt that 'Kildare … need have no fear of the disclosures which such a return would involve'. The O'Mahony, a former Irish Party MP for North Meath, was born Pierce Charles de Lacy O'Mahony, in Kerry, and involved himself heavily in countrywide recruitment. His brother, David, was Secretary to the Co.

Kildare Hunt Club.[13] The O'Mahony delivered many of his speeches in Co. Kildare. At one particular meeting in Staplestown in October 1915 he asked locals to decide if

> ... they were going to leave ... men, who were risking their lives and shedding their blood in defence of our homes and those we loved, unaided ... Now when they had the opportunity of fighting to preserve their nation, why did not they come forward and join. For how could man die better than facing fearful odds. For the ashes of his father and the temple of his God.[14]

The recruiting campaign, however, like much of Britain's policy in Ireland, was mismanaged from the start. Despite John Redmond's support for the campaign, the great bulk of the Irish Party stood aloof from recruiting and exhibited a general apathy towards the war. Very few rank-and-file Irish MPs threw themselves wholeheartedly into the recruiting campaign. Recruiting officials were usually landlords, gentlemen and officers of the Protestant Church who were of strong unionist opinion. They went about the county haranguing farmers and labourers with strident criticisms and threats of conscription. The middle classes in particular were targeted, as their numbers were not as high as the labouring classes in joining the war effort. The *Kildare Observer* claimed that the upper and lower classes had produced the most recruits and that the middle classes 'can hardly said to have made any sacrifices at all'. Figures were not available to show how even one town in Kildare had 'done its bit', but the *Observer* said the workers of Naas – those regarded as the 'lower classes' – had done their duty nobly and abundantly. Of the eligible fifty-one men of military age from The Naas Workingmen's Friendly Society, twenty-nine had joined the colours.[15]

The war attracted those who did not have much in the way of employment to leave behind. The towns of the county were felt to be keeping up their numbers, most notably Athy, which as early as November 1914 had contributed 400 men to the army, many of them members of the local National Volunteers.[16] However, recruits for the war effort also came from places with no ties to the

British army. Seven brothers from Ballitore served in the war, all of whom, like their father Michael, were agricultural labourers. Ballitore was not typically a recruiting ground for the British army; it had suffered ravages from the crown forces in the 1798 rebellion and once had been home to a large pacifist Quaker population. Michael, Laurence, Christopher, John, James, William and Peter Delaney all served with various units during the war. William was killed in action on 13 March 1916, while Michael and Laurence were later wounded.[17]

The British authorities were often critical of Irish recruitment and it was felt that the countryside, particularly the farmers, were falling behind in terms of recruitment numbers. A slow take-up was noted in rural areas by 1915. The harvest ended in October and recruits from this sector were expected to rise, but this did not occur. Farmers gained much from the price increases during the war and prospered well. They did not need the separation allowance in order to feed their families. A wealthy farmer or shop owner would not voluntarily leave a progressive business behind for something that might result in his death. An article in the *Kildare Observer* read:

> If England wins with her present army and navy then she wins without the assistance of the 'respectables' (middle classes). No doubt the middle class will be overjoyed in one sense at this result. Will it feel, in the stocktaking which must follow the war, that it has acted creditably? Will it feel comfortable in going into the streets and cheering with those who have won?[18]

According to statistics published in the Irish media there were 119,000 farmers' sons and 79,000 labourers eligible for service and recruiters were asking for 50,000 of them to fill up the ranks of the Irish regiments.[19] The following extract from a recruiting meeting at Monasterevan in the month of February 1916, published in the *Kildare Observer*, reflected the general feeling of many at the time: 'The labouring class have done remarkably well, and the gentry have also done their bit. But there are two classes still that did not do their bit – the farmers' sons and the young commercial men.'[20] However, in the same breath the *Observer* reported that a few farmers' families had rallied to the colours and that four Spooner brothers had joined the Army, and handed over the management of their 160-acre farm to Messrs Goff and Co., Newbridge, until they came back.[21] Apart from recruiting advertisements the local newspapers also carried list of casualties and accounts of the carnage at the Front – hardly an incentive to join the colours.

Some districts had a high percentage of recruits and in the Athy district alone – which included Grangemellon, Kilberry, Ballaghmoon, Castledermot, Johnstown, Kilkea, Moone, Fontstown, Kilrush, Monasterevan, etc. – it was said that up to mid-1915 over 800 men had already joined the colours. Chairman of Kildare County Council, M.J. Minch, said that the county had done very well in contributing recruits and,

> … taking the district of Athy alone over 800 men have already joined the colours from the district. So far as I can see there are few men that are eligible to join the colours who are free at the present time.[22]

In Celbridge, Sergeant Moore, RIC, told the *Freeman's Journal* that a list published by a local committee at the opening of the war showed that fifty men had immediately joined up, but since then at least 150 had followed suit. He said that almost every available man in the Celbridge, Maynooth and Leixlip district had answered the call without the aid of recruiting meetings. Sgt. Moore said that four young men from one Celbridge household were serving, while three each from four other houses in the district had enlisted. He said: '… perhaps in no other district of its size in Ireland has there been such a spirited response to the call of the army as shown by Celbridge.'[23] Landowner Colonel Claude Cane, of St Wolstan's, Celbridge, reaffirmed this point with a statement the following week: 'Celbridge has as good a record as any place of its size in the United Kingdom.'[24]

The CCORI was established to extend the recruiting programme and more specifically to tap areas in Ireland that had previously provided few recruits. A key part of this process was encouraging civilian effort in support of the voluntary recruiting campaign. The council used large-scale recruiting tours to spread its message and relied on star speakers such as Tom Kettle, a former Home Rule politician and member of the Irish Volunteers, and Michael O'Leary, winner of the Victoria Cross.[25] The 1915 recruitment drive appeared to have some success during the first eight months of the year when from January–August 37,000 men enlisted. However, the rate then fell, with only 12,000 men enlisting from September 1915–March 1916.[26] It was deemed a quite successful year as 689 men from Kildare joined the British army in 1915 – the second highest recruitment rate in Leinster – Dublin being the highest, with 12,529 recruits. Of the 689 Kildare recruits 390 were known to be members of the National Volunteers. The men were predominantly Catholic – 611 Catholics to seventy-eight Protestants.[27]

Two recruiting topics used by recruiters under the aegis of the CCORI were the idea that Ireland could be united and reports of atrocities from 'gallant little Belgium'. The first stories of German atrocities appeared in Irish newspapers on 20 August 1914, although massacres of civilians and burning of towns had begun on the second day of the Belgium invasion. In late August German troops killed 248 civilians and burned down 2,000 buildings, including the renowned university and library, in Louvain, a town with a centuries-old association with Irish Catholicism. The atrocity reports included lurid stories of impaled babies, mutilated children and murder and rape of members of religious orders. One particular recruiting speech told of the 'absolute fact that at the present time there are in or near Dublin fourteen Belgian refugee nuns who are about to become unwilling mothers following German soldiers ravages while marching on Belgium'. This statement was untrue, but at the time it certainly served its purpose; to rouse its listeners into joining the British army in defence of the nuns and in the defence of Catholicism. These horrific stories were published to create a sensation and motivate men to defend those less fortunate than themselves.[28] When the German army did commit atrocities the stories were greatly exaggerated. Soldiers repulsed by stiff Belgian resistance vented their frustration and shot civilians out of hand in the first days of the war. Men, women and children, of all ages, were accused of helping their troops and betraying German positions or taking an active part in the 'Belgian resistance'. In total 6,427 Belgian and

French civilians are known to have been deliberately killed by the German army during their 1914 operations. Only a handful were clergy, killed along with their congregation.[29]

Many men returning from the Front in late 1914 and early 1915 spoke of German barbarity towards civilians. Few, if any, witnessed such incidents. According to the *Kildare Observer* Lce. Cpl. James Moran (Timahoe), home on leave from the Western Front, confirmed the stories of German atrocities. However, no detail was given in the report.[30] Michael White (Rathasker Road, Naas) was wounded in the fighting at Cambrai in late August 1914. While hospitalised in a converted church Pte. White witnessed a German aeroplane dropping 'a black disc suspended by a cord over the church for the purpose, I suppose, of giving the range to the artillery. A few minutes later the steeple of the church came tumbling down and some French doctors and nuns were killed amongst others. This is not hearsay, as I saw it with my own eyes.'[31]

German action on the high seas had a more shocking effect. The sinking of the *Lusitania* in May 1915 by a German submarine off the coast of Ireland outraged the Irish, British and American public. Coming only three years after the tragic sinking of the *Titanic*, the attack on the *Lusitania* seemed like a re-enactment of the natural disaster. In what the *Kildare Observer* called Germany's 'crowning act of barbarism' by firing on a non-military ship without warning, the Germans had breached the international laws known as the Cruiser Rules.[32] Although the Germans had reasons for treating the *Lusitania* as a naval vessel, including that the ship was carrying war munitions and that the British had also been breaching the Cruiser Rules, the sinking caused a storm of protest in the United States. The continuation of unrestricted attacks on US shipping also influenced the decision by the US to declare war on Germany in 1917. Of the 1,959 passengers and crew aboard *Lusitania* at the time of the sinking, 1,195 lost their lives, including 128 Americans and eighty children.[33] Among the survivors of the disaster was a young man named Thomas McCormack, a native of Killina, Robertstown. Being a good swimmer he made no effort to reach any of the lifeboats, leaving space for the women and children. Shortly before he was rescued McCormack noticed that the greater number of those who were floating about in life-belts, especially women and children, were either dead or dying. He kept afloat for about an hour-and-a-quarter until he found a lifebelt and was then rescued by a trawler.[34]

There are no statistics to show whether the sinking of the *Lusitania* had any effect on Irish recruitment. As in Britain recruitment slackened off during the summer and autumn of 1915, followed in winter by a brief recovery attributable to more effective co-operation between the Irish Party, the Irish Executive (under Lord Wimborne) and the CCORI. However, by October 1915 serious rumours of conscription circulated throughout Britain and Ireland, because the voluntary system could no longer live up to former expectations.[35] Nevertheless, the recruiters continued their work. The O'Mahony, Colonel St Leger Moore, Judge Wakely, Charles Colley Palmer and other prominent gentlemen addressed a recruitment meeting beside Carbury Castle. Col. Moore said he was proud of Kildare and proud of the share Kildare men had taken in the war. Within an eight-mile radius of his home there had been fifteen officers killed or wounded, and forty-nine men were at the Front. The O'Mahony pointed out that of the 125,000 Irishmen in the British army, 26,000 of them were National Volunteers who had answered John Redmond's call. As a nationalist he had fought the British government all his life, but this time the British government was in the right and the Irish people always stood with those in the right, he said. The chairman of the meeting, Charles Colley Palmer, said that Belgium had been cultivated like a garden before the 'dreadful' Germans invaded, but now many of its fine churches were in ruins. He said that if the Germans came to Ireland they would treat the Irish worse than the Belgians, because of the resistance put up by the Irish regiments in combat. Mr Palmer added that his eldest son was a major in the army and his grandson was in the Inniskilling Dragoons. He gave the use of the local courthouse for recruiting purposes, but only two volunteers came forward as a result of the meeting.[36]

In total 46,000 men enlisted in Ireland in 1915. Terminal decline ensued in early 1916, and by April the daily rate of enlistment had fallen below sixty. These fluctuations applied in both Ulster and the southern provinces, as well as in Britain. Until early 1916, when conscription was applied to Britain but not Ireland, the daily rate of enlistments in Ireland followed almost the same curve as that for the army overall. Enthusiasm for the war was never as great in Ireland as it was in Britain as only about 10 per cent of Irishmen of a military age went to war, compared with about 25 per cent in Britain. Many believed that Ireland should remain neutral, and even before the Easter Rebellion recruitment had begun to decline. In government circles the problem of Irish recruitment was becoming one of general concern. Only 19,000 men enlisted in 1916; 14,000 in 1917; and fewer than 11,000 in 1918. By then the country was not providing enough recruits to replace the casualties in Irish regiments. Many Irish battalions were disbanded or amalgamated for want of men. The only alternative seemed to be to extend conscription to Ireland.[37]

One of the largest recruiting meetings was held at Newbridge on the evening of 31 January 1916. Mr T. O'Connor, J.P., Chairman of the Town Commission, presided. Sir Keith Fraser made a vigorous appeal to men to come forward and keep up the strength of the Irish regiments. Several officers and enlisted men were on hand to appeal to the crowd to join the ranks, but it was local man, Captain Joseph Henry Greer of Curragh Grange, who got the loudest cheer. In his short address Capt. Greer said that the officer who had recommended Michael O'Leary for the Victoria Cross was his son, Eric Beresford Greer. It was reported that a large number of recruits were enrolled for service.[38] (Lieutenant Francis St Leger Greer, 2nd Irish Guards, was killed in action, on 1 February 1917, aged twenty-three. He was a recipient of the Military Cross. His brother, Lieutenant-Colonel Eric Beresford Greer, 2nd Irish Guards, was killed in action on 31 July 1917. He had been awarded the Military Cross and the 1914 Star.[39])

Barbara Synnott, a member of the landed gentry, undertook a personal recruiting drive at the request of the Central Recruiting Office. She decided to help the war effort by participating in the recruitment campaign because she was of good social standing in Co. Kildare, having lived at Furness, Clane, with her husband, Nicholas, a local administrator involved in various public works, since 1898. Barbara maintained a diary of her recruiting drive from 24 January to 2 February 1916. She had a slightly optimistic view about some of the men she interviewed, and a tendency to describe those who would not volunteer as being in favour of conscription. It was her lack of insight into the minds of the men she canvassed that led to the failure of Barbara Synnott's recruiting drive. As far as can be ascertained from her diary she did not succeed in persuading any men at all to enlist. She called to the homes of many potential recruits in the Naas, Kill, Rathmore and Furness areas and spoke to over seventy men, urging them to enlist. Two or three men did make unsuccessful attempts to join up. The abrupt ending of her diary on 2 February 1916 seems to signal the end of the recruiting drive.

The excuses of those canvassed were many. One said he would rather see his son shot by the Germans at his own door than let him go to the Front where so many were killed at once. Another said his mother needed him on the farm. Barbara Synnott had difficulty locating some of the men on her list. One potential recruit said he did not 'wish to join because he was afraid of the bullets & the bayonets' and had never fired a gun in his life and had no desire to do so. He was not the only honest man. A farmer said he had odd jobs to do and did not want to leave his wife, but recommended that the recruiters should take 'another fat farmer's son' working farther up the canal. Several men gave no reason why they would not enlist; a few said they would wait until they were conscripted. It was quite obvious that there were many men in a county deemed to be loyal who were not interested in any way in joining the British army.[40]

The *Kildare Observer* editorial of 5 February 1916, in noting that there were many men of military age in Naas who had neither received official circulars or being canvassed personally, said: 'That the time will come when, as in England, every man will be compelled to do the duty he has so far shirked...' The editorial asked if the old Irish spirit of generosity, justice and heroism was still evident. It was, but to a lesser extent.[41] A certain war weariness had set in. The casualty lists were too long and so many young men had disappeared forever from the landscape with very little gain. The battles at Loos and Ypres in 1915 and the disastrous Dardanelles campaign had decimated the Irish battalions.

The last British and Dominion troops evacuated the Gallipoli peninsula on the 7/8 January 1916 after enduring an eight-month campaign in which they suffered 198,340 casualties. The 10th Irish Division alone suffered 2,017 fatalities at Gallipoli.[42]

The Easter Rising and its aftermath also contributed to a fall-off in recruitment in Kildare and the rest of the country. About a dozen local men were arrested in the days following the rebellion and the MPs for the county, John O'Connor and Denis Kilbride (IP) sent a letter to the Provost Marshal asking for their release: 'The county did well for the army … and I assure you the continued internment of the Kildare men is making our position more difficult.' O'Connor quoted one of his constituents, an instructor in the National Volunteers, who said that of the 125 men in the Volunteers from Robertstown, Littletown and Allenwood, eighty-five of them had joined the army and that a district that had done so well should be entitled to some consideration.[43]

In Lord Wimborne's report on recruiting issued in January 1916 the figures given were that there were 20,708 Irishmen serving in the British army prior to the outbreak of war. After the declaration of war 17,804 reservists and 12,462 special reservists rejoined, making a total on mobilisation, of 51,046. Subsequently three new divisions of twelve battalions each were organised, making, with the original ten battalions of the regular forces, a total of fifty-two Irish battalions.[44]

It was felt that the country could contribute more men, and statistics compiled by the Registrar-General of the number of men of military age afforded an interesting study. The total number of men of military age was 547,827, of which 245,875 were indispensable for purposes of labour; 33,221 had joined the armed forces since the date of the National Register (1915); and 107,492 were returned as physically unfit. It was estimated that 161,239 men were available for military service, but only 130,241 had so far joined up by November 1916. The total number of men of military age in Leinster was 101,936. The proportions of enlistment in Leinster since the outbreak of the war in comparison with the number of military age was 25 per cent and in Co. Kildare – the highest figure – it was 20 per cent, higher even than the Dublin area, which stood at 16 per cent. Of the 8,275 men on the register in Co. Kildare, 3,436 had been estimated as indispensable for labour; 537 had joined the armed forces since the date of the National Register; the number given as physically unfit was 1,791, leaving the number still available for service as 2,581. Kildare topped the list of Leinster counties with regard to the number enlisting since the date of the register.[45]

This new drive for recruits proved a colossal effort to avert conscription in Ireland. However, very few recruits actually came forward in the first weeks following this surge. By 1917 figures prepared for the Cabinet showed that the percentage of male population represented by enlistment was down to 4.96 per cent in Ireland, compared to 17 per cent in England, Scotland and Wales.[46] But whereas the government had introduced conscription in Britain, it did not dare do so in Ireland, especially as the public mood had changed following the Easter Rising. After the huge casualties of the summer and autumn of 1916 the three Irish divisions failed to replace men who had fallen. Their ranks were replenished with British conscripts. Numerous other Irish battalions experienced losses and recruitment problems. Their ranks, too, were topped up with British conscripts. Ireland had been exempted from the Military Service Acts of January and April 1916, but in 1918 in their relentless search to fill the gaps in the ranks a further Military Service Act enabled conscription to be introduced in Ireland by proclamation.[47] This was another political blunder by a government that was out of touch with events in Ireland. The 'conscription crisis' produced massive popular protests and united all strains of Irish nationalism in one camp.

5 1916: KILDARE REBELS

Captain A. E. Warmington (Naas) was killed in Dublin during the Easter Rebellion. Photo: Brian Munnelly.

THE YEAR 1916 was seen as a pivotal year, one when the armies of Britain, France and Germany were bled white, one that saw two of the most decisive battles of the war – Verdun and the Somme. In Ireland 1916 was also a crucial year, when an armed insurrection against British rule was staged in Dublin during Easter week. The Easter Rising was mounted by Irish republicans with the aims of seceding from the union of Great Britain and Ireland and establishing an independent Irish Republic.

Nationalists formed the Irish Volunteers in November 1913 in response to the formation of the Ulster Volunteer Force which had been organised in January 1913 to prepare for defence against the implementation of Home Rule. In mid-November 1913 the socialist James Connolly called upon his fellow trade unionists to form a military force to protect workers in the Dublin Lock-out. The outcome of his proposal was the Irish Citizen Army, a band of around 200 members who were mainly socialists and trade unionists.[1]

With the formation of the Irish Volunteers there was a major revival of nationalist feeling in Kildare. Units of the Irish Volunteers were organised in nearly every parish in Co. Kildare during the early months of 1914; the first units being formed in Naas, then Athy and Monasterevin. By August the strength of the Volunteers in the county had increased to 6,000 and a County Kildare Committee for the Irish Volunteers was then founded. The first meeting of the Committee of the Irish Volunteers was held in the Town Hall, Naas on 26 August 1914. The attendance comprised representatives from most of the units in the county.[2]

The increase in nationalist activity alarmed the British, but with the outbreak of war in Europe that same month the attention of the military establishment was directed towards preparation for combat. Home Rule was suspended until the war was over and in September John Redmond, MP, called upon the Irish Volunteers to come to the assistance of Britain by joining the British army, a proposal rejected by militant nationalists. The Irish Volunteers split, with the majority following Redmond and becoming known as the National Volunteers. The minority, dominated by the Irish Republican Brotherhood (IRB), kept the title of Irish Volunteers and began preparing for an insurrection while Britain was fighting in Europe. Only five Kildare companies, Naas, Maynooth, Kill, Prosperous and Athgarvan, remained loyal to the Irish Volunteers. The auxiliary organisations, Cumann na mBan and Fianna Éireann, which largely supported the dissidents, also became involved in preparations for an insurrection.[3]

In early 1916 a meeting was held in Michael O'Kelly's home at Gleann na Greine, Naas, to prepare for local action in support of a general rising planned for Easter week. Instructions had been received from Volunteer General Headquarters that the Kildare units were to be 'used as outpost groups between the Curragh Camp and Dublin when the outbreak took place'. Kildare volunteers had been assigned the crucial task of preventing British troops from the Curragh reaching Dublin. GHQ expected the Kildare volunteers to provide 100–150 men to demolish railway lines, roads and other communications, such as telegraph and telephone wires between Dublin and the Curragh. The RIC barracks at Sallins and Kill were also to be attacked, but as there were only five understrength companies in the area that plan was abandoned. The main plan was to destroy the railway-bridge over the canal outside Sallins to prevent troops from the Curragh getting to Dublin. Once these objectives had been completed the Kildare Volunteers were to march to Dublin to join the rebels. On 19 April, Tom Byrne, an ex-soldier with military experience from the South African War, brought news from Dublin that a nationwide rising was to take place on 23 April at 6 p.m. The 'manœuvres', however, were unexpectedly cancelled.[4]

Despite this, many men mobilised with their individual companies, but stood down in the confusion. The Maynooth Company mobilised and after getting word of the Rising, its commanding officer, Domhnall Ua Buachalla, led a thirteen-man contingent from Maynooth to Dublin to take part in the fighting. On Tuesday morning of Easter Week the fourteen Kildaremen marched in formation down into the city and when they came in sight of the General Post Office (GPO), in Sackville Street, there was a great cheer, as the men there had been expecting them. Rebel leaders Pádraig Pearse and James Connolly greeted them at the door. The men were given tea, eggs and cigars and according to Tom Harris (Prosperous), were addressed by Connolly, who said, 'It didn't matter a damn if we were wiped out now as we had justified ourselves.' Patrick Colgan (Maynooth), recalled: 'We entered the GPO by the main entrance. Comdt. General Connolly was at the door. As we entered he shook each of us by the hand and smiled his welcome to us.'[5]

In Dublin the Irish Volunteers and the Irish Citizen Army began the Easter Rising at noon on Easter Monday, April 24, when they commandeered dozens of buildings and positions throughout the city. Eoin MacNeill's countermanding order caused as much confusion there as in the countryside and only around 1,600 men, women and children mobilised for action. From the steps of the commandeered GPO President of the Provisional Government, Pádraig Pearse, read the Proclamation that he had helped compose, announcing the setting up a provisional (temporary) government.[6]

The Maynooth volunteers fought in the GPO and in outlying defensive posts at Parliament Street; other Kildare volunteers fought elsewhere. George Geoghegan, a bandsman in the Citizen Army, was killed in the fighting at Dublin Castle. He was a thirty-five year-old married man with three children. Born at the Curragh, he lived at Cork St, Dublin, and was employed at the

Inchicore Railway Works. However, the majority of Kildare casualties were members of the British forces. Reserve battalions from several Irish regiments were used in the first few days of the fighting and as British reinforcements rushed into the city Captain Alfred E. Warmington, (Naas) serving with the 10th Royal Irish Regiment, was one of the first fatal casualties of the Rising. He was shot dead on Easter Monday in the fighting at the South Dublin Union. Thirty-five officers and men from Irish units in the British army were killed during the Dublin fighting. Among them was Private James Duffy (Carrisvilla, Co. Kildare), 3rd Royal Irish Regiment, who was mortally wounded on the first day of the Rising, while Private William Mulraney (Hodgestown, Donadea), 8th King's Royal Irish Hussars, was another fatality.[7]

Violent street fighting continued until the afternoon of 29 April when Pádraig Pearse offered to surrender his forces to spare the people of Dublin further bloodshed. At 3.30 p.m. Pearse met Brig.-Gen. Lowe at the top of Moore Street. Captain Henry Eliardo de Courcy Wheeler, of Robertstown, who was serving on the Curragh with the Army Service Corps, accompanied Gen. Lowe. Capt. Wheeler, a Kildare native, was the son of Surgeon William de Courcy Wheeler, who was on duty at Dublin's Mercer's Hospital during the Rising. Pearse was driven to a meeting with Gen. Maxwell where he signed the surrender document. Capt. Wheeler accompanied Elizabeth O'Farrell, who had served as a courier and nurse for the GPO garrison, to Moore Street with Pearse's order to surrender.[8]

Around 450 people died in the Easter Rising; eighty rebels, including fifteen executed, 132 military and police, and around 240 civilians.[9] Forty of the dead were children, and coupled with the point that many families had men serving overseas with British forces it was understandable that the populace of Dublin were angry. One of the most tragic stories of the event concerned John Francis Foster, age two years and ten months, who was killed by a stray bullet, while in his pram near Father Matthew Hall, on Church Street, Dublin, on Easter Monday, 24 April. He was one of the first victims of the Rising and his death certificate said: 'Shot through the head at the level of the ears.' His mother Catherine 'Kate' Foster (née O'Neill), 18 Manor Place, Stonybatter, Dublin, was present when the youngster was killed. This was the second tragedy in the family, as the child's father, Rifleman John Foster, (a native of Dowdenstown, Ballymore Eustace) serving with the 1st Royal Irish Rifles, had been killed in action at Auber's Ridge, France on 9 May 1915.[10]

The *Kildare Observer* carried several editorials condemning the Rising, while those of the *Leader* and the *Nationalist* were more sympathetic. On 2 May 1916 the *Observer* printed a special edition of the paper to cover the Rising. Their 'Special Correspondent' reported that:

> All other means of transport being denied me I set forth for Dublin from Naas on Sunday morning, having seen the telegram from the Castle to the Naas police confirming the reported surrender of the rebels. I was informed under these circumstances that I should very probably require no passport to enable me to enter the city, and therefore did not even take the precaution of bringing documents that would prove my identity to the satisfaction of anyone challenging my bona-fides. En route I met many cyclists and pedestrians coming from the direction of the city but none seemed to know anything definite about the situation there. I first questioned a couple of cyclists near Clondalkin. They told me that the fighting was still 'terrible'.

The reporter ventured into the city and was given a pass by the military at a checkpoint at Dolphin's Barn. He visited most of the battle sites and reported that snipers were still firing at the military. The *Observer* editorials took a pro-British stance and expressed outrage at the betrayal of the soldiers at the Front and at the disruption of trade and commerce.[11] The *Leinster Leader*'s attitude to the rebellion was at first one of horror, but this soon turned to sympathy. The *Leader* placed the blame for the Rising on the Unionists in the north who had spurned constitutional methods. The editor and two other members of staff were arrested in the first week of May and taken to the military barracks in Naas. Seumus O'Kelly, then living back in Naas because of ill-health, temporarily assumed editorship of the *Leader*.[12]

There was very little sympathy with the rebels in the chamber of Kildare Co. Council, Mr John Healy proposed the following resolution:

> That we, the members of the Kildare Co. Council, strongly deprecate the recent deplorable action of a section of our countrymen in resorting to force of arms. At the same time we strongly appeal in what we consider the best interests of this country and the Empire as a whole to the Government to extend the greatest possible clemency to the rank and file, who, we believe, were deceived into taking part in the rising. That we take this opportunity of again recording our unabated confidence in Mr J. E. Redmond and the Irish Parliamentary Party, and thoroughly endorse the attitude they adopted during the crisis we are passing through.[13]

In the ruined capital there was little sympathy either for the rebels as they were marched away to captivity. Amongst those who jeered and spat at the prisoners were the Dublin separation women. This group of Dubliners were bitterly hostile to the rebels and British soldiers had to literally defend the volunteers from physical violence. Both the rebels and the military had strict policies against looting and several civilians had been shot by both sides in the act. The great majority of civilian casualties, however, had been caused by military action – indiscriminate bombing and shooting. Nevertheless, the separation women vented their anger at republicans only, and it is understandable why. Many of the women were wives, widows, sisters or mothers of British soldiers and while their menfolk were fighting and dying at the Front 'these Sinn Féiners' had stabbed them in the back.[14]

Between 3 May and 12 May fifteen rebel leaders were shot, including all seven who had signed the Proclamation. The fact that these executions took place so quickly – the first only two days after the last rebel surrender – and then were dragged out over ten days had a powerful effect on public opinion. The Rising had angered most Irish people, but the executions turned their anger gradually against the government and produced more sympathy in the country than the actual events themselves. It also slowed down recruitment to the British army. At a meeting of the Naas Board of Guardians Michael Gogarty refused to endorse a resolution from New Ross Board of Guardians, until it was amended. Gogarty said:

> Now when the thing has come like a blaze and has been damped out, the extreme penalties meted out by those in whose hands the power has been placed has shocked a number of people outside of this miserable organisation. When other rebellions arose – when England was engaged in the war and a rebellion arose in South Africa it ended with one man being executed. Here, in Ireland, twelve men have already paid the penalty of death, and think now the manner in which the people of Ireland have sincerely supported England in her hour of trouble this is no time for vengeance on a poor and misguided body. If they proceed as they have begun they will sow the seeds of another rebellion, and it is the same sad story over again. In the past when misguided men risked their lives as in vain an attempt as this has been, the stories of the awful punishment meted out to them have lived long in the memory of the people, and I therefore ask that this resolution will recite our expression of the help that mercy will be shown, now that the country has settled and the blaze has been extinguished.

The New Ross resolution was rewritten and passed by the Naas Board of Guardians. It said:

> That this Council desires to express its strongest condemnation of the wickedness and insanity of the recent rising of Sinn Féiners in Ireland, and that it heartily approves of the attitude of Mr John E. Redmond and the Irish Party, and reiterates its complete confidence in them, and trust that Mr Redmond will continue his efforts in securing clemency for those misguided

Irishmen who took part in the unfortunate business.

It was decided that copies should be sent to MPs John Redmond and John O' Connor. Joseph Dowling said, 'Send it to the Lord Lieutenant, as he is the man when we are asking for leniency.' Michael Gogarty, expressing the mood prevalent in the country, replied: 'We are not asking for it, we are demanding it.'[15]

Some days after the Rising Michael O'Kelly was in a group of prisoners who were marched to the East Wall to be deported to England. By this stage public opinion had changed considerably and onlookers shouted greetings and threw packets of cigarettes to the prisoners. Patrick Colgan also experienced the same mood from civilians and said there were many who acted in a friendly way. The effects of martial law had taken their toll on public support and even loyal citizens needed a written permit to go about their business. As suspected republicans were arrested and marched away under armed military guard sympathy began to swing in their favour.[16]

There was, of course, little or no sympathy for the rebels at the Front. The Royal Dublin Fusiliers had suffered particularly badly during the same week as fighting erupted in the Irish capital. Fourteen men from Co. Kildare were killed at the Front from 25–29 April, ten of them serving with the 8th and 9th Royal Dublin Fusiliers.[17] These units were subjected to a German gas attack at the Battle of Hulluch, near Loos on 27 April, suffering heavy casualties. This was the 16th (Irish) Division's first real test of battle. The morning was dry and warm with a moderate easterly wind; perfect conditions for a gas attack.[18]

Casualties were horrendous. Lieutenant Wallace Lyon, of the 7th Leinsters, was given the gruesome duty of collecting and burying the dead. 'They were in all sorts of tragic attitudes, some of them holding hands like children in the dark.' He arranged for the burial of sixty corpses in one large shell hole. Lyon and his men found themselves pestered for the next five days by 'half-poisoned rats by the hundred'.[19] Lt. Charles Weld (Downings, Prosperous), 7th Leinsters, said: 'It was a ghastly sight. Hundreds of men who were gassed lay three deep in the firing step. They had died in terrible agony with faces all purple from the gas. Many others not yet dead gasping out green foam. This is about the most fearful sight I have yet seen.'[20]

Two days later, on the morning of 29 April, the Germans launched another attack under cover of a heavy gas release on the Hulluch front. The Irish lost 100 killed and 180 were wounded before the wind changed and brought the gas back over the German lines where it inflicted greater casualties. The 8th Royal Dublin Fusiliers alone lost 183 men killed in the two attacks. The high rate of casualties was blamed on the 'bad gas discipline' of the Irish troops. One officer claimed Irish soldiers cut holes in their masks so they could smoke their pipes. English and Scottish senior officers said the Irish were too wild and their gas discipline lax. However, the gas sack helmets used at the time were of inferior quality and would only reduce, not prevent, the possibility of asphyxiation and many of the dead were found with their gas masks on.[21]

Shortly afterwards, the Germans, in front of the 8th Royal Munster Fusiliers, erected placards in connection with the Easter Rising to taunt the Irish troops. The Munsters reportedly responded by singing 'God Save the King', and later that night raided the enemy trench and brought back the offending placards in triumph.[22] The British authorities, however, tried their best to contain news of the Rising. All army leave to Ireland was stopped on 27 April, while mail from home with news of the Rising was possibly censored. But the Irish at the Front were soon aware of the events of Easter Week.[23]

The *Kildare Observer* printed a letter detailing an unnamed Naas soldier's opinion of the rebels and the Easter Rising, headlined as 'A voice from the trenches':

> Private W._____, writing to a friend in Naas, says;-
> B.E. Force, France
> 6th May, 1916
> Dear Jim, - Just a few lines hoping they will find you in the best of health. I am still in the pink and on the land of the living. I have just arrived at the base, but expect to go up the line again soon; we don't know the day, nor yet the hour, but hope to have a few weeks here. We are just beginning to have the fine

weather here now, and it's near time it did buck up and give us a chance of finishing the war this summer. I believe from the way things are shaping, we intend to have a very good try of making a job of it this year. I for one hope it will be successful, as we are not very keen on sticking another winter in the trenches. What do you think of the Sinn Féiners. They are a right lot of rotters – after ruining Ireland. You should hear the boys out here 'giving out the pay' about them. It's a pity we could not get hold of at least a couple of thousand or so. I would guarantee them a rough half-hour, and a peep into Kingdom Come at the end of it. I believe, from the papers we see, that half the city is destroyed and can hardly ever be replaced. We have had no letters from there since it started, and I need not tell you all the boys are very anxious about their friends and relatives. I also hear that there are a lot of women and children killed. No death would be bad enough for the fellows who caused all this. How did it effect you in Naas? I suppose the shops are only allowed to open at certain times under martial law, but I hope things will resume their normal way in a few days time. If you can possibly do it, send me out a few papers about them. Thank God, the National Volunteers had more sense or we were done altogether. I hope its bad effect won't interfere with Home Rule...[24]

While many Irish soldiers had no sympathy with the rebels, when they heard of the executions of the leaders their views changed. Tom Barry, later an IRA leader, was serving in Mesopotamia when he heard of the Easter Rising. He later expressed what was perhaps the general feeling of Irish soldiers when he wrote: 'It was a rude awakening, guns being fired at the people of my own race by the same army with which I was serving.'[25]

Col. Anthony Weldon (Kilmoreney, Athy) was in command of troops in the administration area of Limerick and Clare during the Rising. A shrewd commander, he took precautionary measures designed to cope with an outbreak of rebellion, but carried out with the object of preventing irritation to 'law-abiding' citizens. In August 1916 at a meeting of Athy Poor Law Guardians, Sir Anthony explained that he had studied the mind-set of Irish revolutionaries in Limerick. The most unkind word he could say of them was that they were misguided. He did not say that they were rogues or traitors, merely from his point of view they were mistaken.[26]

Irish Guardsman Bill Dunne (Colbinstown) arrived in Dublin during Easter Week unaware of the uprising. He had been wounded in February 1916 and spent some time in a Scottish hospital before being discharged on home leave. Bill Dunne was surprised to find all the public houses closed during what would normally be trading hours. 'Any chance of a drink?' he asked a man he met outside one licensed premises. The man looked at Bill Dunne's uniform with an expression of incredulity and explained to him that all the pubs and shops were closed because of fighting in the city. 'The best thing you can do with that uniform on you is get out of the city as quick as possible,' he said. (Teenager Neville Fryday, home on leave and wearing his uniform, was not so lucky. He was shot dead in the city centre at the beginning of Easter Week.)

Bill promptly took his advice and was lucky to catch a train out of the city making his way to Colbinstown station.[27] His views on the Rising are unreported. Co. Kildare had witnessed little activity during the Rising, but arrests of suspected republicans continued throughout the weeks that followed until there were around two dozen men interned, prompting John O'Connor, MP, to visit some of them in Wakefield Jail, England. As the Naas Board of Guardians had condemned the Rising, but asked for clemency for the prisoners, he wrote to Mr Michael Gogarty, Poor Law Guardian, Naas, informing him of his visit and that he had asked the Provost Marshall, Richmond Barracks, to free certain prisoners as they were innocent of any part in the Rising.

> Sir, - I hereby report result of my visit yesterday to certain prisoners at Wakefield.
> Re Tim Dunne, James Dunne and Andrew Dunne, Dublin and

Allenwood. – Three brothers. Tim owns a barge and turf bank in Dublin, fetching turf from the Bog of Allen by canal. James and Andrew work their father's barge from bog with turf. Had come to Dublin with barge loaded, and were lodging with their brother when arrested. These men had nothing to do with the rebellion and should be released forthwith.

Re Nicholas Byrne, Naas. – A school teacher. Went to Teachers' Congress on Easter Monday; returned to Naas on Saturday; taught in school until following Friday; arrested. Manifestly could have nothing to do with rebellion.

John Fitzgerald, Newbridge. – Was at Newbridge Sunday, Monday and Tuesday; went to Curragh Camp Wednesday to work as bootmaker to the military; arrested. Had nothing to do with rebellion.

M. O'Kelly, Naas. – Editor 'Leinster Leader.' At home all the time of trouble. Had nothing to do with rebellion.

E. Moran, Lewis Moran, Ballysax. – Two brothers; arrested on 29th. Had nothing to do with rebellion.

Together with my colleague, Mr Denis Kilbride, MP for South Kildare, I ask for the release for these men above mentioned, as well as of all others from the Co. Kildare. It has been highly injurious to the cause of peace, contentment, and a growing loyalty that these arrests should have been made. The county did well for the army, and in this connection I enclose an extract from a letter received by me to-day by a constituent. For the present, the amazing stupidity of the Government has made recruiting impossible in our constituency, and I assure you the continued internment of the Kildare men is making our position more difficult.

I, therefore, with my colleague, appeal to you, even in the interest of the Government, to release all Kildare men without further delay, - I am yours faithfully,

John O'Connor

Copy of extract from letter mentioned above:

> Thank God, Sinn Féiners in this district are nil. I was the
> instructor of the National Volunteers here – 125 men from
> Robertstown, Littletown and Allenwood. Eighty-five young
> fellows of this number have joined the army. This is a record for
> a country district. We are all loyal followers of your party. These
> figures can be verified by the police. Surely such a district that
> has done so well is entitled to some consideration.[28]

Opposition to Government policy continued to grow, even from Redmond
and John Dillon, who expressed his admiration for the rebels in the House
of Commons. After a visit to Dublin Prime Minister H. H. Asquith sent the
Minister for Munitions, David Lloyd George, to Dublin to offer immediate
implementation of Home Rule to the leaders of the Irish Party. He proposed
that the Home Rule Act of 1914 should be brought into operation 'as soon
as possible' for the twenty-six counties, the six northeastern counties to be
excluded. This was officially a temporary arrangement, as understood by
Redmond. Lloyd George however gave the Unionist leader Edward Carson a
written pledge that Ulster would not be forced into a self-governing Ireland.
His intention was to see that neither side would find out before a compromise
was implemented. A modified Act of 1914 had been drawn up by the Cabinet
on 17 June. The Act had two amendments enforced by Unionists – permanent
exclusion and a reduction of Ireland's representation in the Commons. But
when Lord Lansdowne made it brutally clear in a speech on 11 July that
partition of the country would be 'permanent and enduring' Redmond
washed his hands of the proposals and accused the government of treachery.
He was left to nurse the belief that he had dealt the popularity of his party a
fatal blow, one which was decisive in sealing the future fortunes of the Home
Rule movement.[29]

When the proposals of partition and Lloyd George's double-dealing
became public knowledge nationalist feeling began to harden. Many public

bodies, including those in Co. Kildare, protested against the Home Rule proposal. Sympathy and support for the rebels continued to rise, and for most nationalists even Home Rule was no longer enough. At the same time news from the Western Front was grave. The Somme offensive of July 1916 was bogged down. While gaining a few yards the British army had suffered catastrophic casualties. On the first day of the offensive alone, they had lost 20,000 men. Thirty-three men from Co. Kildare lost their lives during July 1916 – fourteen on the first day of the Somme alone. In total 183 men from Co. Kildare died in 1916 compared to 220 in 1915, which was the worst year for Kildare servicemen. A further 187 died the following year in the horrific slaughter at Passchendaele, Messines and Cambrai.[30]

The reason the death toll for Kildaremen fell was quite simple: there were fewer and fewer men from the Short Grass at the Front. By mid-1916 there were fifty-four Irish infantry battalions on active service, but it was recorded that 45,000 men were needed to bring them up to strength. The solution was to disband the Irish divisions, amalgamate them, or reinforce them with English troops. Most of the proposals were politically sensitive and the army council decided to opt for the latter solution. In November 1916 the first draft of English recruits reinforced the 6th Royal Irish Regiment of the 16th Division. Irish recruitment was practically vanishing.[31]

In December 1916 John Redmond made an impassioned plea to Lloyd George, now prime minister, to release the prisoners as a Christmas gift to the Irish people. Bad publicity and the swing in public opinion forced the Government to reconsider their Irish policy and on 21 December an amnesty for the prisoners was declared. The return to the prisoners to Dublin on 23 December was in marked contrast to their deportation some months earlier. The men of Easter Week returned as heroes to a public whose attitude had completely changed. Domhnall Ua Buachalla, released from Frongoch Internment Camp in Wales, said, 'There was a noticeable change in the people now, and I received a royal welcome reception on reaching Maynooth.'[32] Within a year of the Easter Rising republican nationalism was to emerge as the leading force in Co. Kildare political life.

6 WAR PROFITS

Catherine (from Newbridge) and John Doyle (Royal Dublin Fusiliers) pictured c. 1915.
Photo: Veronica Heavey.

WARS COST MONEY and create great profits for suppliers of foodstuffs, livestock, machinery and armaments. Economically, the First World War created an impressive boom in Irish agricultural prices, and high profits in agriculturally derived industries. However, there was much resentment at the imposition of production quotas and the enforcement of tillage rather than pasture farming.[1]

The growth of capitalism in the late nineteenth century inevitably pushed the world towards state rivalry, imperialist expansion, conflict and war. Britain was no longer, as it had been in the mid-1800s, the 'workshop of the world', nor indeed its major import market. On the contrary; her relative decline was obvious. A number of competing national industrial economies now confronted each other. Under these circumstances economic competition became inextricably part of the political, even military, actions of states. States were obliged to guarantee the development of powerful national armaments industries to carry much of their technical development costs, and to see that they remained profitable. In the 1900s private armament producers accounted for 60 per cent of the supply contracts for the British armed forces. By 1914 Armstrong Whitworth armaments employed 20,000 men – or over 40 per cent of all metalworkers on Tyneside – at their main works in Newcastle, not counting those in the 1,500 smaller firms who lived by Armstrong's sub-contracts. In Germany Krupp, the major manufacturer of cannons, employed 70,000 in their works. These giant industrial concentrations thrived because of the armaments race of governments, leading one British journalist to call WWI the 'war of steel and gold'.[2]

The war also brought economic gains to Ireland. Between 1914 and 1918 Ireland, and indeed Kildare, experienced a period of unprecedented prosperity. Despite the huge loss of part of its population – through death and emigration – the war had huge beneficial effects on the Irish economy. Goods traditionally produced in and exported from Ireland were heavily in demand. The war not only provided more jobs, it created a generally favourable economic environment for Ireland. However, in the opening months of the war jobs were adversely affected. The Irish tourist industry was badly hit and Belfast shipbuilding suffered dislocation as reserve soldiers were called up and workers left for industrialised locations in Britain. Non-essential trades suffered most and unemployment was high in some quarters.[3] Agriculture, still the country's dominant economic activity and employing 43 per cent of the active population (52 per cent of males) at the time of the 1911 census, benefited from the temporary removal during the war of much of the foreign competition in the British markets. The German submarine campaign against Allied trade routes substantially increased shipping rates and made certain sea-lanes, particularly the Atlantic and the North Sea, physically hazardous. Because of this many of Ireland's traditional competitors, particularly those from Continental Europe, found it more difficult to supply the British market. Britain was forced to depend more on its own and Ireland's agricultural resources than it had before 1914.[4]

The cost of living rose sharply on the outbreak of war, as food prices quickly increased. In Belfast and Dublin the cost of a 4lb loaf of bread increased by a halfpenny between August and October 1914.[5] An immediate domestic impact of war was hardship. In addition to the call up of male breadwinners, short time, dismissals and lost wages, prices began an inexorable rise as the war economy took hold, demanding high production, long hours and fewer goods in an inflationary spiral. For many of the labouring class military service was a chance to escape from poverty and unemployment. While certain skilled soldiers could get up to 6s a day in the army, the basic pay for ordinary soldiers was 1s. The wages of most men was increased by the payment of at least one allowance. As an example an extra 6d a day was paid to those with special shooting proficiency, with the result that very few men received just the basic 1s and 1s 9d was closer to the norm. This amounted to wages of approximately 12s 3d a week. In addition boots, clothing and rations were provided, or allowances paid in lieu. At home the family's situation was further improved because the man of the house was not consuming food or adding to expenses at home, while his wife received 12s 6d a week, an extra 5s for one child, a second child 3s 6d, and the other children 2s. Separation allowances were paid to dependents of single men who had been earning a wage prior to enlistment. A pension was also payable in the event of a soldier being killed. The pay of enlisted men was a comparative pittance compared to officers. For example a subaltern got 7s 6d a day, a 2s lodging allowance and a field allowance of 2s 6d.[6]

The demands of the military, however, produced economic dividends of a sort. The mere fact that by April 1916 there were 150,000 Irishmen on active service, of whom two-thirds had joined up since August 1914, meant a considerable influx to Ireland of separation allowances and other remittances.[7] Poverty remained a scourge of the working class and the rural poor, but income for farmers, large and small, rose. Farmer, trader and manufacturer did well during the war years. The conflict boosted the agricultural economy and those involved in agriculture reaped considerable benefits. Working-class families bore the brunt of food shortages and increased prices as wages failed to keep pace with war–time inflation. By the end of the war food prices had doubled though agricultural produce was nearly double what it had been in 1913. This must be placed in the context of price and wage inflation.[8]

Increased food prices, especially on necessities – tea and bread – affected many and were exasperated by heavy taxation to fund the war. Food prices went up 'consistently and monotonously'. The increases were felt in Co. Kildare where the price of agricultural produce such as butter, milk and bacon increased considerably – butter had risen to 3*d* more per lb, in 1916, than one year previous. Eggs were beyond the reach of the ordinary person. The texture of bread changed considerably during the war to try and make it less expensive. From the beginning of 1917 white flour was largely substituted with whole grain and the Irish people objected strongly to this, believing the new bread to be inferior in taste and quality. Kildare people lamented the loss of the white loaf, and food scientists tried, in vain, to convince buyers that wholemeal bread was in fact more healthy than the white loaf. The authorities were determined to strictly enforce the law with regard to the sale of bread by weight and at Petty Sessions courts throughout the county 'bread prosecutions' were regularly heard.[9]

While news of the war dominated, ordinary life continued for the majority of Kildare inhabitants. The lot of the poor improved, but the cost of providing for them rose. At the finance meeting of the Naas Board of Guardians, held on 14 July 1915, the Clerk announced that the number of inmates in the workhouse during the week was 172 as against 226 for the corresponding period last year, a decrease of fifty-four. The general average of providing for an inmate was 8*s* 4*d* in contrast to 8*s* 11*d* in 1914; in the infirmary 6*s* 4*d* as against 4*s* 1*d* for the previous year; the fever hospital, 19*s* 3*d* against 14*s* 3*d*; in the hall, 8*s* 10*d*, as compared with 3s. The number in the infirmary was ninety-one as against 101 in 1914. The first item on the agenda was to consider the question of continuing the extra allowance of 1*s* per case, per week, to recipients of outdoor relief. There were 200 cases and the cost of the extra allowance was £10 a week. The Chairman, Mr Gogarty, said he did not know what the views of other members might be, but he felt that the extra sum allowed to outdoor relief recipients for some months past ought to be discontinued, taking into consideration the fact that they were now in the best season of the year, and later on there might be greater hardships.

He had noticed only that day that a War Savings Committee had been appointed for Ireland, whose duty it was to educate the public generally to the necessity of saving. Mr Wolfe said there was not as much fuel required at that time as at other periods of the year, and, further, people did not require as much food in the summer as in the winter. The Chairman said that if the extra allowance was taken off it could be introduced again around November. Mr Cusack said the people who were providing the relief were likewise affected. Mr Saunders likewise proposed that the extra relief be discontinued until November. Mr Shiel said there was too much employment in the country at that time for inmates to be worse off than they were. He said there were people in his district who were getting outdoor relief who could get work, but would not do it. Only the two voted for a proposal to continue the extra relief, and the original motion to discontinue the relief until November was therefore carried.

At the suggestion of the Government, an Irish War Savings Committee was formed in the summer of 1915, consisting of eleven members, one of whom was Matthew J. Minch, Chairman of Kildare Co. Council. (M. J. Minch had three sons in the service – one at Aldershot, in England, and two more serving with the Connaught Rangers.) The objects of the Committee were to impress on the public:

1. The necessity for effecting economies during the war.
2. The desirability of investing the results of these economies in the War Loan.

It was urged that if thrift was not exercised, the country would be impoverished at the conclusion of the war. The Committee said that any savings that could be made should be invested in the War Loan, of which a very large part would again circulate amongst the very classes to whom the appeal was made, much to their profit and advantage.[10]

Most sections of Irish industry also benefited from the war and the short-lived boom which succeeded it. Between 1914 and 1918 linen was in much demand for military purposes: tents, haversacks, towels, hospital equipment and aeroplane fabric. Shipbuilding also saw a great expansion during the war. The huge losses caused by the German U-boat campaign led to a substantial increase in the demand for replacement shipping. Five munitions factories were set up – in Cork, Galway, Waterford, and two in Dublin. Many food-processing industries, dairy products, biscuits, and flour milling also experienced a period of buoyant demand. The boom was admittedly not universal. The brewing and distilling interests were damaged by heavy increases in excise duty – thirteenfold in the case of beer, fivefold in the case of whiskey.[11] By 1918, Irish brewing output was half of what it had been in 1916. A belief that drinking was unpatriotic while there was a war on was central to this. In Britain war workers were deemed to be drinking too much and its effects were causing loss of production, due to absence, accidents, etc. Over indulgence and excessive drinking was frowned upon and consequently pub opening hours were reduced, beer was watered down, and the buying of a round of drinks was banned.[12]

In Kildare farming was of particular importance. As the largest earner in the county, farming was essential for the economic viability of Kildare. Political leaders and the media consistently called upon Irish farmers for increases in the amount of tilled land, citing the fact that the countries at war were amongst the world's greatest grain producers. For some years to come these countries would not be able to supply even their own wants but would have to depend on others for their necessities. Corn and flour prices would, of necessity, increase and farmers would be only acting in their own personal interest as well as that of their community in general by sowing as much wheat as they could and making immediate preparations for tilling more of their land. An extension of tillage would also solve the problem of the decline of pig raising in Ireland and confer many other benefits on the country.[13]

The statistical return for Co. Kildare in 1915 was up on previous years. The yield for turnips was 191,760 tons as against 162,150 tons in 1911; mangels 39,351 in 1915 against 37,021 in the previous year; cabbage yield in 1915 was 3,623 tons, while for 1914 it was 3,208 tons.[14] Land under tillage experienced a significant rise from 1916, but following persistent calls for increased tillage, the government finally decided to compel farmers by the introduction of compulsory tillage for Ireland in 1917. All occupiers in Ireland of ten acres or more of arable land were required to cultivate 10 per cent more of their plot than they cultivated in 1916.[15]

The tillage question continued to dominate, not alone among the farming community, but generally. In January 1917 a *Leinster Leader* reporter had a 'chat' with an unnamed prominent north Kildare farmer, who said:

> As far as I can see the farmers at present are prepared to fall into line and assist in the production of the necessary food stuffs. The matter has been brought home to them – the real necessity of tillage, and they are already making arrangements to break up in the coming spring such a proportion of their lands that they would not dream of doing only a few years ago. I have been speaking to several and the tillage spirit is being taken, I might say, in a pretty enthusiastic way by the average farmer. I hold, for instance, some 220 acres of land not far from the town of Kildare, and I was always accustomed to till of that ten to twelve acres every year, but I am tilling 20 acres at the very least this year.

The farmer said that if he could procure enough labour he would till 12.5 per cent of his land. He continued:

> From what I know the Kildare farmers are inclined to till and are very anxious to till, now that they see it will pay them to do so, while at the same time they will feel they are contributing to the common good. It has been brought home to the farmers that there is a certain duty required of them. They realise that if the land is not tilled to a far greater extent than formerly, not alone, will the people, especially, the poor of the towns suffer, but even the farmers will suffer if they do not do their duty as far as the tilling of the land is concerned.

He added that the farmers of Kildare 'will do all in their power in the year that has opened to provide all the food stuffs that can be expected of them'.[16]

The Department of Agriculture announced that the Tillage Order had been received as satisfactory as they hoped except for five counties, including Kildare, where 'there is something still to be desired'. However, Kildare was essentially a grazing county and was unequipped for extensive tillage. The North Kildare Farming Society argued that if grass land was to be broken up for tillage purposes a considerable number of tractors, ploughs and horses, along with men to operate them, would be needed. Because of the taking of horses for the army, animals suitable for this work were practically unavailable. Ploughs were also unprocurable. The Society secretary, Frederick Devere, wrote to the Chief Secretary asking for the release of horses which were not urgently required for military purposes to the Kildare farmers, but the reply was negative. Devere had earlier written to the Government and the Department of Agriculture informing them that if mares taken for military purposes were not replaced on Irish farms the horse-breeding industry would be in serious jeopardy. An offer to accept injured war horses was rejected by the Department of Agriculture, which was afraid of introducing equine disease to the country.

Implements for tillage were costly and many small farmers could not afford them. Some wealthier landowners ordered tractors on their own account, but there was also a shortage of machinery. At a meeting of the Co. Kildare Agricultural Committee in January 1917, Mr Synott drew attention to a report that the Government was making arrangements to provide farmers in England with the use of farm tractors and ploughs for tillage purposes. He asked why the needs and claims of Irish farmers who were trying to comply with the Tillage Order were being ignored. If England was to rely on Ireland for the production of an increased quantity of food then Irish farmers should also be supplied with machinery and transit facilities. Synott said:

> If the farmers of North Kildare are given reasonable facilities to overcome the extraordinary and exceptional difficulties in with which they are confronted, they will be found at least as willing as those of other parts of Ireland, to comply with the demand for the extension of tillage. Everywhere throughout the district the ordinary ploughs are to be seen at work, and their number

is only limited by the fact that more cannot be procured to perform the impossible.[17]

Kildare landowners and farmers were not found wanting in contributing to the Tillage Order. Small holders in the vicinity of Kill acquired 100 acres from Lord Mayo at a reasonable rent to cover tillage, grazing and meadow land, while Clongowes College broke up additional land for tillage, hiring a tractor from a South Kildare farmer to do so.[18] The year marked a revolution in the farming life of Co. Kildare – tractors appeared in many places for the first time. Despite misgivings by many farmers compulsory tillage actually provided more profit. Tillage prices were better than cattle prices, but until proved otherwise many farmers were reluctant to change. (When they did invest, few were unwilling to change back to their previous trade.) North Kildare was confined to grasslands, in striking contrast to the state of affairs prevailing in the south of the county. The land in South Kildare was lighter and more suitable for tillage, while that in the north of the county was heavier and more remunerative as grazing land. Many of the farmers in North Kildare had not fulfilled the requirements for the year, but the Tillage Order required an additional 5 per cent of tillage for the coming year. This left some with 15 per cent of tillage to be earned out in cases where none was undertaken the previous year – the full 15 per cent had to be undertaken in 1918 – where those who did the 10 per cent required of them in 1917 would have to do half as much more additional tillage during 1918. Some farmers had sowed wheat that failed and had to re-sow the land with oats. The year was not a good one for wheat and the experience in Kildare was not exceptional. However, some remarkable fields of wheat were grown in North Kildare, results which justified continuing the venture in 1918. The *Observer* noted that 'if the state of things agricultural that now prevails were instituted ten or twenty years ago in Ireland the country would have been the better for it'.[19]

Farmers were often in conflict with the government for its attempts at price control and the amounts and the method in which it paid farmers for their produce. A Requisition Order gave the military authorities power to requisition hay grown in excess of the producer's needs. In September 1915 the authorities commandeered upwards of 100 tons of hay from farmers in the Leixlip district. The authorities weighed the hay and the price given was £4 10s per ton; the hay was to be delivered to the North Wall, Dublin, no later than 1 October 1915. This practice was used only against farmers who were found offering hay for sale and who, upon inspection by government officials, were unable to show that they required their full crop for their own use.[20]

Because Britain imported two-thirds of its food Germany believed it could starve the British into submission. The German Admiralty Staff promised that Britain would have to sue for peace 'within five months', but their calculations were a little optimistic. Even though they were sinking 600,000 tons of shipping a month in 1916, the Germans had underestimated Britain's ability to expand their own wheat production, ration food in short supply and import food from its nearest neighbour.[21] By 1916 the German submarine campaign and naval requisitioning of most merchant vessels had cut Britain off from many of its traditional food suppliers, providing Irish farmers with the irresistible opportunity to make good profits. Ireland, though slightly affected by food shortages and rationing, prospered by providing Britain with food stuffs. By 1917 British and Irish producers supplied 90 per cent of the country's beef needs compared to 60 per cent before the war.[22] Exports to Britain of bacon resulted in major increases in the price of pork in Ireland per hundred weight, which rose from 88s 9d in 1916 to 151s 9d in 1919. Dairy was central to trade in the country. In general the price of milk, cheese and eggs experienced significant price rises during this time. Milk went from 4d per gallon in 1914 to 14d in 1920.[23]

Farmers, naturally, reaped the rewards generated by food scarcity and high prices. Irish producers were operating very much in a seller's market. The government attempted to control prices, but there is strong evidence that the regulation schemes were less successful in Ireland than in Britain. By 1918 over 90 per cent of pigs were being sold at above regulated price levels and in the case of beef the controls had broken down completely. The consequence was that agricultural prices rose consistently faster than the cost of living index. Furthermore one of the most important items of the farmer's expenditure, the annuity payments owed under the Land Acts, were fixed in money terms, and their real value was eroded by more than 50 per cent as a result of the wartime inflation.[24]

Attempts to restrict profiteering by controlling prices generally resulted in the rapid disappearance of some goods from the shops. Generally, price regulation in Britain had only a limited effect in curbing rent and price increases, and it was even less successful in Ireland.[25] In 1917 food shortages became so acute that the government attempted to restrict both prices and exports of certain products, like butter, which was prohibited from export. Serious food shortages developed in Ireland, especially of sugar, bread and potatoes. To prevent the exporting of potatoes from the country and to avert capitalists from cornering the supply and exploiting consumers the government fixed prices for potatoes at 115s per ton for the main crop, 120s for those delivered in February and March 1917 and 130s for the remainder.[26]

James Gaul (Fair Green, Naas), contractor for the supply of potatoes to Naas Workhouse, stated in January 1917 that in consequence of the fact that there were no potatoes for sale in Naas and the neighbouring markets and having no crop himself, he was unable to supply those ordered. He asked that he be relieved of his contract, adding that the price of potatoes had risen enormously since he was declared contractor at £5 per ton in March 1916 to more than 100 per cent. Gaul was relieved of his contract at the end of March 1917. He had been supplying eggs and chickens to the workhouse since at least 1909, and continued to do so. Owing to the failure of contractors to supply potatoes it became necessary to give the workhouse inmates bread in lieu.[27]

The Ministry of Food was set up in December 1916, but was largely ineffective until June 1917, when Lord Devonport was replaced as minister by Lord Rhondda. Alarmed by the appearance of food queues in many cities, the government introduced the rationing of sugar, and began to build up a system of regional and local food distribution. It was not until April 1918 that a nationwide system of meat rationing was in place, and only three months later that all basic food staples were being rationed. Britain faced a stark choice – grow more food or starve.[28] Allotments were also introduced, in Britain and Ireland, for the people to feed themselves. A meeting of

Naas No. 2 Rural District Council in March 1917 said they had only four applications for allotments, but no offers of land for such. One councillor said it was deplorable that 'Naas was surrounded by a ranch', but there was no land available for the people to till.[29]

Enforcement of marketing regulations was hampered by its inability to construct an effective system of control outside the cities, and by constant bickering between the Ministry of Food and the Irish Food Control Committee. Sinn Féin claimed in September 1917 that a famine was imminent. The republican organisation saw an opportunity to embarrass the government and mould their politics to reflect the everyday concerns of the people. Sinn Féin clubs, assisted by clergymen, carried out the supervision of local food supplies of which the government had proven itself incapable. By February 1918 Sinn Féin had set up food committees in several counties, which established markets selling cheap turf and potatoes to the working classes.[30]

Naas republicans bought a ton of 'Shamrock' potatoes from a local farmer at a price that would enable them to be retailed at 8d per stone. They rented the front room of Terence Mahon's licensed premises in Main Street, Naas, and installed scales, weights, scoops, etc. A few members of Sinn Féin were installed to weigh and sell the potatoes. The system adopted was that a purchaser would call to the Sinn Féin club rooms in the Town Hall where the quantity of potatoes required was paid for and a slip of paper showing the weight and price was duly given. This slip of paper was presented at the 'shop' and the potatoes handed over. When the poorer classes of the town heard of the prices there was a steady stream of customers calling to the Sinn Féin shop, including many separation women who were not particular friends of republicans.[31]

The authorities were quick to react, arresting several republicans involved. At Naas Petty Sessions court Michael O'Kelly and Alphonsus Sweeney, Naas, were charged under the Defence of the Realm Act with having, on 9 March 1918, sold potatoes by retail without having a licence from the British Food Controller. The same defendants, with the addition of Stephen Garry, James White and Thomas J. Williams, all of Naas, were charged with a similar offence on 16 March 1918. After the evidence was given Michael O'Kelly said, 'I do not recognise the jurisdiction of this court at all. I am a citizen and soldier of the Irish Republic, and don't recognise this court.' At the announcement of this statement there was loud clapping by his supporters in the court. O'Kelly in answer to a question by the justice, Lord Mayo, of why he was selling potatoes at 8*d* a stone, said the potatoes were being sold to the poor of the town without profit. Alphonsus Sweeney also declared he was a soldier of the Irish Republic and refused to recognise the court. Both were fined 10*s* plus costs or seven days' imprisonment. O'Kelly said he would not pay the fine as a protest, while Sweeney said he would not pay a fine to 'any British authority'.

In the second case James White, Stephen Garry and Thomas J. Williams were charged with a similar offence on 16 March and also fined 10*s*, plus costs or seven days' imprisonment. The cases were adjourned for two months with the undertaking that there would be no sales of potatoes by the defendants within that period, but orders for the payment of fines were made in all cases.[32] Some weeks later another republican, Christy Byrne, was also summoned, but this time the fine was increased to £2. A further batch of summonses were withdrawn as the shop had closed down. All the men concerned were sentenced to serve a week in Mountjoy Jail, Dublin.[33]

Fuel was also in scarce supply. The warring nations, like France and Germany, were not exporting coal, while Britain's coal production fell by 20 per cent.[34] Coal-mining had developed into an important local industry and a colliery operated at Mullaghmore, Wolfhill, in Queens County, which employed over ninety men. To increase output, 200 men were employed in the construction of a railway from Athy to the Wolfhill colliery, but in August 1917 they went on strike. The men were paid 6*d* per hour and some weeks earned 30*s* weekly. They complained that during 'wet time' they lost earnings and with the high price of food in the area they could hardly exist. Some of the men were from the west of Ireland and were housed and provided with beds by the Government. The men demanded 9*d* per hour, because of the shortage of labour for harvest work in the district workers could command 7*s* daily. The strikers were paid off on 16 August and marched through Athy in an orderly fashion, but work resumed at once with an agreement. By May

1918 bridges over the Barrow and the canal at Athy were complete, while a new station had been erected at Athy with engine sheds, platforms, sidings and signalling apparatus. The railway line took several more months before it reached the colliery.[35]

As the U-boat campaign began to impact on imports, Kildare experienced a fuel shortage with the price of coal beyond the means of many working-class people. There were many recommendations to conserve industry – kitchen fires in private homes should not be kept going all day; hall lights should be banned; no artificial light should be allowed to be used in shops after sundown during the operation of the daylight saving regulations; shop windows should not be lighted; church authorities should be asked to arrange for the holding of their services during daylight hours; places of amusement should be closed at or before 10 p.m. unless under special licence.[36]

The *Kildare Observer* of 1 June 1918 reported that many people in Newbridge were supplementing their supplies with turf and there was an increase of turf banks rented near Tankardsgarden. This was an example which might be followed by people in other parts of the county. Assuming that there would be a 50 per cent reduction in coal supplies it was calculated by the *Observer* reporter that twice that of turf would be needed to supplement coal supplies. The following month the media was highlighting the prospect of increased hardship because of the shortage of both coal and gas and reminding domestic users that if they had not made provision to purchase turf to tide them over the winter to do so immediately.[37]

The shortage of coal had a dreadful effect in the county when the Great Flu pandemic swept the land in the autumn and winter of 1918. Coupled with a shortage of gas and the reduction in the water supply these factors contributed to one of the country's highest death rates during the pandemic.

7

THE MEN WHO MARCHED AWAY

Lt. John Vincent Holland (Athy) won the VC at Guillemont in September 1916.
Photo: Kildare Collections and Research Services.

ONE OF THE obvious questions to be asked is 'Why did men volunteer to go to the war?' For the English volunteers patriotism is more usually seen as the typical motive. The Scots were the keenest to volunteer for war. By December 1915 just under 27 per cent of Scottish men, aged between fifteen and forty-nine had volunteered. In total 557,618 men from Scotland served. The Irish, by contrast, were relatively reluctant: only 11 per cent of those eligible enlisted willingly, though recruitment from the northeastern counties was proportionally higher.[1]

The British authorities were often critical of Irish recruitment and superficially at least, there was some ground for complaint. The initial rush to enlist quickly slackened and it became increasingly difficult to fill three Irish divisions (the 10th, 16th and 36th) and keep the dozens of other Irish battalions up to strength. From August 1914 to November 1918 140,456 men joined the British armed forces. At the outbreak of war there were already 20,000 Irishmen in uniform, while within days another 30,000 reservists returned to the ranks. In Britain thousands of Irish-born enlisted. Therefore, around

200,000 Irishmen served in the British forces during the war.[2] Australia, by contrast, with a population similar to Ireland contributed 421,000 men and was the only part of the Empire which did not need to resort to conscription. The Irish suffered 30,000 deaths, Australia 60,000.[3]

For Irish recruits the reasons for enlisting were varied. Idealism was one of the main reasons for many Irishmen saw themselves as subjects of the British Empire and were prepared to fight for king and country. Economics was another major motive. Urban recruiting was more successful than rural because there was less employment available for unskilled and semi-skilled workers. Politics was another motive as both Irish nationalists and unionists believed enlisting furthered their respective political agendas. Peer pressure could also be cited, as well as strong recruiting methods, and a proactive media campaign in Co. Kildare. The Kildare men who marched away to battle came from all walks of life. The majority were from the labouring class. The experiences of William Wilmot, Edward Reddy, James Rogers and John Holland are similar to those of men from all over Ireland. The only difference is that one of them, John Holland, won the Victoria Cross, Britain's highest award for bravery.

WILLIAM WILMOT, ATHGARVAN

On 26 March 1916 Private William Wilmot was killed in action while serving with the Irish Guards on the Western Front. Back home in Co. Kildare William's death was received with shock and sorrow. However, his younger brother, Thomas, had only recently been seriously wounded in revolver practice with the Athgarvan Company, Irish Volunteers. The story of the Wilmot brothers is not unique. Many families in Co. Kildare, and throughout Ireland, had fathers, brothers, and sons serving in both, or either, the British forces and the Irish republican movement.

William and Thomas Wilmot were born four years apart – William in 1892 and Thomas in 1896 – the sons of George Wilmot, a Devonshire-born stoker, and Catherine, or Kate, Wilmot, née Dillon, a native of Co. Tipperary. The Wilmot's lived at Linden House, Athgarvan, and had six children, all of whom were born in Co. Kildare.[4] William was employed as a groom when he joined the Irish Guards on 2 October 1914, at a recruiting office in Naas. There was a height restriction for the Guards regiment and William was recorded as being five foot eight inches tall, 135 lbs, with fresh complexion, hazel eyes and black hair. A day after signing up for three years with the colours William was shipped over to England to join No. 5 Company at the Irish Guards training depot in Warley, Brentwood, Essex, England. He proved to be good at musketry and fieldwork; was well turned out on parade and average at gymnastics. Passing out of the depot as a private soldier William was posted to No. 2 Company, 1st Battalion, Irish Guards, and shipped out from Southampton to France on active service with the British Expeditionary Force on 11 March 1915.[5]

The 1st Irish Guards had been in France since 13 August 1914, nine days after Britain had declared war on Germany. They had fought in the retreat from Mons, and in battles at the Marne and Aisne river, and at Ypres. The Front had since stabilised into trench warfare where they received drafts of replacements to bring the battalion back up to strength. Intended to discourage the Germans from reinforcing their armies opposing a massive French attack towards Lens, the 1st Irish Guards were to experience the true futility of the war they were now fighting. At the battle of Festubert, between Laventie and Richbourg, near Arras in Artois, they were caught by enfilading machine-guns on what had once been flat and open fields. The battalion was cut to ribbons and Private William Wilmot was wounded in the right eye and left buttock. He was one of nearly 400 casualties the 1,100-strong battalion suffered.[6]

William was sent back to a field hospital in Wimereux, a French seaside town between Boulogne-Sûr-Mer and Calais. On 25 May 1915 he was sent to Boulogne for transport back to England and two days later he crossed the Channel. William spent almost two months recuperating in hospital and at the Guards Depot at Warley, in Essex.[7] On 20 July he returned to the front line in France. The 1st Battalion were joined by the 2nd Irish Guards battalion, which became part of a newly formed Guards Division. After a period of training the Guards Division were involved in the Battle of Loos, where again the Irish troops suffered heavy casualties. The fighting dragged on into 1916 and a period of bitter, tedious trench warfare followed. The 1st Irish Guards moved into billets at Brandhoek, near Vlamertingheon on 16 March where they celebrated St Patrick's Day with a huge dinner and inter-company football competitions.

On 23 March the 1st Irish Guards moved into the front-line trenches on the Ypres canal bank in Belgium.[8] It was there three days later, that Pte. William Wilmot was killed instantly by a direct hit on his dug-out by a single 'Whizz-Bang' shell. (The German 77mm artillery shell was commonly known as a 'Whizz-Bang' because of the noise the shell made as it travelled faster than the speed of sound – the soldiers heard the 'whizz' sound, before the 'bang' from the gun itself.) He was buried in Potijze Burial Ground Cemetery, north-east of Ypres, Belgium. In March 1931 the Kildare Board of Health erected a memorial in the Newbridge Parish Cemetery, St Conleth's, on which William Wilmot's name – and that of forty-eight other natives of the area – are inscribed. William was posthumously awarded the 1914–15 Star, the British War Medal 1914–18, and the Allied Victory Medal – which are still in the family's possession.[9]

EDWARD REDDY, RATHBRIDE, KILDARE

On 2 September 1914, a little over a month after the outbreak of the Great War, Edward Reddy, of Rathbride, Kildare, enlisted in the British army for 'the duration of the war'. He was demobilised on 27 July 1919, after four years and 269 days service, in which he had served in three different campaigns. Edward Reddy returned home to Co. Kildare, with three medals – the 1914–15 Star, the British War Medal and the Victory Medal – and the physical scar of a wound to his right hand.[10] Few, if anyone, asked of the mental scars of his four years of war in three of the war's decisive battles fought in some of the world's most unforgiving territory.

Edward Reddy was the youngest son of James and Bridget Reddy, Rathbride. James Reddy, a labourer, married Bridget Nolan on 5 January 1873. They had six children, recorded in the 1901 Census. All were born in

Co. Kildare and baptised in Allen parish: Margaret, 21 November 1880; Mary 3 September 1882; Anne, 26 October 1884; Patrick, 3 April 1887; Simon – only the year 1889 is recorded; and Edward, whose baptism is not recorded. Edward was eight years old in the 1901 Census, so we can assume he was born around 1892/3. In the 1911 Census all three Reddy males are recorded as labourers.[11]

The Reddy family was heavily involved in the local GAA scene and all three sons played football for local teams. Simon lined out for Kildare Round Towers when they beat Eyrefield, by 0-6 to 0-3, in the Co. Kildare 1911 Junior Football Final.[12] On 25 July 1914 Edward and Patrick Reddy played for Milltown against Rathangan in the South Kildare Junior Championship at Maddenstown. Milltown won 0-8 to 0-0.[13] A few weeks later Edward donned British army khaki and on 31 October was assigned to the newly formed 7th Service Battalion of the Royal Munster Fusiliers.[14]

Within ten days of the outbreak of the war Lord Kitchener had called for 100,000 new recruits, and announced that six new divisions would be formed from them. One of these new divisions was the first ever 'Irish' division in the British army – the 10th Irish. The 7th Royal Munster Fusiliers, together with the 6th Munsters and the 6th and 7th Royal Dublin Fusiliers formed the 30th Brigade of the 10th Irish Division. Basic military training on the Curragh was followed by battalion training and then brigade field days. In April 1915 the division moved to Basingstoke, in England, where they practised trench warfare and divisional route marches.[15]

On 9 July 1915 the 30th Brigade of 10th Division, including the 7th Munsters, left Liverpool for the Greek island of Mudros and cast anchor there on 16 July. These troops were the first of the division to reach the advanced base of the Dardanelles operations. Turkey had entered the conflict on the side of the Central Powers in November 1914 and this operation was designed to force the Dardanelles straits, bombard Constantinople (Istanbul) and remove Turkey from the war, opening a short sea-route to Russia.[16]

The Mediterranean Expeditionary Force had landed on the Gallipoli peninsula in April 1915 to secure the high ground commanding the Narrows of the Dardanelles, and to silence or capture the Turkish batteries which barred its passage to the Allied fleet. Unfortunately, the battle was a complete disaster and a new offensive, a co-ordinated surprise landing at Suvla and attack on Sari Bair, was initiated in a decisive bid to break the deadlock. The 10th Division (less one brigade) was to land at Suvla Bay, a name soon to bring sorrow to many Irish, and indeed, Kildare homes.[17]

The 7th Munsters landed on the north shore of Suvla Bay on 7 August and immediately went into action attacking the Kiretch Tepe Sirt Ridge and suffering severe casualties. After capturing the western edge of the ridge the Munsters dug in and then on 9 August attempted to advance, but were repulsed. As Turkish reinforcements arrived hope of an easy victory faded. In the fighting on 9 August Edward Reddy was hit in the hand by a Turkish bullet.[18] On 15 August, a day known in Ireland as 'Lady Day in Harvest', the 7th Munsters advanced taking the north slope of the ridge, but Turkish reinforcements compelled them to retire. Twenty-three members of the battalion were killed. Between 7–15 August the 10th Division lost 114 officers and 3,000 men killed and wounded. The 10th Division had been shattered. A year's preparation and work had been destroyed in a week.[19]

By the 19 August the 7th Munsters were down to half-strength with more casualties being caused by sickness rather than enemy action. On 26 August Edward Reddy was admitted to the Field Ambulance Unit suffering complications due to his hand injury. He was subsequently placed on a hospital ship and arrived back at Hayton House Hospital, Carlisle, on 23 September 1915. A letter addressed to his father, James, said:

> I beg to inform you that your son No. 2006 Private Edward Reddy 7th R. M. Fusiliers was admitted to Hayton House Auxiliary Hospital Carlisle 23/9/1915 suffering from bullet wound right hand (slight).

In February 1916 Edward was fully recovered and was shipped to Salonika in Greece, where he joined the 6th Battalion, of the Royal Munster Fusiliers.[20] The 10th Irish Division had left Gallipoli in late September 1915 and was dispatched to Salonika to assist the Greeks who were under threat from

Bulgaria. In Edward's absence the 10th Division had suffered a severe mauling from the Bulgarians in appalling winter weather. Throughout the spring and summer the Division refitted and retrained. In May the Bulgarians invaded Macedonia and over the next couple of weeks the Munsters were involved in action around the Sturma river. Malaria took a huge toll on troop strength and when few replacements were forthcoming the 6th Munster Battalion was amalgamated with the 7th Battalion.[21]

On 18 August 1917 the 10th Division received orders to move to Palestine.[22] Edward Reddy was admitted to hospital on 22 August suffering from malaria.[23] By the end of the third week of September the division was concentrated in the area of Ismailia on the edge of the Suez Canal. A period of rest and training followed and then it was off to war again. The division had a limited involvement in the Battle of Gaza and was also involved in the capture of Jerusalem in December. By the middle of 1918 most of the battalions were well below strength and many more units were amalgamated, with only one Irish battalion remaining in each of the three infantry brigades of the 10th Irish Division. The other Irish battalions were sent to the Western Front and were replaced by Indian infantry battalions. From then on the Division ceased to be 'Irish'.[24] Edward was transferred to the 2nd Battalion of the Royal Irish Fusiliers on 6 October 1918. By then the war in the Middle East was over.

Edward Reddy was demobilised in Dublin, on 27 July 1919, and returned home to Rathbride, Kildare. His character was noted as 'very good'.[25]

JAMES ROGERS, MILLBROOK, NAAS

James Rogers was born in Naas in 1892 the second eldest of four children to John and Margaret Rogers, of Corbans Lane, Naas. He lived his entire life in the county, except for the brief period when he was a member of the Royal Dublin Fusiliers and later the Royal Irish Rifles. James was listed as a general labourer in the 1911 census. He joined the Royal Dublin Fusiliers as a 'special reserve' at Naas Barracks shortly after the census was taken giving his age as nineteen, when he had actually only just turned seventeen. As a reservist James attended training sessions several weeks a year and was paid accordingly.[26] Reservists were paid between 3s 6d and 7s a week and were liable for annual training camps as well as military duty for up to twelve years after being discharged.[27] Coming from poor economic conditions the money earned as a reservist was vital to a labouring family – in 1914 a labourer's family had a disposable income of only 3s 1d out of a weekly wage of 18s, after the essentials of rent, food, heat and light were paid for. An additional 7s made it possible to rent better accommodation or purchase decent clothes, food and footwear, etc.[28]

With the outbreak of war reservists suddenly found themselves being recalled into the army and on their way to France and Belgium with the BEF. Private James Rogers departed Naas in November 1914 and entered the frontline on 10 December with the 2nd Battalion of the Royal Dublin Fusiliers. He took part in the battle of St Julien in April 1915 – where the Dublins suffered 510 all ranks killed or wounded – and in the second battle of Ypres in May 1915.[29] During this battle James witnessed the first use of chlorine gas by the Germans. James recounted his story to a reporter from the *Kildare Observer* in July 1915 after being sent home to recover from a wound he received in the battle. He described how he was shot in the arm while escaping from a German shell attack at a farm house in which he was taking refuge.

> The bullets were flying all about us. They tore through my coat and shirt just under the left arm. I had this (a Queen Mary Christmas present tin box) in the pocket on the left side of my tunic, and that must have saved my life. It was full of fags at the time. A bullet struck it, and going through the cover, glanced off the bottom of the box. The bullets kept on flying and whistling around us, and then I found myself hit in the left arm. I felt the blood running down my sleeve, but in the excitement I did not mind much.

During his interview with the *Observer* reporter James produced the damaged box which he kept as evidence of his miraculous escape.[30] The 'miraculous' tin box remains a family heirloom, despite the two medals James Rogers received being long since lost.[31]

James described the death of his fellow Kildare men at the battle. He told how he helped bury Mick Keogh, from Kill, and Michael Lewis, from Naas, in one night after the battle of St Julien. Rogers also found the body of his much-liked commanding officer, Col. Loveband, who had been shot dead by a sniper, covered by a tarpaulin in the reserve trench.[32] During his time convalescing James was welcomed by his friends and neighbours as a local hero. However, he could see that the country was changing and that there was not as much support for the war as when he had left. James Rogers returned to the Front and was lucky to survive the following years of bloodshed and slaughter. After the war he worked as a gas fitter, married Kathleen 'Kitty' Cosgrave and raised a family. James Rogers died in January 1947, aged fifty-five.[33]

JOHN VINCENT HOLLAND, ATHY, VC.

At the outbreak of the war John Vincent Holland enlisted as a trooper in the 2nd Life Guards, undergoing his training in Cumbermere Barracks, Windsor. Vincent, as he was known to his family and friends, was the eldest son of John Holland, a veterinary surgeon, and Mrs Katherine Holland, of Model Farm, Athy. Educated at Athy Christian Brothers School, Clongowes Wood College and Liverpool University, he emigrated to Argentina from where he volunteered for service in 1914.[34]

Vincent Holland was gazetted to the Leinster Regiment in February 1915, and proceeded to France shortly afterwards. He was attached to the 2nd Royal Dublin Fusiliers and received a bayonet wound at Ypres in June 1915. Lt. Holland was known affectionately by soldiers from Athy as 'Mr Bin' who wrote to him from France asking him when he recovered to return and lead them again. He returned to the Front and was attached to the 7th Leinsters as Battalion Bombing Officer and served at Loos and Hulluch and later recounted how proud he was of his Athy soldiers.[35]

At the Battle of the Somme the Leinsters were engaged in desperate fighting at the storming of Guillemont and Ginchy, and for his conspicuous bravery and devotion to duty he was mentioned in despatches and awarded 'The Parchment Certificate of the Irish Division.'[36] The battlefield at Guillemont was ghastly. The sunken road and the ground behind was full of German dead; the ground in front full of British dead. By 4 o' clock in the morning of 3 September 1916, the battalions were ready to attack, but no rations had come up on the previous evening owing to the intensity of the German artillery fire and so many had to start hungry when the bell rang to go over the top. Precisely at 12 noon a terrific bombardment was opened up by the British artillery, heavy and light, and this was followed by a creeping barrage from their 18-pounders behind which the Leinsters were to advance. The companies of the 7th Battalion went over in perfect lines through the enemy shelling and so eager were the men that they advanced into the zone of their own barrage. This impetuosity met with its well-deserved reward. The Germans were taken completely by surprise, and before they could leave their dug-outs, or get their machine guns into position, the Leinsters were on top of them. Here the bombers under Lt. Vincent Holland played a splendid part. Not content with bombing hostile dug-outs within the specified objective Holland fearlessly led his bombers through their own barrage and cleared a great part of the village in front. He started out with twenty-six bombers and finished with only five men – sixteen were wounded and five killed. 'By this gallant action he undoubtedly broke the spirit of the enemy and thus saved us many casualties when the battalion made a further advance.' So runs the concluding sentence in the notice of the Gazette in which John Vincent Holland was awarded the Victoria Cross for gallantry. Two Distinguished Conduct Medals and six Military Medals were also awarded to the rest of the bombers.[37]

The beginning of 1917 found the 3rd Leinsters at Queenstown (Cobh), training and recruiting. The regimental history noted that 'one of the earliest incidents of importance of that year' was the wedding of Lt. Holland, VC, to Miss Frances Grogan, in Queenstown. At the wedding breakfast the bridegroom proposed the King's health, which was duly honoured, the effect, however, being somewhat marred by a guest who opened with 'He's a jolly good fellow.' The singer then switched to the 'National Anthem.' (God Save the King, we assume.)[38] Vincent Holland returned to Athy in February 1917 where he received a presentation scroll from the people of Kildare and also a plate from Kildare Co. Council in the Town Hall on 11 February. This was to acknowledge the honour he had brought to the county by his conspicuous gallantry in the field and the pride felt by his friends at his achievements. A committee representative of all sections of the community had been formed and a large number of subscriptions were received. The scroll was the work of Mr H. Painting, headmaster at Athy Technical Schools. Owing to a family bereavement a public procession with bands was abandoned, but Lt. Holland on arrival was carried by his enthusiastic admirers to the platform amidst scenes of great excitement. His wife, Mrs Frances Holland, received a cordial welcome on making her first appearance in Athy.[39]

Vincent Holland was awarded the French Legion of Honour and the Croix de Guerre. He lost an eye in 1918. After the war he joined the Indian Army and served for some years with the Bengal Lancers. Later he went into the administrative service, serving in East Africa for many years. During WWII he served in Middle East Intelligence and India. His eldest son, Major Niall Vincent Holland, was killed in action in Burma in June 1944 and was posthumously awarded the Military Cross for distinguished leadership and conspicuous gallant service. On the death of his wife, Frances, Vincent entered a monastery but, to his regret, had to leave after six months owing to ill health. He retired to an ex-servicemen's home in Tasmania, until he died in February 1975.[40]

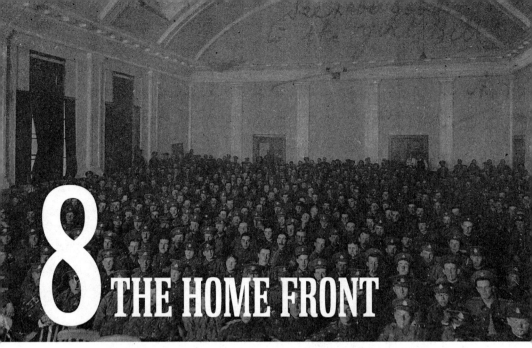

8 THE HOME FRONT

The New Hall, Sandes Soldiers' Home, Curragh Camp. Photo: Kildare Collections and Research Services.

FROM THE MOMENT war was declared on 4 August 1914 everyday life in Co. Kildare was affected. Within hours various local events were called off – the South Kildare Agricultural Society Show, fixed for 15 August, was postponed – the interruption of railway traffic and the absence of horses and cattle was noticeable. Other events were brought forward: the marriage of Captain Philip Yorke, Royal Field Artillery, to Miss Beryl Phillpotts, was celebrated at very short notice at Moorefield Church, Newbridge, because he was under orders to join the expeditionary force.[1]

Almost immediately a National Relief Fund was set up by the Prince of Wales to deal with distress caused by the consequence of war. Various individuals around Ireland were selected to raise money for the fund. In most cases men were selected, but in Kildare the wife of the Lord Lieutenant for the County, Lady Weldon, was selected as her husband, Sir Anthony, was dispatched to Cork to partake in the preparation of troops there. Lady Weldon, by default, became treasurer of the Fund and, as often as possible, submitted a detailed list of those who subscribed to the Fund to the local newspapers. The first list was published on 22 August 1914, with a total raised of £1,430 13s. The largest single amount subscribed was £1,000 by the Duke of Leinster, an unbelievably generous act by the standards of the time. Other donations came from Col. de Burgh, Oldtown, Naas, £25; Newbridge Church Offertory, £20; Col. St Leger Moore, Killashee, Naas, £15; Mrs Henry Mansfield, 44 Sunday's Well, Cork, £10; Naas Presbyterian Church Offertory, £9 3s 5d; United Parish of Donadea and Kilcock, £6 5s; Joseph Smythe, Esq., Greenawn Goura, Naas, £5 5s; Brigadier-General and Mrs Waldron, Melitta Lodge, Kildare, £5; Mrs O'Connor, the Grove, Celbridge, £1 1s; Mr Thomas Lumley, Duke Street, Athy, £1. Donations collected were sent at regular intervals to Buckingham Palace to aid the war effort. The first use of the National Relief Fund was in late August 1914 when gifts of buns and cigarettes were distributed by women to troops leaving for the Front.[2]

There was immediate distress and hardship to families as the bread-winner marched away in August 1914. The Board of Guardians normally issued separation allowances, but in the circumstances of the time, funds were not readily available. The Soldiers' and Sailors' Families Association (SSFA) a long-standing organisation set up to look after and provide for the families of naval and army servicemen, including reservists and special reserve, was required to give separation allowances to those who had not received any money from the Board of Guardians. The SSFA had substantial monies available and provided a stop-gap until government officials were able to mobilise their resources for assistance.

The Naas branch of the SSFA covered a very large area, including Naas, Sallins, Kill, Straffan, Celbridge, Maynooth, Leixlip, Edenderry, Robertstown, Clane, Ballymore-Eustace, Blessington, Brannockstown and Rathmore. The president was Mrs B. H. Barton (Straffan); Hon. Secretary, Lady Burrowes (Barrettstown Castle); Hon. Treasurer, Miss de Robeck, Naas. The committee included Mrs Loveband, Mrs De Courcey Wheeler and Mrs St Leger Moore. These names would appear time and time again in connection with various fund-raising events throughout the war years. Mrs Loveband's husband, Arthur, was killed in June 1916. No separation allowances were received in the Naas district until 17 August 1914, but even by the following week fifty dependents of soldiers had to receive assistance from the Naas branch of the SSFA.[3]

Around the county local authorities made efforts to alleviate the hardship caused by the war. At a meeting of the Celbridge Board of Guardians in early September 1914 it was agreed to provide assistance through the Soldiers and Sailors Families' Association to those dependents of men serving with the British forces who did not already receive a weekly allowance.[4] Subsequently, Celbridge district council established a committee to deal with distress arising from the war. The committee included local women such as Miss Walshe, Lady Kennedy, and the Hon. Miss Lawless among others. In early August 1914 the Local Government Board had forwarded a request to Athy UDC to form a local representative committee for dealing with any distress 'which might arise in consequence of the war'.[5]

From the earliest weeks of the war societies sprang up to cater for the needs of the country and the troops. Some funds focused on a particular regiment, usually linked to a locality – in Kildare it was mainly the Royal Dublin Fusiliers. Because of this connection various local people organised fund-raising aid for the families and soldiers involved. In the retreat from Mons in August 1914 the Dublin Fusiliers suffered heavily and lost many men taken prisoner. Numbers of these had Kildare connections and in October 1914 four separate committees began supplying comforts for the men at the Front or those held as POWs. A Central Advisory Committee of the RDF was formed to co-ordinate the work of the four groups – the Royal Dublin Fusiliers Bureau, the Ladies Committee of the Royal Dublin Fusiliers, the Dublin Women's Royal Dublin Fusiliers Committee and the Co. Kildare Prisoners Committee.[6]

When news of the first soldiers captured reached Kildare a local organisation, the Co. Kildare Prisoners Committee, was formed with Colonel Briggs, OC Naas Military Barracks, as Chairman. The committee was voluntary and without any expense, except for the necessary printing, advertising and postage. There were about 500 RDF prisoners, with 360 at Limburg POW Camp, in Germany. The Co. Kildare Committee sent out fortnightly parcels of food to all the Royal Dublin Fusiliers prisoners at over twenty different camps in Germany. The parcels were sent from Berne, Switzerland, and comprised of one tin of coffee and milk, one tin of condensed milk, 1lb of tea, 1lb of bacon and 1lb of cheese to augment their prisoners' fare, which was understood to be very meagre. Cigarettes, papers and magazines were always on request from the prisoners. The captured men were very grateful for these efforts on their behalf. Pte. Johnny Doran wrote to his wife, Mary, 39 Corban's Lane, Naas, from Sennelager POW Camp in Paderborn, Germany:

> My dear wife – I suppose you must be in a bad way since you got no letter from me, but it was not my fault. I would have written long ago, but we are only getting the privilege now. When you receive this letter I want you to send me a box of cigarettes, as we can't get any smoke here, as we have no money...[7]

In 1916 alone the Co. Kildare Committee dealt with 500 prisoners of the RDF. Various fund-raising events were organised by the Committee to help the men in whatever way possible. Vests, socks, shirts and mufflers and other comforts were received by the Committee and dispatched to soldiers either leaving Ireland, at the Front, in hospitals or as POWs. A fund named 'The Warm Clothing and Prisoners Fund' was set up locally.[8] There was a deep sense of community involvement on the home front during the early phase of the war and musicians, singers and actors provided entertainment and concerts to raises funds. Dances in Naas, Newbridge and Kildare, held by the Co. Kildare Committee in March 1916, raised a total £182 11s 7d. Appeals were made in the local newspapers for relatives to insert the name, rank, number and regiment of Kildare natives who were POWs so that the Committee would have an up to date and comprehensive list of prisoners. On 17 June 1916 the Committee submitted a list of forty-three names of Kildare soldiers held by the Germans – twenty-one were Dublin Fusiliers, while the balance was distributed over Irish and English regiments.[9]

Various other groups organised fund-raising events around the county. In the first week of the war Lady Weldon and the Countess of Mayo requested women in Co. Kildare to assist them making garments from patterns received from the Central Red Cross Society. Various garments were needed and help was required in any of the following ways: donations of money; the loan of sewing machines; the organisation of sewing meetings; or the making of garments at home. Baroness de Robeck was heavily involved in the Naas Branch of the Red Cross Work Guild and helped to raise many consignments of shirts, pyjamas, slippers and other items for men in the hospitals of France and the Middle East. The Naas Nursing Division of the St John Ambulance Brigade subscribed surgical dressings for hospitals at the Front through the Red Cross. Local women were invited to attend classes in making surgical dressing for hospitals abroad and requested to bring 'their own needles, thimble and scissors'.[10]

In December 1915 sub-depots of the Irish War Hospital Supply Depot were set up at Naas and Athy. These depots were directly affiliated with the Joint British Red Cross and St John's Depot and registered under the scheme controlled by the Director General of the Voluntary Organisations. The Technical Instruction Committee granted the use of their workshops and equipment at Naas and Athy Technical Schools and many willing workers gave up their afternoons or evenings manufacturing splints, bed rests, bed tray tables, crutches and other hospital aids which were forwarded to clearing stations, field and base hospitals at the Front. Further sub-depots were later set up at the Curragh, Kildare Town, Monasterevan and a joint venture for Celbridge/Leixlip.[11]

Due to the high number of casualties from the August 1914 fighting and the fact that English hospitals were overcrowded with sick and wounded Major William James Honner, High Sheriff, issued an appeal to the inhabitants of Co. Kildare for offers from all who could manage to house convalescent soldiers who had been discharged from hospitals, but required food and rest. The appeal was addressed to all classes. Positive answers were quickly forthcoming and all enquires on the matter were to be addressed to his daughter Miss Colleen Cliff Honner, Ardenode, Brannockstown, Co. Kildare.[12]

The first batch of wounded soldiers returning from the Front to recover and convalesce arrived in Naas in the second week of July 1915. Nearly all were from the Dublin Fusiliers. The men spent time in either the Naas Military

Hospital, located in the town barracks, or in the local hospital. The Board of Guardians for the county hospital had approved the building for military use in October 1914. The Curragh fever hospital had also been donated to the military for the duration of the war. The *Kildare Observer* reported on entertainment organised by the townspeople for the troops, which broke the monotony of hospital life for the wounded men.

> On Thursday in the Town Hall, Naas, a very pleasing entertainment was given to the wounded soldiers who are at present in the Naas Depot Military Hospital. The entertainment was in the hands of a local committee of lady organisers and the presence of the band of the Royal Dublin Fusiliers added much to the enjoyment of the occasion. The hall was crowded with military and the surrounding gentry were in force.[13]

In March 1917 the *Kildare Observer* carried a story of a meeting in Naas chaired by the Countess of Mayo, Palmerstown House. The meeting heard that country houses at Moorefield (Newbridge), Craddockstown (Naas) and Firmount (Clane) were being inspected with a view to opening a convalescent home for wounded Irish soldiers brought back from the war zone. The thousands of wounded returning from the Front overwhelmed the capacity of the military hospitals in Ireland and a number of big houses around the country were pressed into service to cope with the never-ending flow of casualties. It was eventually agreed to rent Firmount from its owner Major Henry. Funds were subscribed for the purpose by the ladies and gentlemen of the county. A committee was formed which furnished the house, raised funds for its upkeep and provided entertainment for the patients. The Firmount Military Hospital opened on 2 May 1917 and twenty-five patients were sent there from the Curragh hospital, with which Firmount was affiliated. By 10 July 1917 the hospital had forty beds ready, which were constantly full with an average of thirty-eight patients every day.

Firmount catered for two types of patients – those of the Expeditionary Force and those from the Garrison, or Home, Force. The majority of the cases were from the Garrison Force. The average stay in the hospital was three weeks, except in cases of gassing or chronic cases. The hospital proved to be well suited for the men's needs, as they improved quickly upon arrival. From the time it opened in May 1917 to its closure in February 1919, 600 patients passed through the hospital. Fortunately, there were no deaths reported. The general behaviour of the men was good and some made their way to the nearby village of Clane to have a few drinks and socialise. Among the patrons of the hospital were Lord and Lady Mayo, Colonel and Mrs St Leger Moore, General and Mrs Walker, Mr and Mrs C. Odlum, and Canon Craig.[14]

While it came as some comfort to the families of Irish soldiers in France and Belgium that they were well-looked after by the populace, in return any help in Ireland would be much appreciated by those whose homes were in the direct path of the war. Shortly after the invasion of Belgium Ireland was requested to arrange hospitality for some of the Belgian refugees displaced by the occupation of their country by the German army. Arrangements were made with Boards of Guardians within easy reach of Dublin for the use of portions of the workhouse premises as temporary receiving and distributing depots. Celbridge Board of Guardians was among those requested to take in Belgian refugees.[15]

The *Kildare Observer* reported that Mr Robinson, Inspector of the Local Government Board (LBG) attended Celbridge Workhouse, on 16 October 1914, and discussed the question of providing for some Belgian refugees – seventy-two men, women and children – with the Board of Guardians. As a result a provision proposed by Mr George Wolfe, seconded by Mr John Healy, and resolved: 'That in our opinion the appeal of the Distress Committee of the Country on behalf of the Belgian Refugees is worthy of the support of the people of the Country.'[16] Mr Wolfe said it was unnecessary to enlarge upon the resolution, because they all knew everything about the question – what these patriotic people had lost by their heroic action and the upholding of their national honour. Appeals for vacant homes to be opened up for the refugees was made by Mr Healy, while Mr Wolfe said furniture of any kind would be thankfully received by the Committee.[17]

Thirty-six refugees arrived in Celbridge on 21 October 1914 to be greeted by the inhabitants of the village who stood at their doorways waving Belgian flags in greeting as they passed. Belgian flags floated from windows, lamp posts and gates, with here and there a Union Jack displayed. The refugees – thirty-two men and four women – were warmly received at the workhouse by the Master, the Sisters in charge, the clerk and many others.[18] The refugees were treated differently than those already resident in the union and were not subject to ordinary workhouse rules. They were not given the same rations and all clothes supplied were new and of a different material and pattern to ordinary workhouse clothes.

The cost of maintenance for the refugees was recouped by the Local Government Board out of the parliamentary grant for the war effort in Ireland. Efforts were made to raise funds for the Belgian Refugee Committee in Kildare. Locals helped to cover costs with church collections and a public dance organised by the Naas National Volunteer Nursing Corps held in Naas town hall.[19] Employment was found for many of the Belgians who stressed that they were anxious not to take any positions which would interfere with local labour. The refugees said they all intended to return home after the war. Two refugees, Gustavo Eggermont and Irma Hoare, married in the Celbridge parish church in November 1914. The two had been employed in a flax mill in Ghent before the war. The ceremony was performed by a Belgian priest assisted by Rev. J. Dunne, P.P. The event was given great press.[20] A report on the death of one of the refugees was also given prominent position in the local press. Jean de Kock died on 18 February 1915 leaving behind a wife and five children in the workhouse. He was buried – with Belgian burial custom – in Donaghcumber Cemetery, Celbridge. A Belgian priest, based in Dublin, and Rev. Frs Dunne and McGough officiated at the funeral. De Kock was a painter and had been ailing for a month before he died. All the Celbridge Belgian community and many locals attended the funeral.[21]

Celbridge was only a temporary home for Belgian refugees before they were transferred elsewhere around the country. The de Burgh family housed eight Belgian guests from January 1915 in their big house in Oldtown demesne, Naas, as did several other Kildare families throughout the war.[22]

New arrivals were constantly coming in and replacing those who had left, some for as far away as Kerry. The refugees were all eventually consolidated at Dunshaughlin workhouse and the last eleven refugees left Celbridge for their new residence in Meath on 27 March 1915. According to the *Kildare Observer* they all regretted having to move and were profuse in their expressions of gratitude for the treatment they received in the Kildare village.[23]

Fifteen refugees went back to Belgium to enlist and subsequently found themselves in the front lines. The Clerk of Celbridge Union, F. Shortt, received a letter from one, Oscar Motte, which stated:

> It is with the greatest pleasure that I received your very welcome letter. I am always glad to receive a few lines from my dear Irish friends. I don't forget you for all you did for me – for all the Belgians – and in particular for me.[24]

While there was little progress on the front lines, considerable headway was being made on the home front. Housing was a big priority for local authorities. A scheme of six two-storey houses, on the Dublin Road, in Naas, was completed in late 1914, by Naas UDC, at a cost of £1,750, while the Main Street, from the Dublin Road bridge to Fair Green, was tarred for the first time in July 1915 at a cost of £30. The media claimed that some local bodies were still indulging in unnecessary building, street improvement or lighting, and other forms of municipal activity which, at that time, amounted to extravagance. With the object of stopping what they called this form of waste, the Local Government Board refused to sanction borrowing by local authorities, but if works were undertaken without recourse to a loan, it had no effective control. The Dublin Road housing scheme had been started before the European conflict arose and so had to be finished, while a similar project in Athy did not manage to get off the ground.[25]

Athy UDC had applied for a loan of £7,000 from the Local Government Board for the purpose of erecting a scheme of forty houses on several sites, after Dr John Kilbride, Medical Officer of Health, reporting to the Local Government Board inquiry, said there were at least 200 very unsanitary houses in the town. Eleven of the houses examined consisted of one room, about twenty houses consisted of one room and a loft, while the remainder consisted of a kitchen and one room. All these houses had very small windows, in some cases not capable of being opened, and all of them were very deficient both in ventilation and sunshine. The yards in all cases were very bad. With very few exceptions there was no provision made for any sanitary accommodation. Tenders were advertised on 15 June 1914 for the erection of only thirty-seven working-class dwellings on four different sites.

At a meeting of Athy UDC, on 2 November 1914, a letter dated 29 October 1914 from the Secretary, Office of Public Works, Dublin, was read with reference to the application of the UDC for the loan of £7,000, and stated that

> the Lords Commissioners of His Majesty's Treasury have intimated that they are not disposed to grant loans during the present crisis, except for urgent purposes, and as the purpose for which this loan is sought, does not come within the category of urgent purposes the Board do not think that it would be of any use to proceed with the application.

Following receipt of the above letter the UDC passed a resolution which they forwarded to the Local Government Board saying that the building of these houses would be 'the best means to avert any distress that might arise during the coming winter in consequence of the war, a local representative committee has been appointed by the council to deal with much distress which seems impending, and we respectfully and firmly urge upon the Treasury the necessity of advancing to us the necessary housing loans applied for, a loan which we could have obtained earlier in the year, but which was not applied for until now, to meet the serious situation which has been foreseen.' At the suggestion of the Engineers the UDC decided to postpone the building of working-class housing for the foreseeable future. Unfortunately, for those living in substandard housing the pressure on housing stock remained because of the almost complete suspension of house-building caused by the war.[26]

Those in the 'big houses', however, would find that the war would impinge on their social life as well as that of many of their offspring who were fighting and dying at the Front. The drafting of horses into the Army's Remount Department meant that countrywide stocks were low. The Kildare Hunt was threatened with collapse as it was supported by military funds. Many of its members had gone off to war and this led to lack of support. However, Kildare Co. Council and Naas Urban Council stepped in. Naas UDC provided the Hunt Club with a favourable lease of premises in the Town Hall. The Co. Council agreed to solicit the public to support a fund for the Kildare Hunt Club. A large part of this generosity stemmed from the fact that the Hunt Club brought a lot of money into the county's economy.[27]

Sadly, many of the officers who hunted with the Killing Kildares and Newbridge Beagles were amongst the war's casualties: Lieutenant-Colonel Sir Evelyn Ridley Bradford, nephew of Ned Talbot-Ponsonby (Master of the Kildare Hunt) and Charles Fitzclarence (Kill), who won a Victoria Cross in the Boer War, were killed in September and November 1914. Sir John Milbanke, another Victoria Cross holder who lived at Mullaboden, was killed at Gallipoli, as was James Johnston, Deputy Ranger of the Curragh. Nineteen-year-old Gerald Hans Aylmer, of Kerdiffstown, died near Arras in April 1917. Lt. John Horace Kennedy was killed while serving with the Connaught Rangers in Flanders in January 1915, while Lt. Ronald Kennedy died of wounds in August 1917. Their cousin, Edmond de Vere Percy, Viscount Glentworth, a pilot in the Royal Air Force and heir to the Earl of Limerick, was killed in May 1918. Lt. Richard Francis Nugent, son of Hon. Richard Nugent of Stacumny, Celbridge, and a grandson of the Earl of Westmeath, was another well-known figure at Kildare hunt meetings and enlisted with the Scots Guards. During an attack on German trenches, Nugent was fatally wounded and taken into the enemy's front-line trench where he was treated. He died on 18 December 1914 and German troops then sent word to the Scots Guards allowing them to collect the bodies of Lt. Nugent and others who had been killed.[28]

In a county which is synonymous with horses the War played havoc with one of Kildare's most famous sporting activities. One of the earliest government actions to affect the thoroughbred county was the occupation of the Stand House, the Curragh, which disrupted horse racing. On 1 August

1914 the Turf Club received an alarming request from Captain King, the Deputy Assistant Director of Remounts: he wanted the use of the Stand House for fourteen officers and 100 men, and the use of the racecourse for 5,000 horses. The stewards of the Club, meeting at Baldoyle, Co. Dublin, were not at all pleased with this news and suggested alternative arrangements, only to be told by army headquarters two days later that under the Army Act the military had the power to seize and use any land premises it wished. It was added that 'care would be taken to avoid damage to the course and stands'. The next day, the premises and courses were handed over to the War Office. Because of the military occupation the Curragh September Meeting, regarded as one of the most important of the year with its traditional Kildare Plate and Turf Club Cup, was abandoned – the first time this had happened in 125 years. The military occupation of the Curragh Stand House ceased from 17 October 1914, so the Cesarewitch, Grand Prize and Royal Whip could go ahead as scheduled. Racing began to settle down to war time as the military returned to the Stand House and the stewards offered free admission to officers and their wives for the October meeting.

British racing was disrupted to a far greater extent than it was in Ireland leading to a 'racing invasion' by trainers and jockeys from Britain. The British invasion also involved horses – 150 animals in all – and since they were concentrated in the Curragh area this had the effect of pushing up training costs through increased rents, labour charges and fodder prices. Trainers who had paid one guinea a year per horse in training on the Curragh from 1842 saw that charge rise to four guineas by 1918. In addition the war-induced inflation brought new strains and expenses to the Turf Club itself. As early as October 1914, the ground staff sought a wage increase and a half-holiday on Saturday. In 1915 the government introduced the Entertainments or Amusement Tax, which was levied on admissions to places of public amusement, like racecourses. The number of places, meetings and racing days naturally contracted during the war, caused strain to the Turf Club, owners, trainers and jockeys. Yet wherever racing was held, it seems to have been well attended.

On 27 April 1917 the War Cabinet prohibited all racing in the United Kingdom as of 6 May. Although the decision was presented on economic grounds, it was in fact based on moral and propaganda considerations – a newspaper campaign had indicated that racing and attendance at racing was unpatriotic. Negotiations between the senior Turf Club steward, Lord Decies, the Minister for Food, Lord Devonport and the Chief Secretary Mr Duke secured a limited number of days for the Curragh. The Irish Breeders, Owners and Trainers Association (IBOTA), under Edward 'Cub' Kennedy, of Bishopscourt, Kill, held a protest meeting in Dublin. Kennedy reminded his audience that 15,000–20,000 people worked in the breeding and racing industries in Ireland and that they had provided 300,000 horses for export since the war had begun. The IBOTA demanded that the racing stewards secure sanction for Mullingar, Roscommon, Gowran Park, Thurles and Limerick Junction, as well as for the Curragh and the metropolitan courses. Lord Decies explained that Dublin Castle had only sanctioned Tipperary and the Curragh and the IBOTA had to accept that the Turf Club had done its best. While continued pressure extracted permission for Gowran Park in June, it was not until 4 July 1917 that the crisis eased and the government withdrew the April edict.

The resumption of racing did not result in a complete return to the way things were and the 1918 season still required government sanction and resulted in a restricted programme. Coal shortages, and therefore railway restrictions, were the primary cause of the curtailments.[29] The war also had a dramatic effect on National Hunt racing at Punchestown, outside Naas, and while the 1916 Rebellion did not prevent Punchestown going ahead and nor the attendance expected to be large it proved satisfactory enough. Needless to say, there was an absence of 'that gaiety and brightness' which the meeting was accustomed to in prewar times and 'the Hunt Stand bore a particularly empty look'.

The General Strike, called on 23 April 1918 by the Irish Congress of Trade Unions as part of the resistance against the extension to Ireland of conscription, coincided with the first day of the Punchestown Festival (traditionally the third week of April) that same year. Although, according to the *Irish Field*, there was 'total dislocation of business throughout the country for a whole day', the 'great Kildare steeplechasing carnival' still managed to go ahead, though thousands missed out on it as a result of the suspension of rail services. Petrol rationing had been introduced after the Easter Rising and most racegoers from around the country depended on rail travel. Determined not to miss out, many racegoers wisely caught the last trains on the previous evening, which put a severe strain on all available accommodations.[30] The *Kildare Observer* concentrated on the high points of the festival, like the Flag Day organised by the Countess of Drogheda for the Co. Kildare Committee's Royal Dublin Fusiliers Fund, which was held on both days of Punchestown, and 'notwithstanding the very scant attendance in the enclosures, realised the handsome sum' of £73 103s.[31]

World War I was the first media-driven war. By this stage governments were well aware newspapers had the power to influence the conduct, and possibly the outcome, of the war. Some Irish newspapers were censored or suppressed for anti-British feeling, including *The Irish Worker, The Volunteer, Irish Freedom* and *Sinn Féin*.[32] One of Kildare's most vocal supporters of the war was The *Kildare Observer*, a conservative newspaper, published in Naas, in 1879 at 56 Market Square, by the Grey family. The politics and land troubles of the late 1880s saw many nationalist provincial papers start up in opposition to Anglo-Irish newspapers. The *Leinster Leader* was first published in Naas in mid-August 1880, with the aim to 'strenuously and faithfully maintain the great principles of Irish nationality and liberal progress'. The *Leader's* main competitors were the *Kildare Observer* and the *Leinster Express*, published in Maryborough (Portlaoise) since 1831, but in 1883 another nationalist paper entered the competition when P. J. Conlan, who had worked on the staff of the *Leinster Leader*, set up his own newspaper, at Carlow, the *Carlow Nationalist*, later known as the *Nationalist and Leinster Times*.

The strongly nationalistic views of the *Leinster Leader* editor, Michael O'Kelly, were reflected in the paper, especially in reports concerning the British army and its war effort, which were considerably muted compared with those of the *Kildare Observer*. In October 1914 O'Kelly wrote a long editorial on 'Ireland and the war' in which he attacked the 'unholy lust of capitalism and others' and argued that Ireland's quarrel was with Britain and not Germany. The *Observer* on the other hand tended to cover every aspect of the war from the minute to the mundane.[33]

As the war progressed newsprint grew more expensive and the price of ink and other materials grew sharply. Paper became scarce and newspapers smaller in terms of page numbers, to try and avoid putting the cover price up. The *Kildare Observer* went from a standard eight pages to a six-pager from the end of May 1917, while the *Leader* dropped to a four-pager in April and then went up to a six-pager in June 1917. In Britain paper rationing was introduced in 1918. Ireland, too, suffered a paper shortage and an experiment to make paper pulp from peat was unsuccessful. Most Irish papers doubled their cover price during the war.[34] In Co. Kildare the price of newspapers did not go up until the last year of the war. The *Leinster Leader*, *Kildare Observer* and *Nationalist and Leinster Times* were all 1*d* in August 1914, but on 2 March 1918 all three newspapers increased to 1½*d*. The *Nationalist* went up to 2*d* on 22 June 1918, with the *Leader* and *Observer* following suit two weeks later on 6 July 1918.

The *Kildare Observer* was not the only publication to preach support for the war effort. *The Clongownian*, the periodical of Clongowes Wood College, Clane, Co. Kildare, published yearly in June, lavished praise on past pupils who joined the armed forces. Its June 1915 volume devoted sixteen pages to the war. It printed a list of former Clongownians in the Army and Navy, letters from former pupils at the Front and a list of men in the army honours, killed and wounded in action, and taken prisoner. At that time ten former pupils had been killed, twenty-one wounded and eight taken prisoner; 321 were 'listed as being in the Army or Navy', which included British, French, Australian and Indian forces. Special masses were said for Clongownians at the Front each week and the 'Boys' offered their Holy Communion on Mondays and their Rosaries on Sundays, Tuesdays and Thursdays for the same.[35]

In June 1916 *The Clongownian* reported a figure of 455 former pupils on active service with a death toll of twenty-eight and forty-five wounded.[36] The following year the Easter Rebellion was ignored, but *The Clongownian* did acknowledge that past pupils fought on either side. (The 1966 anniversary celebrations of the Easter Rising were also completely ignored.) It reported that a total of 516 men were on active service with the 'Army and Navy', with fifty-four killed, two missing, seventy-two wounded and nine POWs. Forty had received military awards, with sixty-four Mentioned in Despatches.[37]

Several famous 'old Clongownians' were killed as the war progressed and lengthy articles about them were included in the periodical. Captain Tom Kettle was killed leading a company of his men on 9 September 1916 at Ginchy, during the Battle of the Somme. Kettle had been a Clongowes pupil from 1894–7. Major Willie Redmond was also killed leading the men of his beloved A Company of the 6th Battalion, Royal Irish Regiment, in an attack on Messines Ridge on 7 June 1917. The Wexford MP was a pupil of Clongowes from 1873–6 and a brother of John Redmond.[38] Father Willie Doyle, chaplain of the 16th (Irish) Division, was killed on 17 August 1917, during the Battle of Passchendaele. Fr Doyle, a Jesuit priest, was not a pupil but was founder and editor of *The Clongownian*.[39]

However, Michael Joseph O'Rahilly, known as The O'Rahilly, another distinguished Old Clongownian, killed during the Easter Rising was not mentioned. The O'Rahilly was prominent in the Irish Volunteers, but the loyalty of the majority of Clongownians was to Britain. Proportionally, more Old Clongownians died in the Great War than Old Etonians. Annually *The Clongownian* recorded the names and experiences of those serving and dying in the British armed forces.[40]

The Clongownian of June 1918 reported seventy-eight former pupils killed, eighty-seven wounded, one Victoria Cross (John Vincent Holland) and thirty Military Crosses awarded.[41] The following year *The Clongownian* reported a total of 604 men were on active service, with ninety-three killed.[42] The loss to the country was immense: a generation of educated men of position and talent were wiped out. As the war drew to a close it was clear that the Ireland for which many Clongownians had died would be a changed place.

9 WOMEN AND THE WAR

Mary 'Polly' Dunne, from Foxhill, Athy, trained at St Albans Hospital in England, with her two sisters, Kitty and Josie. Photo: Mary Rose Everan.

DURING THE WAR, and because of it, the role of women in Irish society changed completely. The war brought women from the domestic to the public sphere. More opportunities for women opened up in the labour market and their expectations changed dramatically. Many Irish women were actively involved in home-front activities, but the most significant and visible contribution by women was in the area of nursing. Nurses during the war consisted of two kinds: professionals and temporary volunteers. The trained nurses usually had several years' experience in hospital and district work, whereas the Voluntary Aid Detachment (VAD) nurses only received a three-month first-aid course with the Red Cross or St John's Ambulance. In August 1914 a ship full of trained Irish military nurses set sail from Dublin to hospitals in Britain. By the middle of the war, nurses trained in Dublin's Mater Hospital were working in Britain, France, Salonika and Palestine. In 1915 the Irish Local Government Board reported a slight shortage of trained nurses, due to nurses volunteering for the war.[1]

Mary 'Polly' Dunne, from Foxhill, Athy, trained at St Albans Hospital, in England, with her two sisters. Polly nursed in the 2nd Northern General Hospital, which was a military hospital, in Leeds, from 1917 to 1919. The first eighty wounded men arrived at this hospital after the Battle of the Marne in September 1914. There were sixty officer beds, 2,039 other ranks and over 57,000 soldiers were treated there. She then nursed in the Linden Auxiliary Hospital, in Stillorgan, Dublin, a military convalescing hospital. Polly received the Royal Red Cross Medal for her nursing during the war.[2] The Royal Red Cross was a military decoration awarded for exceptional services in military nursing and on 28 October 1916, the *Kildare Observer*, reported that:

> The King, at an investiture at Buckingham Palace on the 4th inst. decorated Sister A.M. Tweedy, of the Curragh Camp Military Hospital, with the 'Royal Red Cross', 2nd Class. Mrs Tweedy, who was trained in Richmond Hospital, Dublin, volunteered at the outbreak of the war, joining Q.A.I.M.N.S.R. [Queen Alexandra's Imperial Military Nursing Service Reserve]

Nurses in particular needed periods of rest away from their post, which was provided by Queen Mary's Army Auxiliary Corps Home for Convalescents, in France, and the Edith Cavell Homes, in Britain. Some nurses recovering there had been so badly affected by their experiences that they never returned to the Front. The war took a severe toll on medical personnel at the Front.[3] Nurses also benefited from leave at home. The *Kildare Observer* reported that Nurse B. Manahan, who had been on hospital duty at an unnamed base was home on leave in Celbridge for the past few weeks and had returned to France.[4]

Altogether 239 Voluntary Aid Detachments were established in Ireland, supplying 4,500 nurses for service at home and abroad. The response from various ladies committees was astounding in the organising of training for nurses, fund raising and provision of comforts for returned soldiers in towns all over the country. As the need for hospital beds grew with more and more injured men returning from the war zones, voluntary hospitals were established and regional and country hospitals devoted wards to military personnel. These were essentially run by VAD nurses, St John's Ambulance and the Red Cross.[5]

The VAD employed women as nursing members, cooks, kitchen maids, clerks, house maids, laundry maids, laundresses and van drivers. The Joint Committee of the Red Cross and St John's Ambulance Association was established in September 1915, in which 5,668 women served. In Co. Kildare there were two St John's Ambulance Association divisions, one in Naas and the other in Leixlip. The Naas Division, formed in March 1915, with Miss Evelyn Moore, Killashee, as commandant, had sixty-nine members. Forty-three members served in hospitals in Ireland and Britain, while ten served overseas. The Leixlip Division, under Comdt. Martha Fraser (Lucan), had eleven members.[6]

At a fête held at the Firmount Military Hospital in June 1918 the Matron, Miss Carr, informed Lord Mayo that the VADs had been most satisfactory in their work. Lord Mayo told an assembled crowd of local dignitaries that they owed the VADs of Firmount a deep debt of gratitude. He said it was difficult to get VADs as there were so many varieties of well-paid work open to women now. Lord Mayo said he hoped they were aware that the VADs gave their services free and did a great deal of disagreeable and onerous work and from what he knew of their duties these volunteers had been most versatile and diligent.[7]

Miss Elise Sandes was at Coolmoney Camp, in the Glen of Imaal, when she heard of the mobilisation order after midnight on Sunday, 2 August 1914. She had opened a Soldiers' Home there for the summer. Miss Sandes immediately arranged to return to the Curragh where she knew the demand on her services would be great. Elise Sandes, from Tralee, Co Kerry, was an evangelical missionary whose aim was to provide wholesome recreation for young soldiers to keep them away from pubs. Mrs Perry had opened a Soldiers' Home at Lumville, on the edge of the Curragh, to care for the spiritual and physical welfare of men who were away from home. When she died in 1899 she left her establishment to Elise Sandes, who felt it was to be 'a Home full of light and gladness, and music, and free from the blasphemies and horrible songs which were polluting the air around me; a Home where these men could find warm hearts, always ready to welcome, to help, and befriend them, a Home where they could hear of the only One who could free them from sin, and make their lives glad, and useful and victorious'.

By 1898 her homes had spread to eleven other army stations in Ireland and four in India. In October 1911 Miss Sandes oversaw the opening of her new Home in the Curragh. Another Home was opened shortly after in Newbridge.[8] There were over thirty homes at one stage, eight of them in India. Their only rule they had, was 'Welcome'. (The Curragh Home was the headquarters and stayed open until the 1970s, serving the Irish army. Irish soldiers remember the Home with great affection and appreciation.)[9]

While there was help for soldiers who strayed from the straight and narrow there was very little sympathy for the wives of men at the Front who fell foul of the authorities. Domestic problems increased with the absence of the men, and the court appearances of women became more common. The wives of men at war received a marriage allowance, known as the 'separation allowance', and the women who received this allowance became known as 'separation women'. Sometimes their reputation – due to the anti-social characters of a minority – was rather sullied. The separation allowance was paid to married women and 'was to prove, in so far as it is possible, for the maintenance of the soldiers' home, the support of such members of his family as were in any degree dependent upon him, and to assist in as much as his dependents, other than his wife and children, in the same degree a comfort as were enjoyed by men as the result of his contributions before he joined the forces'.[10]

Army pay and separation allowances provided many working-class families with a regular income for the first time and were much more attractive in Ireland where the standard of living and rates of pay were lower. Some men enlisted just so their wives and families could have the separation allowance. From 1 March 1915 increased separation allowances were announced for the wives and children of married soldiers and for the dependents of unmarried men and widowers. The scale for privates, corporals and sergeants – the most common of ranks was:

Privates and corporals

Wife 12s 6d.

Wife and child 17s 6d.

Wife and two children 21s 0d.

Sergeants

Wife 15s 0d.

Wife and child 20s 0d.

Wife and two children 23s 6d.[11]

What was not said was that if the receiver misbehaved their separation allowance could be stopped. Mary Reilly, from Back Lane, Naas, the wife of a Dublin Fusilier, and mother of three children, appeared before Col. St Leger Moore, at Naas Petty Sessions, for being drunk and disorderly on a public street on 16 August 1915. She was found fighting with a woman of the same name, Mary Reilly, from Friary Road, Naas, whose husband Christopher, also in the Royal Dublin Fusiliers, had died of pneumonia in Kent in April 1915. Constable Murphy stated that this was Mrs Reilly's fifth offence in twelve months. She was a soldiers' wife in receipt of a separation allowance of 23s a week he added. Col. Moore said: 'Isn't it disgraceful that you should go on like this while your husband is at the front fighting?' Mrs Reilly agreed and said she had taken the pledge for life. She was fined £1 1s and costs and seven days to pay or face a month in jail.[12] Mary Reilly, however, did not refrain from alcohol for long and made several more court appearances, and served a total of four months in jail, before she again took the pledge after she was given one more chance by Major Thackeray, R.M., who said he did not want to keep sending the 'unfortunate' woman back to jail. Thackeray said he would give her a final chance, but only if she took the pledge forthwith and produced it in court. Mary, accompanied by the RIC sergeant, went to a local priest and returned with the pledge, which she had taken 'for life'. The case was accordingly adjourned. Her adjourned case was called in March 1917, when it was learned Mary Reilly was now in employment and doing well. She was, however, fined for an original charge of window-breaking and ordered to pay compensation at 1s a week.[13]

Within a few weeks of the outbreak of the war 'separation women' were the subject of severe comments from the magistrates' bench. Women, on generous separation allowances, found themselves with plenty of money and time on their hands. This led to a sharp increase of drunkenness, abuse and neglect of children and subsequent appearances before the local petty sessions' courts. Thomas Plewman, J.P., while presiding at the Athy Petty Sessions, commenting on the number of physical assault cases involving females, said: 'Athy is becoming notorious for these women.' Athy, however, was no more disreputable than any other area. Head Constable Hannon admitted that: 'My experience in Athy is that it is not since the separation money commenced to come that you have these cases.'[14]

A correspondent from Woodstock Street, Athy, later took issue with Mr Plewman's remark. In a letter to the local press he gave the following details of the average weekly household expenditure:

7 loaves ------------------- 1/7
¼ lb tea -------------------8d
2 lb sugar -----------------1/-
7 ½ d worth of milk ----- 3½d
1 lb butter ----------------1/4
3 lb meat ------------------3/6
Light and fuel ------------1/6
Rent ----------------------1/6
Total ---------------------11/4½

Leaving, as he pointed out contemptuously, 1/1½ to be spent on 'riotous' living at a time when a pint cost 4d.[15] The correspondent was using the example of a married woman with no children, who received 12s 6d, while 'separation women' who were appearing before magistrates were from all classes of military wives, some of whom were receiving quite substantial allowances.

Loss and loneliness led some women to despair. We can never know what those men who died in the conflict would have achieved in their lives, and equally we will never know what way their spouses' lives would have worked out either. Mary Kelly, from Chapel Hill, Athy, who received a 'large amount of separation allowances' on the death of her husband at the Front was summoned by her mother-in-law, Rose Kelly, for abusive language. Mrs Kelly said her nerves were gone since the death of her two sons at the Front. (Private John Kelly, Leinster Regiment, died of wounds in France, on 23 May 1915; Owen Kelly, also in the Leinster Regiment, was killed in action on 1 August 1915.) RIC Sergeant Hoffman, in evidence, said Mary Kelly was a nuisance in the locality. Mr Plewman said the conduct of women like Mary Kelly would not improve the name of the town. He said he was sorry to see a woman like Mrs Rose Kelly, who had lost two sons in the war, treated like this. Mary Kelly was bound to the peace and received a fine, and a warning from Mr Plewman that if she appeared again she would not get away so lightly. He said this conduct would have to stop, as Athy would not be injured by such women.[16]

The problem was not confined to Naas and Athy, but was widespread. The separation of men from their families exacerbated social problems which had always been there. In January 1917, at Kildare Petty Sessions, Constable McWeeney charged a widow of a sergeant, who died on active service in the summer of 1915, with cruelty to her four-year-old daughter. The woman was living on a pension of 16s per week – a not unsubstantial sum. Like many women in her predicament she drank a lot and hung around with 'bad company'. She was noted as being of 'bad character' and had received a 'severe warning' when she had appeared at an earlier court sitting for another offence. On this latest occasion the widow was sentenced to a month in jail and her daughter sent into care.[17]

Separation allowances allowed women to spend money that they never had before and drapers' shops and groceries reported brisk business, much better than before the war. Pubs, of course, did see an increase in business, but this was generally because, there was more money available. At the annual meeting of the Athy branch of the Society for the Prevention of Cruelty to Children, the organiser for Ireland, Miss Cecilia Power said that on the whole soldiers wives were behaving splendidly and that reports that they were drinking excessively was slanderous. She said women were not accustomed to having so much money and when they went to the post office to draw their allowance they were surrounded by a 'crowd of harpies waiting outside' and those who were weak succumbed to peer pressure to stand a round of drinks in a public house. Miss Power said the Society had suggested that a guardian should be appointed in such cases to open a bank account for women who were really not such 'bad cases' but did not know how to manage money properly without the guidance of their husbands.[18]

There is no doubt some separated wives did not handle the parting from their husbands well, but the majority of women did acquit themselves in the face of such adversity. It was a hard situation and most women rose to the occasion. At the sitting of Kildare Petty Sessions in April 1916, Mrs Margaret Smeaton, Claregate Street, Kildare, charged her husband, Private Charles Smeaton, with ill-treatment. The defendant was brought from the Curragh Military Hospital. In the course of her evidence Mrs Smeaton said that on one occasion her husband threatened to choke her and put his two hands across her neck. Her neck was swollen as a result. Margaret Smeaton said she gave her husband no reason to do this, but he threatened her life. The couple had been married two years and had two children.

In his defence Pte. Smeaton said it had been reported to him that his wife was associating herself with a sergeant-major, while her sister was keeping company with a member of the Flying Corps. He said his wife had been causing trouble since the beginning of their marriage. Charles Smeaton said he asked his wife to visit him at the hospital, but 'she preferred the company of the sergeant-major'. The Chairman, Mr Thackeray, said they would have to put a stop to this conduct and put Charles Smeaton under a rule of bail of £10 and two sureties of £5 or go to jail for a month. Pte. Smeaton was subsequently handed over to the military authorities.[19] There were, presumably, many cases of infidelity while husbands were away at the Front. However, some infidelities during the war years, as we shall see, led to more serious charges.

The women of the middle and upper classes were very active during the war years. Apart from the recruiting process the Irish aristocracy and their families involved themselves in a wide variety of civilian organisations and activities. Most of these were aimed at raising funds for good causes – to assist families, businesses or industries which had been damaged by the war.

Titled women played an important role in these activities; many of their men were away and relief work was considered appropriate for them. Some gentry were directly involved in war work: Lady Weldon, Kilmoroney, was engaged on several committees providing comforts for prisoners and the wounded; Miss Evelyn Moore, of Killashee, rallied volunteers to work in the war zones; Baroness de Robeck sought funds to send hot-water bottles and cigarettes to the wounded soldiers in France. Various committees were set up throughout the county to raise funds for a multitude of purposes: the hot bag and cigarette fund, prisoner-of-war comforts committee, hospital supplies committee, literature for prisoners committee, etc. In North Kildare an egg committee was set up and schoolchildren were asked to bring in one egg a week for prisoner-of-war comfort. The children inscribed their names on the eggs and these were sent to Germany. Dances, concerts, fêtes, field days, golf and tennis tournaments were also run to raise funds.[20]

The ladies committees were responsible for distributing Christmas presents for soldiers' children in December 1914. The *Kildare Observer* reported that Mr F. V. Devere, Hon. Secretary of the Co. Kildare Distress Committee, had at the request of the Local Government Board, furnished them with a list of the children of servicemen who were abroad with the object of securing a 'proportion of the American gift of Xmas presents for children of the county'. (At that time in Ireland the giving of presents was limited to the upper classes.) The list contained the names of 645 children – 311 boys and 334 girls – of some 250 servicemen. The ladies committees, consisting of members of the Soldiers' and Sailors' Families Association, coupled with others who had knowledge of the people for whom the gifts were intended, were responsible for the distribution of the 'presents' to those on the list.[21]

Other committees, like the Co. Kildare Ladies Working Guild sent comforts to soldiers, while the ladies of the Ascendancy helped the wounded by collecting sphagnum moss, which was renowned for its healing properties and used in hospitals for dressing wounds.[22] Women also conducted letter writing, organised meetings and engaged in newspaper publicity. In addition to appeals for subscriptions and donations of clothes, women used their positions and property to assist the war effort. Miss Dowling opened a depot at 50 Main Street, Naas, to receive gifts of vegetables, fruit, eggs, etc., which were much needed for the soldiers at Firmount Convalescent Hospital. An advertisement in the *Kildare Observer* said: 'The smallest contributions will be most acceptable, and will be acknowledged in local papers.' A car based at the hospital arrived at Miss Dowling's every Thursday of the week to collect donations.[23]

But it was not only the 'loyal' women of the county who were active during the war years. In early and mid-1914 nationalist women organised branches of Cumann na mBan (Council of Women) in Naas, Athy, Kildare Town and Newbridge. The aim of Cumann na mBan was to advance the cause of liberty and to assist in arming and equipping the Irish Volunteers.[24] These militant women clashed regularly with the separation women and at a recruiting meeting in Athy's Emily Square, the soldiers' wives loudly booed the republicans and angrily shook their 'ring papers' at them. The 'ring papers' were the separation allowance books held by each servicemen's dependent wife or mother and so called because of the impression stamped in each book on payment of the weekly allowance.[25]

Nationalist women protested against what they perceived to be wrong – i.e. recruitment for the British army – and were also prominent in the anti-conscription campaign. On 2 June 1918 a meeting of the ladies of Rathangan and district was held at Rathangan for the purpose of forming a committee to protest against conscription. Mrs S. J. Malone presided, and Miss Kathleen Murphy and Miss Pearl Murphy were appointed hon. secretaries. A committee was formed to arrange a procession on the following Sunday.[26] With the campaign against conscription in full swing there would be plenty of time for protest and counter-protest.

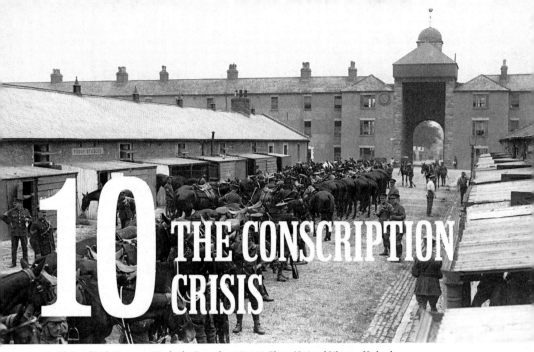

10 THE CONSCRIPTION CRISIS

8th Royal Irish Hussars in Newbridge Barracks c.1914-18. Photo: National Library of Ireland.

BY THE BEGINNING of 1918, the Great War in Europe had been raging for three and a half years, most of the time in a condition of bloody stalemate on the Western Front. Russia had given up and Germany was still undefeated. The Battle of the Somme, in 1916, and the Battle of Passchendaele, in 1917, had inflicted horrendous British casualties. Recruitment had dropped off drastically. The British army was striving to maintain its strength by yearly reinforcements from the new 'class' of recruits, the young men just reaching draft age. That source of manpower, however, could not keep the ranks of the army filled; nearly all its units were far below strength. The French army was facing the same predicament. The only bright spot for the Allies was that the United States had declared war on Germany. Consequently, the Germans realised that their only remaining chance of victory was to defeat the Allies before the overwhelming human and material resources of America could be deployed. The German army, substantially reinforced following the end of the war on the Russian front, launched the 'Spring Offensive', a series of attacks along the Western Front.

The first day of the offensive, 21 March 1918, was the worst day of the war for Kildaremen – twenty-four were killed in action on that day alone. A further thirteen lost their lives in the following week. The massive German onslaught hit the undermanned British lines where a wedge could be driven through the Anglo-French front. The initial impact was so devastating that in certain sectors the entire force in the British 'Forward' and 'Battle' zones was eliminated. Some battalions were virtually annihilated, ceasing to exist, except for a few stragglers and prisoners. The war diary of the 12th Royal Irish Rifles stated: 'The battalion itself was gone, killed, wounded and prisoner.' The 15th Royal Irish Rifles' diary was even more succinct: 'Battalion surrounded. 22 officers and 566 men missing.' For the Germans the feeling of success was instant and overwhelming. They had broken through at several points on the front of the British Fifth Army. After two days Fifth Army was in full retreat.[1]

The offensive was big news in the local press, with both the *Leinster Leader* (30 March 1918) and the *Nationalist and Leinster Times* (6 April 1918) featuring the crisis in their editorial. The *Nationalist* reported:

> News of the terrible battle raging on the Western front is being
> followed with keen anxiety in South Kildare, especially in Athy,
> practically every family having relatives in the army.[2]

Deputy vice-chairman of Athy Board of Guardians, Sergeant Michael McLoughlin, 10th Royal Dublin Fusiliers, was wounded during the March battles and was hospitalised in England. He wrote to a friend:

> I was fighting a rear guard action for eight days before being hit,
> and I consider myself lucky. Ned Nolan (Castledermot) is all
> right, but poor Kepple was killed. He died fighting to the last.
> We were outnumbered at least 20 to 1.

Private John Keppel, Craigue Hill House, Carlow, was an ex-employee of Messrs Jackson in Athy, and the news of his death was received with regret by a wide circle of friends, according to the *Nationalist and Leinster Times*.[3]

On 9 April the Germans began a second offensive, which likewise had a powerful initial impact. Indeed, at one time there was a genuine fear that Britain might have to evacuate her troops from the continent and that the war might be lost. The British army suffered 38,500 casualties on the first day of the March offensive. Between 21 March and the end of April the British army lost over 300,000 men.[4] Among those missing was Thomas Cahill, son of Naas publican, Catherine and the late John Cahill. Thomas Cahill had enlisted in the Irish Guards from the Royal Irish Constabulary in January 1915. He was awarded the Military Medal in June 1916, and was commissioned as a second lieutenant in February 1917. Tom Cahill was home on leave in Ireland in January 1918 and after spending some time in hospital in Rouen, France, suffering from bronchitis he was sent to the Reinforcement Depot, awaiting unit assignation. It seems he was in transit from the Reinforcement Depot to the front line when the German attack was launched on 21 March. He was reported as killed in action, but on 9 April another report said he was 'at present in hospital'. This note added to the mystery of Thomas Cahill's death. It was dated 9 April, two weeks after his official death, and was signed by a captain. This note was returned with other correspondence to his sister, Lizzie, in Naas. Based on this note his sister continued for years to believe he might still be alive, perhaps suffering from shell-shock, based on this note. Another letter was sent to Lizzie from Talavera Barracks, in Aldershot, England, concerning an amount of 40s 2d which Thomas apparently owed to the Army. As Lizzie was by then married to republican Stephen Garry, and both were strong supporters of Sinn Féin, it is unlikely the British army ever received the money owed.[5]

With the massive casualties caused by the new offensives and manpower exhausted, Britain looked towards Ireland for men to replace those lost. Conscription had been introduced in Britain in 1916, but John Dillon, the leader of the Irish Party after John Redmond's death in March 1918, had insisted that only an Irish parliament could make such a serious decision for Ireland. 'All Ireland will rise against you,' Dillon warned British premier Lloyd George. And he was right. Overnight the entire atmosphere in Ireland towards Britain changed. Nationalists in Ireland united against conscription and Home Rulers and Sinn Féiners formed a committee to resist its implementation.[6]

At the weekly meeting of Athy Board of Guardians, Mr Heffernan proposed a resolution emphatically protesting against any form of conscription being applied to Ireland without the mandate of the Irish people, claiming that no nation had a right to conscript another nation against its will. He said that the policy pursued by the British government was entirely in disagreement with its declared principle of fighting for the self-determination of the smaller nations of the world. Continuing, Mr Heffernan said that Ireland was under the iron heel of a 'pledge-breaking government and they were led on by blood-thirsty English members and some of the English press, who advised them to have no arguing, but to shoot'. For Home Rule they wanted this country to hand over the young men, he said, but he knew that no Irishman would think of making a slave of their people even for the best Home Rule Bill that could be passed. Mr Heffernan thought they should call on the clergy of all denominations to raise their voices against the slavery that was to be attempted against the Irish people.[7]

On 28 March the war cabinet considered whether conscription should be extended to Ireland and the related question, on what date was the new military service bill to be introduced into parliament. Lloyd George and some prominent members of his cabinet were in favour of extending conscription to Ireland and simultaneously introducing a scheme of home rule based on the Irish Convention's report. However, they knew that conscription would not be popular in nationalist Ireland and the Ulster unionists had already flatly rejected the scheme of home rule sponsored by a majority in the convention. Moreover, there was an awkward technical problem to be faced: the Military Service Bill could not be delayed, but a home rule bill based on the recommendations contained in the convention's report, which was bound to be a lengthy and complicated measure, had still to be drafted.

On 9 April, in a powerful and energetic speech Lloyd George surveyed the war situation and introduced the military service bill. As soon as the prime minister sat down John Dillon tried to move an adjournment and during the next few days the Irish nationalist MPs in a series of impassioned speeches denounced the proposal to impose conscription in Ireland.[8] Despite the objections of the Irish Party, the Military Service Bill was passed by the House of Commons on 16 April. The government proposed to introduce compulsory military service in Ireland for all males between the ages of eighteen and fifty-one. In protest, John Dillon led the Irish Party out of the House of Commons and home to Ireland. Two days later a huge meeting was held in Dublin's Mansion House. Almost every strand of Irish nationalism was present – Sinn Féin, the Irish Party, Independent nationalists, Labour and the Irish Congress of Trade Unions. An anti-conscription pledge was drawn up to be signed at church doors the following Sunday.[9] It read:

> Denying the right of the British Government to enforce compulsory service in this country, we pledge ourselves solemnly to one another to resist conscription by the most effective means at our disposal.[10]

The Catholic prelates met in Maynooth College, and issued a strong condemnation of forced conscription:

> We consider that conscription forced in this way upon Ireland is an oppressive and inhumane law which the Irish people have a right to resist by every means that are consonant with the law of God.[11]

The participation of the Catholic Church in opposition to conscription was particularly significant by virtue of their previous inaction on nationalism and the differences within the Hierarchy concerning political involvement and the expression of political views. Efforts by the British Foreign Office to have Pope Benedict restrain the Irish bishops failed. The Hierarchy believed their role to be crucial in cementing opposition and preventing chaos.[12]

Father Patrick J. Doyle (later P.P. of Naas) recalled a meeting of the priests of Kildare Diocese to organise against the implementation of conscription.

The meeting duly came off in a dingy cinema in Kildare [Town], but the majority of priests were not prepared to face the crisis with the realistic outlook that had been manifested in Carlow, and the meeting adjourned without any decisive course of action being decided upon. Light relief during the meeting was afforded by a timorous cleric who feared a nigger in the wood-pile, and made a vigorous search of the tawdry scenery and surroundings of the stage in the fear of finding some hidden spy.[13]

On 21 April the pledge against conscription was signed by nearly the whole of nationalist Ireland, Catholics signing at the chapel door. Protests meetings against conscription were held throughout the country. Kildare was no different. Some of the anti-conscription meetings were the largest gatherings seen since the days of the Land League. Large gatherings were held in Naas and Newbridge, while Naas UDC and Naas Rural District Council (RDC) pledged their opposition to conscription. At a huge protest in Naas the Chairman, D. J. Purcell, read the words of the anti-conscription pledge, which the crowd affirmed by standing bare-headed with their right hand upraised.[14]

At what was described as 'a monster meeting of the people of Athy and South Kildare and also from the adjoining districts in the Queen's Co.' held in the Square, Athy, on 21 April, resolutions were passed protesting against the unconstitutional and tyrannical attempt to enforce conscription without the consent of the Irish nation. Those assembled listened as the speakers reiterated claims that no nation had a right to conscript another against its will; the Government policy was in complete disagreement with its policy of fighting for the self-determination of small nationalities. Irishmen were congratulated in overcoming their differences and presenting a united front to the enemy. Another resolution was passed to resist conscription in every way that seemed feasible.[15]

The Irish Trade Union Congress organised a one-day general strike in protest against conscription. The whole country, with the exception of Belfast and its surrounding counties, closed down for twenty-four hours on

23 April, with only banks, the law courts and government offices operating that day. Because the issue was not an industrial one the issue was one of nationalism not socialism, many employers backed their workers, though some threatened lockouts or dismissal if employees participated. The success of the strike was remarkable, not least because it was organised within two days and despite heavy press censorship.[16] The strike coincided with the first day of the Punchestown meeting and many of the workers who supported the strike headed to the races. However, the local newspapers reported that the day was a bad one for bettors, and many probably wished they had stayed at home. Workers protested at hundreds of meetings across the country. In Kildare Town 2,000 people assembled in the Market Square and headed by a band and a banner with the inscription 'The Voice of the Workers' elected a defence Committee by ballot. The local G.P., Dr Laurence Rowan, topped the poll with 200 votes.

A special meeting of Kildare Co. Council passed a resolution condemning conscription as 'oppressive and an outrage on the national rights of the country. We therefore record our emphatic protest against its enactment and resolve to oppose it by every means in our power'. Matthew J. Minch presided as chairman and despite the fact that his sons had joined the colours he said he could not agree with conscription saying he was opposed to coercion in any shape or form.[17]

Many people were prepared to go further than voicing their opposition and recruits flocked in their thousands to the Irish Volunteers, pledging to fight all attempts by Britain to introduce conscription. Michael O'Kelly said:

> It was considered that the anti-conscription committees set up could also be utilised to turn to advantage the conscription threat by acting as recruiting agencies for the Volunteers. All parties were, for the time being, united in the common purpose of defeating conscription.[18]

The conscription crisis changed the challenge to the authorities from open defiance of volunteers, who often, like O'Kelly and his comrades in the Sinn

Féin potato case, invited arrest to shelter preparation for military conflict. By the autumn the Volunteers had 100,000 members.[19] In Co. Kildare Commandant Patrick Colgan (Maynooth) said:

> We gained many new recruits into the Volunteers during the threat, the majority of whom left the organisation when the threat had passed. The instruction to Volunteer units was to resist conscription. Looking back on that time, we were not in Kildare, at least, in a position to do more than offer passive resistance. We had fewer arms then we had in Easter Week.[20]

Opposition to conscription gathered pace into May as a new Irish executive was installed. Sir John French replaced Lord Wimborne as viceroy, or lord lieutenant, while Edward Shortt, an expert on national-service problems, succeeded Henry Duke as chief secretary. The new executive was expected to administer Ireland firmly, but French and Shortt began by insisting that in Ireland, as in Great Britain, the introduction of compulsory service must be preceded by a recruiting campaign whereby men could enlist voluntarily with an obligation to come if called up later on. The war cabinet agreed, and discussed a proclamation to be issued by the viceroy calling for recruits. Shortt also gave his support to an unusual plan to encourage Irish soldiers to join the French army, while persuading the Catholic hierarchy in Ireland to support conscription. However, both parts of the plan collapsed due to infighting within the government and the military establishment.[21]

French and Shortt were not only confronted by the great anti-conscription agitation, but also by the disturbed condition of much of the country. John O'Connor and Denis Kilbride, the Parliamentary representatives of North and South Kildare respectively, were the principal speakers at a very successful meeting held in the Town Hall, Newbridge, on 5 May 1918. There was a very large attendance, and the proceedings were characterised by great enthusiasm and determination. Peter Kelly, Treasurer of the local branch of the Irish Party, who presided, said it was a gratifying sign for the success of their movement to see so many townspeople present united under the old flag of the United

Irish League.[22] Not only was the defiance of authority loudly expressed at anti-conscription meetings, but recruiting and drilling by the Irish Volunteers was constant.

Nervous of growing unrest, and still not giving up on conscription the government undertook to quell the backlash. As Sinn Féin was publicly perceived to be the key instigator of anti-government and anti-conscription feeling, the new Lord Lieutenant, Sir John French, claiming evidence of a treasonable plot between Sinn Féin and Germany, ordered the arrest of seventy-three leaders of Sinn Féin and the Volunteers, on 17 May. However, Kildareman Eamon Broy (Rathangan) worked as a confidential clerk in the G Division – the intelligence section – of the Dublin Metropolitan Police and tipped-off the republican leadership of the impending raids. Some, like Michael Collins, avoided arrest, while others, like Arthur Griffith and Eamon de Valera, allowed themselves to be captured for the adverse publicity. The heavy-handed response by the authorities did little to defuse the conscription crisis. In fact, a lack of evidence meant the rumoured 'German Plot' was viewed with suspicion outside official and unionist circles. As the authorities refused to produce the evidence the arrests actually aggravated opinion and increased support for Sinn Féin.[23]

Even the conservative *Kildare Observer* referred to the arrests and the plot as an 'alleged plot', saying though there had been many arrests throughout the country 'no indication has been given by the Government as to the nature of the plot, and it is alleged in Sinn Féin circles that there is no justification for the allegation, and that it has been made to prejudice Ireland in the eyes of the world, but particularly those of America'.[24] A large meeting held in the Market Square, in Naas, in protest against the arrests and deportations of the republican leaders was addressed by Fr O'Brien, C.C., Kill, who said: 'That we protest against the action of the British Government in arresting our leaders, and denounce their action in deporting them without trial or sufficient evidence, and that we regard the published statement of the Government indictment as a miserable concoction with the object of defaming our leaders and movement in the eyes of neutral countries.' Arthur O'Connor (Celbridge) also addressed the meeting. He was among those earmarked for arrest, but who evaded capture after the tip-off from Eamon Broy.[25]

There was in fact, some truth to the British allegations. Information gleaned by British intelligence was that the Irish-Americans and particularly, the irrepressible Kildareman, John Devoy, had renewed their contacts with Germany a few weeks after the Easter Rising and that there had been discussions about further landings of arms in Ireland. There was also a report that German weapons had been sent to Ireland, but failed to arrive. Apart from a steady exchange of messages between Irish-Americans and the Germans, there were indications that U-boats had been in contact with agents off the west coast of Ireland. When Joseph Dowling, a former British army POW and a member of Roger Casement's ill-fated Irish Brigade, was arrested after landing on the Galway coast from a German U-boat, it provided Britain a pretext of a 'German Plot'. According to the British, Dowling claimed the Germans were planning an expedition to Ireland, but he in fact had been sent by the Germans on their own initiative to try to discover whether there were any prospects for a rising. However, there was no sign of a concerted 'plot' and no evidence that the Sinn Féin leaders were in any way implicated.[26]

By June 1918 it had become apparent to most observers in Britain and Ireland that following the entry of the United States into the conflict the tide of war had changed in favour of the Allied armies in Europe. A proclamation, which called on Ireland 'to play her part fully and freely in the world struggle for liberty' by supplying 50,000 recruits by 1 October, was issued at the beginning of June, with 11,700 men expected from the recruiting area of Dublin, Kildare, Wicklow, Carlow, Meath and Louth.[27] But by 20 June the Government had dropped its conscription and home rule plans, citing the lack of agreement of the Irish Convention.

The Irish Convention had been proposed in June 1917, by Lloyd George to John Redmond, to address the apparently intractable Irish question and other constitutional problems relating to an early enactment of self-government for Ireland. From the introduction of the Third Home Rule Bill into Parliament in 1912, efforts had been made to find a compromise, and though the outbreak of war in Europe distracted attention from Ireland, the Easter Rebellion compelled the British government to treat Ireland as a grave and immediate problem. The Convention met for the first time on 25 July 1917 at Trinity College. It was to be composed of representative Irishmen from different political parties and spheres of interest but from the beginning was boycotted by Sinn Féin.[28] Nationalist, Matthew Minch, Kildare Co. Council, and unionist Lord Mayo (Palmerstown), were the only Kildare representatives on the ninety-five-man committee.[29]

Matthew J. Minch, scion of the well-known Athy grain merchant family, was elected to the first Kildare Co. Council in 1899, and later became chairman of the Council. Minch first came to prominence when he was elected to the South Kildare constituency as an anti-Parnell candidate for the Irish National Federation in 1895.[30] Although a committed nationalist Minch was chairman of the Co. Kildare Recruiting Committee, and had three sons in the service, but also became chairman of the Co. Kildare anti-conscription committee.

Lord Mayo was one of Southern Ireland's leading unionists. He was born Dermot Robert Wyndham Bourke and became the seventh earl after the death of his father, Richard Southwell Bourke, Earl of Mayo and Governor-General of India, who was assassinated at the Andaman Islands' penal settlement, on 8 February 1872. In 1890 Dermot Bourke was elected as a representative peer for Ireland in succession to the sixth Earl of Milltown. It was from this period that Lord Mayo's deep interest in the social and industrial well-being of his native country began to take a practical form. His ambition was to promote a widespread and more intelligent knowledge of Irish history and antiquities, to create a truer appreciation of art as applied to crafts, and generally to raise the level both of labour and of social life. With such objects in view, he was a founder member the County Kildare Archaeological Society, established at Palmerstown House on 25 April 1891.[31]

To proceed with conscription and home rule faced with intense hostility in the south and defiant opposition to home rule in the north, seemed to Lloyd George 'folly', and on 25 June he announced that the government was not going to introduce the home rule measure in the immediate future. With conscription and home rule indefinitely postponed, the government's Irish policy was in total dissaray.[32] While officially conscription was postponed, in reality it had been abandoned. The British authorities were finally dissuaded from introducing conscription simply because they realised that it would require more troops to police conscription than its enforcement could produce. The Chief Secretary, Henry Duke, remarked that conscription would be tantamount to recruiting Germans and that additional troops would have to be sent to Ireland to enforce it.[33] Despite the turn of events men continued to enlist and from 1 June to 11 November 1918 the army gained 11,797 recruits from Ireland.[34] The *Kildare Observer* even reported on a 'very successful recruiting meeting' in Naas as late as 19 October 1918.

The strength of resistance made it impossible to impose conscription – confronted with the united political and religious front, the signing of the anti-conscription pledge by hundreds of thousands, and the success of the general strike made the depth of opposition quite clear. However, the legacy of the conscription crisis remained. Support for Britain and the war effort continued to decline, while that of Sinn Féin and Irish independence continued to rise. The conscription crisis spelled the end of home rule as a popular cause. From then on only self-determination would be accepted.

11 END OF DAYS

Sgt. Maj. Joseph Bermingham (Kilina), second from right, celebrating the end of the war.
Photo: Author's collection.

THE THIRD GERMAN offensive of 1918, unleashed on the Chemin des Dames and the Aisne river on 27 May, came within fifty miles of Paris before it sputtered to a halt from exhaustion and the arrival of massive French and American reinforcements. American troops entered the fray in substantial numbers for the first time, fighting to halt the Germans at Cantigny, Château-Thierry and Belleau Wood. The German army had lost its race against time – one million Americans had swelled the Allied ranks. On 8 June General Ludendorff launched a fourth offensive on the Western Front, again with the goal of taking Paris, but this time the offensive withered after just four days in the face of French counter-attacks. A subsequent offensive along the Marne was halted by fierce French, British and American resistance on 15 July. The following day the Allied supreme commander, Marshal Foch, launched a counter-offensive. By August the Germans were back where they had started their offensive in the Champagne district, north of the Aisne, in May.[1]

With the American Expeditionary Force (AEF) were many newly arrived Irish immigrants, some of whom were born in Co. Kildare. Corporal Frederick

Fleming, who enlisted in New York, was killed in action, in France, on 29 July 1918, serving with the 165th Infantry Regiment – the former 'Fighting Irish' 69th Regiment – 42nd Division, AEF. He was the son of the late Sgt. Fleming, RIC, and Mrs Fleming, Sallins. A few weeks later, another fatal casualty occurred. Sergeant Christopher Byrne (Rathangan), 305th Infantry Regiment, 77th Division, AEF, died from effects of gas poisoning on 27 August 1918.[2]

During the summer, as French and American troops counter-attacked, soldiers from all sides began to succumb to a mystery new illness – a deadly strain of influenza. Troop losses from the epidemic soon exceeded combat casualties, especially weakening the hard-pressed German army. The illness was swiftly dubbed 'the Spanish Influenza', as Spain, free from wartime censorship, was the first country to announce an outbreak, and many people believed it originated there. The disease possibly originated in China as a bird flu, hit the United States in March 1918 and by early summer 1918 had become widespread over Europe, brought there by newly-arrived American troops. But throughout its course the disease was surrounded by uncertainty as to its cause and ignorance as to a possible cure. It was a twentieth-century version of the Black Death, affecting over a billion people, more than half the global population. Worst affected was Asia, especially India, which suffered 12.5 million deaths out of a total of 21.5 million worldwide. The countries most heavily engaged in the war lost in flu fatalities (in descending order): Russia 450,000, Britain 228,917, Germany 225,230, France 166,000.[3]

A dark spectre stalked the country – the 'last Irish plague' was an almost constant presence in Ireland from June 1918 to May 1919. Co. Kildare had the highest death rate in 1918 – 3.95 per thousand – a total of 263 deaths. The Great Flu was such a horrifying disease that people thought it was the end of the world. Doctors were not even agreed as to the name of the disease – it was referred to as a scourge, influenza, the 'plague of the Spanish lady' or the 'Black Flu'. Very few called it a pandemic. The disease became known as the 'Black Flu' because one of the complications was blood poisoning, leading victims to appear to turn black. Strangely, the virus was attracted to people between the ages of twenty and forty, reversing the usual trend of other flu epidemics where the old, very young and infirm were the normal victims.

It killed marginally more males than females. Physicians were faced with a disease that presented symptoms and complications which had never been experienced before in dealing with ordinary influenza or pneumonia. It was highly infectious and deadly. It appeared in Ireland in three waves: summer and autumn/winter 1918 and spring 1919. The first wave originated in Belfast in early June 1918 and the first recorded instance in Co. Kildare was in Athy on 13 July 1918.[4]

Because of the wartime ban on emigration to the United States there were more young people in the country than usual. The disease spread through human contact and the railway system brought it to every corner of the country. Mass troop movement helped spread the disease. Many of the worst-hit areas in 1918 were among those which had returned high enlistment figures. Ulster, Dublin, Wicklow, Carlow and Kildare raised the highest number of recruits for the war effort and while Ulster endured the highest number of flu casualties during 1918, all of the latter counties were among those worst hit by the first two waves of the disease, with Dublin county borough and Kildare heading the list. Out of all the rural towns, Naas suffered the most, with the flu accounting for just under 25 per cent of all deaths in 1918, while in Athy, just over one in five deaths were due to influenza.[5]

Naas was hit badly from September–November 1918. By October 20, according to Dr M. R. Morrissey, there were about 1,000 cases in the town out of a population of about 4,000. He estimated a total of 1,420 in Naas and district by 26 October.[6] Nine deaths were recorded in Naas in September; forty-three in October and eleven in November. Mary Pearse was eighteen years old at the time and lived at Loughwee, Naas. She remembered the epidemic and the fact that coffins could not be made quickly enough. The deceased were wrapped in blankets, or sheets, and sometimes carried to the graveyard in people's arms. Sometimes a handyman would make a stretcher with two planks of wood and use this to get the bodies to the graveyard. Mary recalled how she would help with the laying out of some of the victims. They were buried in the clothes in which they died, and the women laying the bodies out would just wash their faces and brush their hair. The bodies would not be touched with bare hands; gloves were a luxury and hands were covered with socks; a scarf covered the face of the women laying out the victims. She recalled an entire family of Higgins (Kilcullen Road, Naas) had been wiped out – father, mother and all the children.[7]

The epidemic touched the lives of many republicans around the country. The RIC reports contain numerous reference to Volunteer funerals occurring over the course of 1918 and the Inspector for Kildare was able to report with satisfaction that in November 1918 there was 'no activity noticed among the IVs [Irish Volunteers] at all, most of its members have been ill with "flue"'.[8] Schools in all the districts affected were closed as a precautionary measure and were followed by the postponing of many functions and public gatherings. Pubs and shops also closed. The medical authorities agreed that the public authority should prohibit any public gatherings and that the bodies of people who died of the disease would be speedily interred and that no wakes were to be held for fear of spreading the germs. Efforts were made to educate the public on the means of preventing the spread of the disease. The *Kildare Observer* suggested that locally Kildare should follow the lead of the military authorities who forbade troops to frequent theatres and other places of amusement in Dublin.[9]

The North Kildare Farming Society show, which was to be held at Naas on 29 October 1918 was postponed owing to the prevalence of influenza in the district. A communal kitchen was set up in Naas Town Hall and gifts of potatoes, onions and carrots were donated.[10] The worst affected month in Naas was October, as the *Irish Times* reported:

> The influenza epidemic during the past week has spread to an alarming extent in Naas and district and several deaths have occurred from complications mostly among young people during the past few days. In some cases entire families have been stricken down. Several cases at the weekly Petty Sessions Court had to be adjourned owing to the inability of policemen who were suffering with the disease to be present. The local schools have been closed for the past week.[11]

The *Leinster Leader* described how they were unable to publish notices in respect of several 'lamented deaths', due to the fact that so many of their staff had the virus.

> Since then the list of fatal cases has been augmented upwards, with more than a dozen deaths occurring in the town of Naas alone at the beginning of the week. A gloom seems to hang over the affected districts and this is accentuated in Naas after nightfall by the absence of business and of the usual lighting of shops and street lamps. The employees of the Gas Works like those in other institutions have suffered from the ravages of the disease and in almost every district business has been interfered with.[12]

The newspaper praised the work done by local doctors, clergy and the St Vincent de Paul. The paper also stated that some terrible cases had been witnessed during that week of several members of the same family suffering from the virus occupying the same small apartment and in some instances the same bed. There was a fear that gas could not be supplied for the full winter and consumers were requested to cut consumption by half. All shops were asked to close at 7 p.m. and all public houses to close by 8 p.m. Saturday opening was to remain the same.[13]

At a special meeting of Naas UDC on 29 October the Chairman, D. J. Purcell, said before proceeding with the business of the meeting he thought it was only right that he should refer briefly to the gloom which overshadowed the town for the past fortnight owing to the ravages caused by the prevailing epidemic. In some cases whole families had been stricken down, and there was scarcely a family that had not had a sufferer. Sorrow had entered many homes, and death claimed numerous victims. In one place it was the bread-winner, in another it was the mother of helpless children, and in the majority it was the young man or the woman, the hope of the future. There were several peculiarly pathetic cases, and it was no wonder that sadness was on every brow. He did not need to tell them that the clergy were untiring in their ministrations to bring comfort and consolation to the afflicted and mitigate their sufferings. Everything that medical science and skilled nursing could suggest was done to stem the onward march of the disease. The members of the St Vincent de Paul Society and others imbibed with the highest sense of Christian charity did everything they could to counteract the possible effects of the awful visitation. The sympathy of the Council went out wholeheartedly to the bereaved ones of all classes, and they sincerely hoped that the Divine Comforter would console the sorrow-stricken, and speedily restore to their families those labouring under the terrible disease. With these few remarks, he proposed a resolution expressing the Council's profound regret, and their deep condolence with the relatives of the departed of all sections without distinction.[14]

The virus usually appeared in an area, peaked in three weeks and then moved on. By mid-November the epidemic in Naas was abating as the *Leinster Leader* reported:

> A feeling of general relief and hopelessness has to a considerable extent replaced the depression which has prevailed in our midst ever since the epidemic became malignant in Naas, now that there are definite indications of its abatement. The number of fresh cases are steadily declining and most of those which have been regarded as serious are progressing favourably. Those who have survived and who have escaped the epidemic have every reason to be thankful and grateful to the splendid devotion of our doctors.[15]

Influenza appeared in Newbridge around the middle of October and the *Leinster Leader* reported that since then a large number of people had been seriously affected. In one unnamed 'small court there were 16 persons reported to be suffering during the week'. The schools in the town were closed to help prevent the spread of the disease, while meetings of the Town Commission and concerts at the Curragh were also abandoned. Doctors, public transport employees, and shopkeepers were very vulnerable and many shops closed their doors. Priests and clergymen were also in the front line and many of them died. On 24 October 1918, Reverend Father Kevin J. McLoughlin, O.P., died from the effects of influenza. He was thirty-two and a Professor of English Literature in Newbridge Dominican College.

Ten people from the town died of influenza in October and another dozen or so in November. In mid-November three sisters in one family caught the disease. Katie Reddy became ill on Friday and died on Saturday. Her sister, Mary, also died before her sibling's funeral. Mary Reddy was engaged to be married and the ceremony was to take place immediately after Christmas. The funerals to the New Cemetery were very largely attended. Another sister, Annie, was also seriously ill with the flu, but recovered. The girls were the daughters of John and Mary Reddy, Edward Street. John was a car owner and his two sons, Patrick and John, also worked as car drivers. At a meeting of the Town Commissioners the Chairman said they all deeply regretted the sad deaths, which had occurred as a result of the recent epidemic in their midst, but they were glad to know there were no new cases being reported. They recognised the valuable services of the medical officers, who had worked so hard and unselfishly and who were so successful in coping with the epidemic in the district.[16]

At a meeting of Athy Board of Guardians the following resolution from Galway Union was read and adopted:

> That owing to the gravity of the Influenza Plague and the admitted shortage of Medical aid in this country, we demand the immediate release of all Medical Practitioners interned or imprisoned, so that their services may be availed of in this awful crisis.

The 'Plague' – as it was referred to in the Athy Union Minute Books – also spread to Castledermot and Monasterevan. Nurse Harmon was employed to assist Dr Brennan, in Castledermot, but as influenza raged through Monasterevan the Local Government Board regretted that they were unable to supply a doctor for the district to replace Dr McKenna, who was ill. A horse and cart went around Monasterevan district each day delivering milk procured from local farmers, while the Convent undertook to distribute milk, beef tea, gruel and other products, which would help combat the disease. Dr O'Neill, of Athy, said he was unable to get to Monasterevan as he had his hands full with calls in his own district. The Relieving Officer for Monasterevan was asked to employ any nurse available in the area.[17] Monasterevan and Kildare Town were 'in the grip' of the epidemic and doctors in the area were hard-pressed to cope. The *Leinster Leader* reported that 'a number of strong people in the prime of their life succumbed to the disease in the district'. Private Michael Keegan of the Connaught Rangers was home on leave when he contracted the flu and died of pneumonia, in Monasterevan, on 1 October 1918.[18]

In Athy Miss Minnie Murphy was appointed as 'Nurse of District, with such voluntary help as may be obtained, to visit the sick and render all possible assistance'. The Board of Guardians also arranged with the Relieving Officer, Mr Cleary, to establish a communal kitchen at Athy Technical School to distribute beef tea, milk, gruel, etc. A Committee of Ladies made arrangements to cook the necessary provisions for distribution to the sick poor.[19] At the end of the epidemic, which lasted six weeks, Mr Cleary, R.O., asked 'for some honorarium or bonus in connection with the extra hard work' he had to perform during the period, stating that he was out night and day giving relief to the sick and arranging for the burial of the dead. The application for a bonus was refused.[20] (Naas Poor Law Guardians awarded their relieving officers a bonus of £3 each in respect of extra services discharged by them during the epidemic.) Meanwhile, Dr T. F. Higgins, Ballitore, applied for payment at the rate of £2 2s per day for acting as temporary medical officer of Kilcullen Dispensary District for four weeks during the absence of Dr Barker, who was – lucky for him – on holidays. Dr Higgins said he had to attend over 1,000 cases of influenza in his four week sojourn and was duly awarded the payment, along with the ordinary remuneration of £4 4s per week, already sanctioned for that period.[21]

Urban areas suffered more than rural districts and the epidemic took a heavy toll throughout Naas, Newbridge and Athy. The poor were naturally the most severely affected. Their chronically unsanitary dwellings provided a suitable environment for the propagation of the disease, while they also suffered from a lack of fuel, as well as milk and eggs; the former being scarce, while the latter were, owing to unprecedented prices, unaffordable. The *Kildare Observer* reported that the death rate in the Naas district during the height of the epidemic was very heavy, perhaps heavier, than in any district with the same population in Ireland.[22] Athy Board of Guardians reported fifty deaths in a three-week period.[23]

The third and final wave of the epidemic broke out in the spring of 1919, mainly in the north of the county though it was reported as being less fatal, but more contagious, than the other instances. Naas reported many cases, but few fatalities. A serious outbreak of influenza occurred in the Clane and Timahoe North Dispensary District requiring the assistance of a medical practitioner. After advertisements Dr W. N. Alexander, Rathmines, Dublin, was engaged at £6 6s per week.[24] Four extra nurses were engaged in Celbridge Workhouse owing to the large number of influenza patients admitted to the hospital from the Lucan, Celbridge and Straffan districts. A particularly sad case involved the Dillon family of Hazelhatch, who were stricken with the flu. The mother died at home, while five members of the family were removed to the workhouse, three of whom died.[25] The epidemic was gone by March 1919 leaving hundreds dead in its wake. By the time the epidemic had finally passed the Register General maintained that 20,051 certified deaths could be directly attributed to the Great Flu in Ireland a figure he admitted was conservative, as it did not include deaths from pneumonia, or other diseases, resulting from influenza.[26]

The Registrar General statistics indicated that Co. Kildare suffered the highest county rate of death from influenza per head of population in the country, even surpassing the more industrial towns in the north. The death rate in Co. Kildare from the Great Flu in 1918 was 3.95 per thousand head of living population, a total of 263 deaths; the following year the county death rate from influenza dropped to 1.95 per thousand living, or 126 deaths. In Leinster only Dublin came close to the 1918 Kildare death rate, at 3.70, while Belfast county borough had a death rate of 3.85. The county's death rate from influenza was 389, indicating that 2.5 per cent of sufferers died. That is about a quarter of the population in Kildare, or about 15,500 people, caught the disease.[27]

On the Western Front things had taken a turn for the better. Marshal Foch's grand offensive, which eventually compelled the Germans to appeal for peace, began in late September. By the end of the month the much vaunted Hindenberg Line, the last line of German defences on the Western Front, was breached by the Allies. In October the German government approached the United States with a request for an armistice. By 3 November, a revolution had broken out in Germany and six days later the Kaiser abdicated.[28] It was wet, dank and cold when the German delegation signed the terms of the ceasefire that ended the greatest war in world history on 11 November 1918. The war lasted 1,568 days.[29] At the fighting fronts, as soon as the news had been absorbed and digested, one question was on the lips of all the men who had done so much to bring about the Armistice: When would they go home?

The *Kildare Observer* (16 November) printed a copy of the terms of the Armistice and ran an editorial headlined 'The triumph of right'. There was little mention of the war except for a report on the peace celebrations and some small notes on military awards recently given. The *Nationalist and Leinster Times* (18 November), had an end of war report, but no mention of local peace celebrations; the 'Kildare Notes' section was more concerned with the flu epidemic. The paper's editorial was on the forthcoming General Election. The following week's issue again made no mention of the war, but contained an open letter from the Bishop of Kildare and Leighlin, Patrick Foley, titled 'The end of the war and the conscription menace.'[30]

With the suspension of hostilities all recruiting for the armed services was immediately suspended under the Military Services Act. The last Kildare man killed in action was Able Seaman Robert Williamson (born in Celbridge), who went down with his ship H.M.P.M.S. *Ascot*, on 10 November 18. The *Ascot* was a paddle minesweeper, which has the dubious honour of being the last British ship lost in WWI. One day before the armistice was signed, she was torpedoed by UB67 off the northwest coast of Scotland.[31]

With the arrival of the news in Naas of the signing of the Armistice a Union Jack was hoisted over the courthouse. The *Observer* said 'there was a general feeling of relief if there was but little outward manifestation of relief'. Towards evening there was some flag waving by soldiers in the town and many indulged in celebrations and pranks. Soldiers stationed at the Depot came into the streets, singing and cheering, many of them carrying small flags of the Allied nations. The soldiers were in good form. Union Jack flags were hung out of some houses in the town and vicinity. The *Irish Times* reported that in some of the country districts church bells were rung. The same type of celebrations were held in Newbridge and Kildare Town. At a meeting of Newbridge Town Commission a resolution was passed 'congratulating the Allies and of satisfaction at the splendid triumph which had been gained'.[32]

There was general rejoicing at the Curragh Camp and also at Newbridge and Kildare barracks. All parades were declared off for the day with a result that a general holiday was enjoyed by the troops. All over Kildare the military and civilians celebrated.[33] The town of Celbridge was 'brilliantly illuminated on Monday night in celebration of the ending of the war. Bonfires were lighted in the district and on the streets and dancing was kept up until the small hours of Tuesday morning'.[34] The day after the signing of the Armistice there was a seven card race at the Curragh – the main race was the Killashee Plate – and the happy circumstances under which the meeting was held made it a well-attended affair.[35] A Thanksgiving service was held in St Brigid's Cathedral, Kildare Town, on Sunday 17 November. At the 11 o'clock service there was a full parade by the Royal Field Artillery and Cadet Corps.[36]

In Dublin there was major rejoicing, but the celebrations were marred by ugly scenes as soldiers, civilians and republicans clashed on several occasions. The Mansion House, Liberty Hall and Sinn Féin headquarters at Parnell Square were attacked and windows broken by soldiers and civilians. After further clashes on 13 November soldiers were recalled to barracks. Former *Leinster Leader* editor, Seumas O'Kelly, journalist, author and playwright, was working late into the night when soldiers and civilians celebrating the Armistice attacked the offices of the Sinn Féin newspaper, *Nationality*. A man of gentle character O'Kelly was upset by the aggression of the attackers and suffered a seizure. He died three days later, on 14 November. (The *Irish Times* reported that O'Kelly died after a brief illness and made no mention of the attack.) Previous to the removal of the remains from the Church of St Teresa, Clarendon Street, to Glasnevin Cemetery, on 17 November, Requiem Mass was celebrated by his brother, Rev. Father Alphonsus O'Kelly, (Carmelites) O.D.C. A crowd of 10,000 attended the funeral, organised by Sinn Féin. Dozens of uniformed British and colonial soldiers were in the vicinity, but there were no incidents. The coffin was covered with the republican colours. A guard of honour was supplied by the Irish Volunteers, a section of the cycling corps leading the cortége. Numerous wreaths were received from friends, the Sinn Féin Executive, the staff of *Nationality*, of which O'Kelly was acting editor since the arrest of Arthur Griffith; Sinn Féin clubs; the staff of the *Leinster Leader*; the Co. Kildare Gaelic League Executive; Naas (Sean Connolly) Sinn Féin Club and other organisations. His more militant brother, Michael, had taken over as editor of the *Leinster Leader* after Seumas's departure to Dublin.[37]

The Central Powers held 171,000 British and colonial prisoners-of-war and contingents of released Irish POWs began arriving back at the North Wall, in Dublin, from 25 November 1918. Some had been prisoners since 1914. They were from all parts of the country, but included some from Kildare.[38] Private John Ginnane, 2nd Battalion, RDF, a brother of P. J. Ginnane the *Kildare Observer* representative at Athy, arrived home from Russia where he was a German prisoner of war for the previous nine months. Like thousands of other British prisoners, he was sent out to work in all weathers and although registered as being interned in a German camp, he never saw the place, and consequently, never got a letter or a parcel from home. His POW party traversed France, Alsace-Lorraine, Warsaw, and Russia, and large numbers of the men succumbed for want of food and care. Pte. Ginnane was captured on 21 March 1918, the first day of the Spring Offensive. He said,

> After being in Russia for some time my health broke down, so
> that I had to go to the (Lazarette) hospital. Here I had to live on
> elderberry soup and cabbage water, but of course, most of the
> patients being Englishmen and accustomed to plenty of solid
> food, they were dying in large numbers for the want of decent

food. It may interest your readers to know that I never had occasion to raise a fork while a prisoner of war, and of course, such things as knife, spoon, soap, tea, cocoa, coffee, white bread, milk or sugar were all things of the past, and I received no letters or parcels during my captivity. However, thanks to the Red Cross Societies and the Returned Prisoners of War Committee, Dublin, I am now home again, safe and sound, and hope soon to be in civvies again. On the way home I was detained for about a week at Copenhagen (Denmark), during which time several inquiries were put to me about Ireland and Home Rule, but having been out of the country for a long time, I was not able to say much on the subject.[39]

Like the reaction towards the end of the war, which was quite muted in the local media, there were few reports of events concerning the release and return of the dozens of Kildare prisoners. The Great War, it seemed, no longer held the interest of the Irish people.

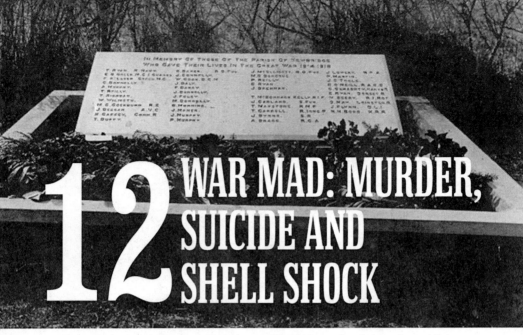

12 WAR MAD: MURDER, SUICIDE AND SHELL SHOCK

The memorial in St Conleth's Cemetery, Newbridge, erected in 1931 for men from the town who were killed in WWI. Photo: Veronica Heavey.

THE VAST MAJORITY of Irish soldiers in the First World War managed to survive the bombs and bullets emotionally and psychologically intact. A significant proportion became psychiatric casualties. The causes were varied: the stresses resulting from being catapulted into a very different military environment, the terror of combat, or more long-term predisposition to insanity. Sadly, the true extent of the problem is unknown since there are no reliable statistics regarding the proportion of Irish soldiers who suffered psychiatric collapse during the war. The chief problem is that the data provided by medical personnel was highly unreliable. Officer's reports tended to avoid using psychiatric terms, preferring 'safer' diagnoses based upon feigned categories.[1] Sixty-five thousand British ex-soldiers received disability pensions because of injury to the nerves, 'neurasthenia', or combat stress; many were hospitalised for the rest of their lives.[2]

The tedium of army life and the terror of battle are just two aspects of military service that create intense psychological stress, sometimes resulting in madness.[3] Mental damage inflicted by constant artillery fire affected many soldiers on both sides. Veterans returned home injured in mind and body. Few were unaffected by the war. There was hospital treatment available for physical wounds, but no cure for the injuries of the mind. Some veterans learned to deal with their problems with time; others were not so lucky and could not come to terms with what had happened in the war. Shell shock was the common word used to describe what is now known as post-traumatic stress disorder. This condition was not understood at the time, and symptoms included fatigue, irritability, headaches, and lack of concentration. Some soldiers who suffered from mental breakdowns, were reduced to shivering wrecks, and could not continue in the front lines. Officers were sent home to recuperate. Ordinary soldiers, however, were not so lucky. Shell shock was not recognised as an official medical problem, and many high-ranking officials thought that the sufferers were cowards who wanted to get away from the fighting. Some casualties refused to follow orders; others committed suicide or deserted. Punishment of these men was harsh, and ranged from court-martial to execution.

Shell-shocked veterans were common in every town and village. Timmy Conway grew up in Naas during the 1940s and 1950s when many of the local veterans of the war were reaching old age:

> I knew them [shell-shocked veterans] from coming into our shop. Nobody wanted them in their premises. They created too much trouble. They had idiosyncrasies, which marked them out. Tommy Lewis was a bit eccentric and would walk up the town as if he was on parade with a walking stick on his shoulder. He would often stand to attention with his stick over his shoulder and go through the drill routine of the British army and astonish his audience with his precision and dexterity. Another man I remember would stand out in the middle of the main street directing traffic. When the Garda put him off the street he would start again further down. I remember men walking up the town; talking to themselves; boxing with an imaginary boxer; shouting orders; jumping when a car passed.

They were the walking dead. Many ended their days in the poor house rejected by the people. Others were tolerated as long as they didn't step out of line. They were an integral part of the town and formed a love/hate relationship with the townsfolk. Children copied and teased them, while shopkeepers were intolerant of them, running them at the first sign of trouble. Their special oddities became more pronounced when drink was taken.[4]

Mick Mulvey worked in his father's public house in Naas, and recalled shell-shocked veterans like Tommy Lewis and Andy Murphy:

Tommy Lewis lived in Fishery Lane. He had a walking stick and used to carry his belongings in a quarter-sized flour sack tied to the stick. He had several sayings, which made him stand out. One was 'Muddy canals and rusty railways,' to which he blamed on the policies of Éamon de Valera and Fianna Fáil. He hated de Valera and during an election poked all the eyes out of Dev's election posters in the town. He was never violent, and would only bang his walking stick on a bar stool. Then he was asked to leave.[5]

Tommy Lewis survived the conflict, but suffered all his life from shell shock, or post-traumatic stress. He died in 1971, aged eighty-five. Three Lewis brothers, from Naas, served in three different units: Tommy as a gunner in the Royal Field Artillery; Michael with the 2nd Royal Dublin Fusiliers; and Patrick with the 1st Royal Dublin Fusiliers. In 1911 Michael and Patrick were living in a two-roomed second-class house at Jigginstown, with their widowed mother, Kate, and three sisters. Michael and Patrick were employed as farm labourers and enlistment in the army was probably an escape from the grinding poverty and the drudgery of work. The whereabouts of Tommy is not recorded in the census.[6]

The three brothers had different experiences in the war. Michael Lewis was killed in action on 1 May 1915, when the 2nd Royal Dublin Fusiliers tried to retake the village of St Julien, which had been lost to the Germans the previous day. Michael's body was not identified; his name is recorded on the Menin Gate Memorial, Ypres, in Belgium, along with 54,896 others.[7] On Sunday 25 April 1915, Patrick Lewis landed at Cape Helles, Turkey, with the 1st Royal Dublin Fusiliers. Before he went to the Dardanelles, Patrick wrote a last letter to his mother from Victoria Barracks, Cork:

My Dear Mother,

Just a few lines to find you in good health as this leaves me at present. I am going in the next draft. I was for the doctor's inspection on Sunday after coming off the Nun's guard. I am going to the first battalion they are in England after coming home from India. I don't know whether they are going to France or where. I hear we are going to Egypt, about fifty of us with the first Battalion. We are going to England to join them. Jim Mc Combs is here. I heard no account of Mike's yet only from your letter. I was sorry to hear of Mr Haydon's death, I wish I had taken his advice about the army.

Tell William Stafford I was asking for him and Patrick Malone. Tell them I was asking for them, tell them I am going out with the first battalion that came home from India. They are in England, we are going in two or three days, it was along time threatening but it has come at last. It will cripple all the young fellows of the world. It is a pity to see them, fine young fellows going around here crippled. Paddy Hackett is in my room he is home from the front I think I have no more to say at present.

Write soon don't delay a minute, in case I would not be here. I don't know the minute I might not be here.

No. 4385 Pte. P. Lewis

B Company 3 R.D.F.

Victoria Barracks. Cork.[8]

Patrick Lewis was killed in action on 11 May 1915 at Cape Helles, Gallipoli, just two weeks after his brother Michael died. Patrick was buried with his fallen comrades in the war cemetery at V Beach, Cape Helles. Lance Corporal Peter Coughlin, 2nd Royal Dublin Fusiliers (Rathasker Road, Naas), mentioned in Patrick's last letter was killed in action in France on 1 March 1917. Both Jim McCombs and Paddy Hackett, mentioned in Patrick's last letter, survived the war.[9]

Naas resident Timmy Conway recalled another shell-shocked veteran, Andy Murphy, who like Tommy Lewis had some peculiar sayings. Andy Murphy was from Newbridge, but lived in Sallins.

> Andy was tall and thin. He wore a hat with a large crown on it making him look like a cowboy as he staggered down the street. He spoke about the tragedies of war and its futility. The recalling of the horror of trench warfare always upset him. He talked about the rats and decaying bodies in the trenches and the terrible fear that ran through him as he awaited the order to go over the top. Andy ended every sentence with 'All along the line, a right one.' This phrase was quickly spoken when sober and nearly incoherent when drunk. It was easy to tell when he was drunk as he staggered from shop to shop supporting himself with his hands on the buildings and muttering the first part of the phrase 'All along the line,' then roaring out 'A right one!' During these periods he was barred from every pub in the town. We would follow him as he occasionally got one foot in the door of a pub only to be told to shove off.[10]

James Berney, Shruleen Lane, Athy, was discharged from the army in August 1916 being no longer fit for service. He was suffering from shell shock and the effects of gas poisoning. During his service his character was described as exemplary by his commanding officer: 'Private James B[i]erney has served his country well, and has been temporarily incapacitated in its defence...'[11] A married man, aged thirty-three, he had two young daughters; three previous children had died. James Berney's occupation was given as a general dealer and he had probably joined the army out of economic necessity. He served with the Scottish Rifles.

Shell shock was by no means the preserve of the faint-hearted or psychologically fragile. It was not just young inexperienced volunteers who succumbed, but experienced regulars and tough veterans. Soldiers suffered severe shock from the impact of near misses or continuous artillery barrages. George Marshall, a US Army operations officer in WWI, wrote on the effects of artillery fire:

> A three-inch shell will temporarily scare or deter a man; a six-inch shell will shock him; but an eight-inch shell, such as those 210mm ones, rips up the nervous system of everyone within a hundred yards of the explosion.[12]

German officer Ernst Jünger, described this feeling in his autobiography *Storm of Steel*:

> I think I have found a comparison that captures the situation in which I and all the other soldiers who took part in this war so often found ourselves: you must imagine you are securely tied to a post and threatened by a fellow swinging a sledgehammer. Now the hammer is swung back for the blow, now its cleaving the air towards your skull, then its struck the post, and the splinters are flying from the post – that's what it's like to experience heavy shelling in an exposed position ... The brain links every separate sound of whirring metal with the idea of death and so the nerves are exposed without protection and without pause to the sense of absolute menace ... Hours such as these were without doubt the most awful of the war.

Jünger had been at war since 1914 and was an exceptionally brave officer, but when sixty-three out of his company of 150 men were killed by artillery on the eve of the March Offensive in 1918 he ran from the spot in terror, then broke down and wept in front of the survivors. If this could happen to a veteran soldier like Jünger it is small wonder so many men on both sides suffered from shell shock.[13]

The tensions and stresses of service at the Front were sometimes exposed in more tragic ways. In June 1916 Lieutenant and Quartermaster William Evans, 5th Leinster Regiment, shot himself dead with his revolver in his office at the Curragh Camp. The forty-seven-year-old married man was worried and overworked and had sought clerical assistance which was not granted. Also at the Curragh Corporal George W. Askew, 17th Lancers, shot himself with his rifle after seeing his brother's name in the roll of honour of his local newspaper. The jury returned a verdict of suicide in accordance with the medical evidence, adding that they believed Cpl. Askew was insane when he committed the act.[14]

The body of Private Edward Noone was taken from the canal at Limerick Bridge, Jigginstown, Naas on 11 March 1916. The coroner reported the body had been in the water for around ten days. His widow, Anne Noone, Swordlestown, Naas, in giving evidence to the coroner's court, said she last saw her husband alive on 14 February 1916 when he was in his usual health. She said he was a little depressed at the thought of going back to his regiment and was sorry to be leaving his children. Anne Noone said her husband was 'sometimes strange in his mind' and had dictated a rambling letter, which was found on his body, addressed to the 'Captain in charge of Beggarsbush Barracks, Dublin', saying that he was threatened and would be drowned if he appeared for guard duty. His wife agreed that the letter made no sense. Pte. Noone had been home on fourteen days leave and when taken from the water was wearing his uniform, without a great coat or cap. His death was recorded as 'found dead in the canal'.

Edward Noone was buried with full military honours in St Corban's Cemetery, Naas. The band of the Royal Dublin Fusiliers played the Dead March, the coffin being borne on a gun carriage covered with the Union Jack. According to the *Leinster Leader* the cortége presented a very impressive and solemn spectacle. A firing party from the Dublin Fusiliers fired the usual three parting volleys over the grave of the deceased.[15]

One veteran, Michael Kelly, inflamed with jealousy owing to rumours of his wife's infidelity, drowned her in the Royal Canal, at Kilcock. On 11 August 1915 Kelly, a private with the Royal Dublin Fusiliers, arrived from the Military Barracks in Cork to where his wife, Mollie, was staying, at her parents' house in Courtown, Kilcock. During the evening the couple argued and Michael Kelly was heard by his sister-in-law to threaten to kill his wife. He accused her of spending all the money he sent to her on male friends, who were staying in the house while he was away. The two went for a walk towards the town and were last seen standing at the Royal Canal bridge. Some time later, Mollie Kelly's body was taken from the canal. Michael Kelly was brought to identify her body and said to Sgt. Dunne, RIC, 'I wish I was shot in France; all my troubles would be over. How will I get on now with my four little children?' When he was then arrested on suspicion of murder Kelly said 'All right sir; I would rather than a thousand pounds that my wife was alive.'

Pte. Kelly was convicted of murdering his wife by drowning her in the canal and sentenced to death. It was later learned that Michael Kelly had tried to hang himself two years previous and that he was possibly of unsound mind at the time and had been tried at Celbridge Petty Sessions for attempted suicide. Kelly's death sentence was commuted to life imprisonment by the Lord Lieutenant in December 1915.[16]

Tragedy awaited others who had survived the war years. Sergeant John Geraghty (Newbridge) was shot dead by another uniformed soldier on the morning of 13 December 1919. Thirty-one year-old Geraghty had enlisted in Naas on 4 September 1914 in the Royal Dublin Fusiliers. John left the Dublin Fusiliers after three-months home service and then re-enlisted in the Royal Irish Regiment. He was transferred to the newly-formed Machine Gun Corps in 1916, where he underwent a six-week training course in Harrowby, England. Following machine-gun training, he was sent via Southampton to the M. G. Base Depot at Camiers, France, and promoted to corporal. A corporal with the Machine Gun Corps would have been in charge of transport of two gun teams with six men to each team. John Geraghty was demobilised in 1919, but then re-enlisted travelling to France with the Hampshire Regiment's 21st Battalion as a sergeant. A letter from John's company commander, Captain Bullick, to his mother, Anne Geraghty, of James's Street, Newbridge, stated that 'the occurrence took place about three o'clock on the morning of December 13th, whilst on duty'. A letter from the chaplain, Headquarters Mess 6, Camp Calais, said 'that he was killed in the execution of his duty while guarding Government stores on the harbour quay in Calais. He was shot through the head and never regained consciousness'.

A letter from Private Jack Connolly, also of James's Street, Newbridge, to John's sister, Catherine Doyle, said,

> I have been asking the men that were on guard with Johnnie how it happened and none of them seem to know exactly how it came about. They say that they heard the fellow who fired the shot ask 'Are you the Sergeant of the guards'. Johnnie of course said 'Yes,' then the fellow fired the shot and hit poor Johnnie, who was taken away immediately to hospital.

Connolly's letter went on to describe how the soldier, Private P. Hennessy, who shot Sgt. Geraghty, was given a severe beating by the men of his detachment and was saved further violence by the intervention of an officer. He described Geraghty as one of the most popular NCOs in the regiment, a sentiment confirmed by John's commanding officer in the letter to Mrs Anne Geraghty. Why Pte. Hennessy shot Sgt. Geraghty is unclear and if he was the intended target and not some other sergeant of the guard, as it is unknown whether he even knew him. John Geraghty died on 14 December and was buried three days later in the Soldier's Cemetery, at La Baraques, near Calais, France. John's medals were sent to his mother in October 1921, nearly two years after his death.[17]

Accidental deaths contributed to a significant proportion of the 'war dead'. Any serviceman who died between 4 August 1914 and 11 November 1918 and even up to 31 December 1919 are termed as 'war dead', even though they might not have been killed in action, or died of wounds received in action. Personnel who died while on active service in other parts of the British Empire are also given the same status. Dozens of men died in Co. Kildare from accidents, suicide, illness and wounds received in action. All of them are listed as war dead.

Australian soldier Private J. J. Hickey was run over by a train near Osberstown, between Caragh and Sallins on 27 January 1918. Walking along the railway line towards Sallins to catch a train to the Curragh, Pte. Hickey was struck by one train and run over by another. He died in the Curragh Military Hospital of terrible injuries. He was buried in Bridgetown Cemetery after his body was released to his uncle, Thomas Hickey, of Ballybrack, Kilmore, Co. Limerick.[18]

In a short period of just over four weeks four men were buried in the grounds of St Brigid's Cathedral Kildare: Private John Ashbie, 12th (Prince of Wales's Royal) Lancers, who died on 9 August 1915; Private George Evans, 5th (Royal Irish) Lancers who died on 28 August 1915; Private Albert Hughes, 2nd/1st Montgomeryshire Yeomanry, who died on 6 September 1915; Private Gordon Walker, 3rd/1st Montgomeryshire Yeomanry, who died on 14 September 1915. Their deaths were recorded as accidental, but it was a harrowing fact that there appeared to be a high percentage of suicides amongst the British forces stationed in Co. Kildare.

Private Gordon Walker died within ten days of having an operation, on the 14 September 1915, at the Military Hospital Curragh. The Montgomeryshire Yeomanry were only recently formed, or rather reformed, at the outbreak of the war and would not have been long in Kildare. But it was the death of Private John Ashbie that raised more questions than answers. The *Kildare Observer* of 14 August 1915 reported on an inquest at the Military Barracks, Kildare, on 10 August, by Dr M. F. Kenna, Coroner for South Kildare on the body of John 'Ashby', a Private in the 6th Reserve Cavalry. John Ashbie's body was found around 5.45 a.m. at the foot of the stairs leading to his room on the morning of 9 August 1915. Apparently he had gone to bed in good spirits the previous evening and was a well-liked, though quiet, peaceable man; he was about forty-five years old and married. Two witnesses were examined. John Fleming had slept in the same room but heard no commotion or dispute nor the door being opened. Shoeing-smith Sydney Baxter slept in the room next door but similarly heard no disturbance though he did not see Ashbie on the night in question. Baxter remarked that Ashbie was 'on good terms with everyone in the regiment'. Dr E. T. Coady was then examined as he was called to the scene around 6.30am. He found a fracture at the base of the skull caused by his accidentally falling down the stairs. There was no other evidence of violence. The jury found in accordance with the medical evidence.[19]

Mark Hickey, who had survived four years at the Front with the Irish Guards died after a squabble on a roadside near Naas, a few years after the war. Earlier in the day, of 18 March 1925, Mark Hickey was drinking in John Nolan's public house, in Naas, when he got into an altercation with John Clarke, a farmer from Mullacash, Two-Mile-House. Mark Hickey later claimed Clarke called him a coward. For a man who had faced death many times this was a serious affront and later on, as he travelled home the short distance to his home at Killashee, Mark Hickey again met Clarke accompanied by another man, Owen Behan, of Bishopshill, Ballymore-Eustace. Words and blows were exchanged; Mark Hickey struck Clarke, who struck him back with his hand, which held a smoking pipe. Unfortunately, for Hickey, the stem of the pipe struck him in the left cheek under his eye. However, Hickey developed septic inflammation of the optic tissues, which then developed into meningitis and was brought to Baggot Street Hospital, Dublin, where he later died. John Clarke was first charged with assault, let out on bail, and then charged with murder. When arrested he said it was 'an unfortunate occurrence'. At his trial for manslaughter, in Dublin's Central Criminal Court, in January 1926, John Clarke pleaded not guilty. In his defence Clarke stated that when he, Mark Hickey and Owen Behan were returning from Naas, the deceased attempted to strike him, and witness, being in the act of lighting his pipe at the time, put up his hand to save himself, and must have struck Hickey in the eye with the shank of the pipe. Clarke said it was only when he reached his home that he discovered his pipe was broken. He was found not guilty of manslaughter and discharged.[20]

Soldiers were quick to use violence in disagreements with republicans and nationalists. During a proclaimed meeting in Naas in late summer 1918 the RIC arrived in force to arrest the republican spokesman, Art O'Connor (Celbridge). Volunteers from Naas, Newbridge and Kill companies surrounded the platform while O'Connor addressed the meeting. The police made no attempt to interfere until O'Connor stepped down from the platform. The volunteers linked hands and formed two double lines to a laneway where O'Connor made his escape. There were some scuffles between police and volunteers. Later in the evening, as the members of Kill Company were leaving Naas, they were attacked by about thirty British soldiers, many of them locals home on furlough. Their wives and girlfriends joined in throwing stones and bottles. Volunteer captain, Patrick Dunne, received a cut to his hand from a knife or bottle, while Volunteer lieutenant, Tom Domican, received injuries to the head when struck by a bottle.[21]

Naas was the scene of another incident during the 'khaki election' of 1918. There had been no general election in Britain or Ireland since 1910, but a lot had changed since then. The Irish population had been radicalised, and a whole generation of young voters, coupled with the sudden influx of women over thirty, dramatically changed the make-up of the Irish electorate. The Irish Party had been dominant for decades, but Sinn Féin were becoming a power to be reckoned with and the IP candidates, John O'Connor and Denis Kilbride, were hoping to pick up extra votes from returning soldiers. In November 1918, amid fears that many soldiers would not be able to vote, O'Connor claimed that there were a large number of military not on the voting register.[22]

Some days prior to polling day, on 2 December, the Sinn Féin candidate for North Kildare, Domhnall Ua Buachalla, arrived in Naas to address an election meeting at the Market Square. There was a large receptive crowd listening to the republican speakers when a crowd of British soldiers and accompanying women congregated at the outskirts of the crowd and began shouting, 'Up the red, white and blue', and 'Up England', and 'Up the khaki'. The soldiers hoisted a Union Jack on a lamp-post outside the post office on the opposite side of the road and Domhnall Ua Buachalla, pointing to it, said this was the flag under which Ireland had to live under, but would soon be replaced by the flag of Sinn Féin. Some youths pulled the flag down and a scuffle broke out between them and soldiers who tried to reclaim their flag. After a few minutes republican stewards restored order, while cheers and counter cheers continued. Eventually, some soldiers hoisted another Union Jack on the lamp-post. The police had to intervene to prevent further incident and the situation calmed down as the meeting was brought to a close. When a republican car parked outside the Royal Hotel some young girls pulled a Sinn Féin flag from its rear, but this was recovered after a few minutes.[23]

Violence from British soldiers and high hopes from the Irish Party made no difference. The declaration of the poll for South Kildare was made at Athy town hall on 30 December 1918. Of the 755 absent voters, soldiers and sailors, only 189 voted. The register contained about 13,900 voters, and 8,649 voted. Art O'Connor was elected for Sinn Féin with 7,104 votes, while Denis Kilbride (IP) received 1,545. The results in North Kildare were: Domhnall Ua Buachalla (SF) 5,979; John O'Connor (IP) 2,772.[24] The election in Kildare, and the rest of the country, apart from the six north-eastern counties, was an overwhelming victory for Sinn Féin. The country returning soldiers came home to was 'all changed, changed utterly'. The train of events set in motion by the election would lead to the Irish War of Independence.

The Newbridge British Legion Band, pictured in 1930, outside their local hall. John Doyle is standing under the second window from the left. Photo: Veronica Heavey.

'We too are among the ranks of the forgotten…' J. V. Holland

FOR THE YOUNG, and not-so young, men from Co. Kildare who had answered the call in 1914–18 the world would never be the same. They had experienced death, danger, cold, fatigue, hunger and disease at first hand and endured events which left indelible marks on their minds and bodies. The country to which demobilised soldiers returned was completely changed: Sinn Féin had achieved a landslide victory in the General Election, and Home Rule had been suspended but realistically was no longer an option. For Britain Irish independence was not an option, either. The return of the soldiers was lost in an atmosphere of republican triumph. Memory of the war was politically contentious. It became an embarrassment to say you had fought for the British Empire and it was perceived that Irish veterans had served in the wrong army in the wrong war. Britain was now the enemy and those who came home kept quiet about their service and put their medals away out of view.

The effect of nationalist and unionist fighting side-by-side had no lasting significance for the country. After the war both nationalist and unionist veterans throughout the country were discriminated against by one side or another. The prospect of 'we're all in this together' proved illusory. Ex-British servicemen remained a forgotten group within the new emerging Ireland. John Vincent Holland, VC, summed up the feeling of many ex-soldiers, in an interview with historian Sir John Hammerton, in 1933, when he said, 'We too are among the ranks of the forgotten.'[1]

Around 100,000 demobilised men returned home to economic and political uncertainty, while another 70,000 opted to stay in the armed forces, or made their home in Britain. Corporal James Delaney (Ballitore), probably decided to stay in the British army, as the *Leinster Leader* reported he was in North Walsham in February 1919 where he was awarded a DCM for 'conspicuous gallantry and devotion to duty'.[2] James Delaney was one of seven brothers in the service, and probably had few employment prospects to come home to.

Denis Lawless, Naas, also opted to stay in the military. He had enlisted in the Royal Dublin Fusiliers in 1916, when he was only seventeen. He served in Salonika and France, where he was wounded in the neck. When the Royal Dublin Fusiliers were disbanded in 1922, he re-enlisted in the Dorsetshire Regiment. Denis served in Egypt, Malta and India, retiring as a sergeant in 1937, after twenty-one years' service.[3]

The majority of returning men attempted to resume normal life in their communities. Like most war veterans they did not talk of their experiences. Far from the honour they were due, they were treated with contempt. Thousands of returning soldiers were wounded, some coughing up their lungs from gas poisoning, others mutilated, missing limbs, confined to wheelchairs, or blinded, all marked for ever. Men mutilated in battle could be seen in every part of Ireland – a dispiriting reminder of 'Britain's' war. British Legion halls in Athy, Naas, Newbridge and Brownstown were havens for veterans where they could meet other ex-servicemen, but many saw out their days in physical or psychological torment, remaining silent about their experiences throughout their lives, because nobody really wanted to listen.

James Doran of Fair Green, Naas, died of wounds on 24 August 1919. He was one of many who lingered after the war carrying the scars and wounds which ultimately cut short their lives.[4] Patrick J. Coughlin from Maynooth suffered the same fate. A former sergeant in the Connaught Rangers, Coughlin died in 1923, aged twenty-nine, from the effects of shell shock and tuberculosis in Newcastle Sanatorium.[5]

Other returning soldiers were maimed, but lived on into their latter years: Tom Alcock, (Athy) Leinster Regiment, lost a leg at Ypres; Darby Delaney also lost a leg while serving with the Royal Garrison Artillery. He died in 1964. Dick Warren, Killeen, Narraghmore, described by a senior officer of the Irish Guards, as 'the finest looking man in the regiment', lost part of his fingers under artillery fire; John Barry Browne, Greenaun, Naas, lost an eye and while recuperating from his wounds in Switzerland, met a Polish nurse, Petronella, who he later married; Thomas Higgins, Fair Green, Naas, lost his left hand at the Battle of Mons, while the famous handballer, George Robinson, lost part of his right hand. Robinson, a private soldier with the Leinster Regiment, who won an All-Ireland handball title prior to the war, was injured when a shell exploded near him. The loss of part of his hand was a devastating blow for an athlete who would never again compete at the highest level in his favourite sport. George was employed for many years as a gate man at the Asbestos factory, in Athy.[6]

Employment was scarce for returning servicemen. Protestant landowners and businessmen, however, were sympathetic to veterans and were quick to hire a man who had fought for 'King and Country'. Various committees, groups and organisations were set up to try and integrate returning soldiers into society. An Employment Bureau, set up early in the war, played a major part in providing soldiers with employment. In March 1916, 221 discharged soldiers were registered to the Co. Kildare Employment Bureau. Kildare Co. Council kept work places open for men who had joined up, and although a good number of men were taken back into their old employment, there were many who required new work. Other methods were used to provide ex-servicemen with aid. The Irish Land (Provision for Soldiers and Sailors) Bill was formulated to enable ex-servicemen to obtain small holdings, while about

3,600 houses countrywide were built with British government funding to house ex-servicemen. However, only a handful were provided for Co. Kildare in Naas, Newbridge, Kildare Town and Athy.[7]

Some veterans were content to return to family life and employment, while others, like Stephen Curran (Dunshane) and Christopher Murray (Moone) joined in the fight for independence. When the National Army was formed in early 1922 it found many willing recruits among WWI veterans. But for some the Irish Civil War was one conflict too many: Sean Nolan (Kildare Town), Peter Behan (Great Connell) and John Wogan Browne (Naas) all died in the 'troubles' in 1922.[8]

John Doyle enlisted with the Irish National Army, attesting at the Curragh Camp on 7 August 1922 and was discharged on 31 January 1923 due to being medically unfit. He was a British army veteran who had served nearly twelve years overseas, before being demobilised in 1919. Born in Fitzwilliam Lane, Dublin, John enlisted in the Royal Dublin Fusiliers, in Naas Depot, in 1904. After eight years overseas service he was transferred to the Army Reserve. John Doyle met Catherine Geraghty, from Newbridge, who was working as a domestic servant in Dublin, some time before the outbreak of the war when he was on Reserve Status. Mobilised for active service in August 1914 John married Catherine Geraghty in Donnybrook Church, Dublin, in July 1915. Shortly after his wedding he was posted to France, to serve in the 2nd Battalion, RDF, as a butcher in charge of rations. When his war service was over in 1918, he returned to Ireland and settled in Newbridge with his wife, Catherine. John and Catherine Doyle's seven children were born in James's Street, Newbridge. John became a member of the Royal British Legion, Newbridge branch, where he served as Club Steward. His eyesight began to fail and he was completely blind by 1932, when four of his children were still very young. John Doyle died in June 1939, aged fifty-eight.[9]

Of the 805 men from the county killed in the war around 100 were born to English soldiers, clergy, etc. The majority, however, were true Kildare men. Thirteen sets of brothers from Co. Kildare were killed in the war, while George and Elizabeth Harding, of Branganstown, Kilcock, lost a son and daughter. Richard William Harding (21), a Lance-Corporal, with the 2nd Royal Irish

Rifles, died of wounds, in France, on 3 July 1916; his sister, Isabel Lois Harding (22), a nurse with the Voluntary Aid Detachment, died in Birmingham, on 15 February 1919. [10]

Some families lost three sons in the war. The Kelly family of Meeting Lane, Athy, received three telegrams from the War Office informing them of the deaths of their beloved sons. Private John Kelly, Leinster Regiment, died of wounds in France on 23 May 1915. His brother Owen, also in the Leinster Regiment, was killed in action on 1 August 1915. The two brothers had joined up the same day. Their younger brother, Denis, later joined the same regiment despite the pleas of his distraught mother who had already lost two sons. Mary Kelly followed him to the railway station on the day she heard of his intention to enlist and in vain searched the train for her son. As it pulled out of the station she stood on the platform in tears. Denis Kelly died of wounds in France on 30 September 1918, aged twenty. [11]

Another Kildare family to suffer the loss of three sons was the Curtis family, of Kilcrow, Athy. Patrick Curtis (28), a private in the Irish Guards was killed in action on 5 November 1914. His brother, John, an acting bombardier in the Field Artillery, was killed on 9 January 1917. Their brother, Lawrence (30), a private in the 5th Irish Lancers, died of wounds on 4 December 1917. The brothers are buried together in Old St Michael's Cemetery, Athy.[12] There was hardly a house in the back streets of Athy, Naas, Newbridge or any other town in the county which wasn't affected by the war.

The effect of the war on Kildare was catastrophic; a whole generation was destroyed that would have produced businessmen, jurists, scholars, administrators and political leaders. The war caused desolation to many of the landed families by the deaths of sons and heirs. The *Irish Times* warned that 'before the war is over many old and respected families will have come to an end so far as their male line is concerned'. While 27 per cent of 30–34 year-old nobles, or peers, were killed during the war this does not represent a 'lost generation', it does reinforce the point that they were worse off than ordinary members of the forces whose rate of loss was one in eight. At times the life expectancy of a lieutenant on the Western Front was six weeks. Thirteen per cent of Irish soldiers mobilised for the war died as a result. Landed families had a very high enlistment rate of 59 per cent, which meant that nearly all of them had family or friends who served. The gentry thus seems to have suffered disproportionately and the closeness of the aristocratic community intensified the sense of loss.[13]

Terence Dooley in his survey of the 'big houses' found that of a total of 215 peers or their sons killed at the Front, twenty-eight were from Irish landowning families. He maintains, however, that three-quarters of those who served returned from the war and that it was an economic factor rather than the losses during the war that was responsible for the decline of the big house.[14] Crippled with debt duties and the loss of a son or two, the end of the war signalled the end of the feudal power of the landed gentry.

In Co. Kildare the 5th Duke of Leinster lost his son, Lord Desmond FitzGerald, a major in the Irish Guards, on the Western Front in March 1916, and a nephew Captain Gerald FitzGerald of the 4th Dragoon Guards, in 1914. Lt. Colonel Thomas de Burgh, Oldtown, Naas, lost his son, Thomas, a lieutenant in the 51st Lancers (Indian Army) in July 1917, and a cousin, John Maurice de Burgh, Royal Navy, was killed in action in 1915. Brigadier General Charles Fitzclarence, VC, who had been born at Kill, was leading the 1st Guards Brigade in November 1914 when he was killed. Second Lieutenant George Hubert Medlicott, of Dunmurry, Kildare, died serving with the South African Infantry in 1916. Capt. R. J. Smith, of Jigginstown, Naas, an engineer, and who merited mention in despatches, and Lt. J. Tynan of Monasterevan, were also killed in action. Captain Harry Greer, of the National Stud, Tully, Kildare, lost two sons: the elder, Col. Eric, aged twenty-five, was commanding 2nd Battalion, Irish Guards; while Lt. Francis St Leger Greer, aged twenty-three, was killed in action in February 1917.[15]

There are 160 war graves in Co. Kildare, of which 103 are in the Curragh Military Cemetery; the rest are scattered over twenty-seven cemeteries and churchyards. In total there are 158 soldiers and two members of the Royal Air Force buried in the county. Of the soldiers, fifty-seven belonged to Irish regiments, the comparatively small proportion being due to the presence of British regiments at the Curragh. Twenty-five of the Irish soldiers belonged to the Royal Dublin Fusiliers.[16] Each death and injury represented a painful loss for family, relations and friends. The end of the war did not bring an end to the pain.

'The Great War for Civilisation' was a senseless and brutal conflict which resolved little in terms of European power struggles. It was really only phase one of a single conflict. The world leaders gathered in Versailles to sign the treaty, but Germany signed only under duress. The Treaty of Versailles was forced upon them without discussion, along with massive war reparations. The treaty deprived Germany of territory, inflicted harsh, humiliating terms and saddled her with backbreaking financial reparations. The seeds of another conflict were sown, simply waiting for a spark. The 'Great War' was the harbinger of a far more brutal conflict and twenty-one years later another European war began, which again engulfed the world.

When the troops returned home in late 1918 and all through 1919, they assumed, along with the rest of the world, that the Great War had been truly the 'war to end all wars'. There was at least one visible change: the Great War had created a more democratic, more equal Britain. Demobilised servicemen came home to a Labour government committed to establishing a welfare state. All men, and some women, had the right to vote given to them by a grateful country. There was hope then for Ireland and perhaps appreciation for her sacrifices during the war. Irish republicans sought to put their case for self-determination, diplomatic recognition and membership of the proposed League of Nations, to delegates at the Paris Peace Conference, but Irish nationalism was unpopular with the Allies because of the conscription crisis of 1918 and Britain had decided to legislate for two home rule states. There would be no peace in Ireland for the foreseeable future, only war. That, however, is another story.

Notes

CHAPTER ONE

1. Neillands, R., *The Great War Generals on the Western Front, 1914–18* (London, 1999), pp.25–9; Fenby, J., *The General. Charles de Gaulle and the France he Saved* (London, 2010), p.55, 57.

2. Hastings, M., *Catastrophe: Europe Goes to War 1914* (London, 2013), p.89.

3. Costello, C., *A Most Delightful Station. The British Army on the Curragh of Kildare, Ireland, 1855–1922* (Cork, 1996), p.275.

4. *Kildare Observer*, 8 August 1914.

5. Ferguson, N., *The Pity of War* (London, 1999), p.164; *Leinster Leader*, 15 August 1914.

6. *Kildare Observer*, 8 August 1914.

7. Hastings, *Catastrophe*, p.112.

8. Athy UDC Minute Book, 4 April 1914–30 April 1920.

9. Denman, T., *Ireland's Unknown Soldiers: The 16th (Irish) Division in the Great War* (Dublin, 1992), p.25.

10. Davies, N., *Europe: A History* (London, 1997), p.1139.

11. Lyons, F. S. L., *Ireland Since the Famine* (London, 1985), p.322.

12. Hastings, *Catastrophe*, p.96.

13. Yeates, P., *A City in Wartime: Dublin, 1914–18* (Dublin, 2012), pp.5–6; *Kildare Observer*, 1 August 1914; *Leinster Leader*, 1 and 8 August 1914.

14. *Kildare Observer*, 8 August 1914.

15. *Leinster Leader*, 8 August 1914.

16. *Kildare Observer*, 8 August 1914.

17. Ibid; Taaffe, F., 'Athy and the Great War', in Nolan, W. and McGrath, T.

(eds), *Kildare. History and Society* (Dublin, 2006), p.589.

18. Costello, *A Most Delightful Station*, p.276.

19. *Kildare Observer*, 15 August 1914.

20. Ibid., 8 August 1914.

21. Costello, *A Most Delightful Station*, p.278.

22. *Kildare Observer*, 2 January 1915.

23. Hastings, *Catastrophe*, p.89.

24. Horne, J. (ed.), *Our War: Ireland and the Great War* (Dublin 2008), pp.66–7.

25. McGuire, J. and Quinn, J. (eds), *Dictionary of Irish Biography* (Cambridge, 2009), pp.238–9. Lord and Lady Mayo, of Palmerstown House were among the leading supporters of the Art and Crafts Movement in Ireland; Lady Geraldine Mayo re-founded the Royal Irish School of Art Needlework in 1894.

26. Yeates, *A City in Wartime*, p.130.

27. Kildare County Council. Minutes of the County Council and its Committees, January–December 1914. Sourced at KCRS, Newbridge Library.

28. Durney, J., *Far From the Short Grass: The Story of Kildaremen in Two World Wars* (Naas, 1999), pp.8–9.

29. *Kildare Observer*, 26 September 1914.

30. Meleady, D., *John Redmond: The National Leader* (Sallins, 2013), p.307.

31. *Kildare Observer*, 16 October 1914.

32. Meleady, *John Redmond*, p.308.

33. Horne, *Our War: Ireland and the Great War*, pp.45–6.

CHAPTER TWO

1. Corrigan, M. (ed.), *Druim Craig:The Ridge of Clay* (Naas, 2009), p.34.

2. Durney, J. *The War of Independence in Kildare* (Cork, 2013), pp.14–16.

3. Costello, C., *A Most Delightful Station: The British Army on the Curragh of Kildare, Ireland, 1855–1922* (Cork, 1996), pp.21–2.

4. Ibid; Durney, J., 'The Dubs come to Naas', County Kildare online electric historic journal, 21 July 2012.

5. O'Donovan, Lt. F. (ed.), *Ní obair in aisce Í. Forty years of the Army Apprentice School. 1956–1996* (Naas, 1996), pp.8, 17.

6. *Leinster Leader*, 12 September 1914.

7. Costello, *A Most Delightful Station*, pp.279–81.

8. Durney, J., 'Newbridge barracks. The first units', County Kildare online electric historic journal, 31 August 2012; Durney, J., *A Bridge, A Town, A People: Social Housing in Newbridge, 1900–1996* (Naas, 2009), pp.13–4.

9. *Leinster Express*, 5 May 1855; Costello, *A Most Delightful Station*, p.23.

10. Muenger, E. A., *The British Military Dilemma in Ireland: Occupation Politics, 1886–1914* (Dublin, 1991), p.3–4.

11. Costello, *A Most Delightful Station*, pp.43–4.

12. Gibson, W. and Nolan, P., 'Military influence on Kildare towns', *The Nationalist Centenary 1883–1993*.

13. Ann Donohoe and Eric Herrievan, 'Price family of Newbridge, 1895–1989', April 1989, sourced at Kildare Collections and Research Service, Newbridge Library, Newbridge, County Kildare.

14. *Leinster Leader*, 24 September 1966.

15. Costello, *A Most Delightful Station*, p.277.

16. *Leinster Leader*, 12 September 1914.

17. Gibson, W. and Nolan, W., 'Military influence on Kildare towns'.

18. Durney, J., Corrigan, M. and Connelly, J., *Hearth and Home: A History of Social Housing in Kildare Town 1889–2009* (Naas, 2012), pp.19–20.

19. Corry, E., 'The Orange Order in Kildare and Laois', *Kildare Voice*, 7 July 2007.

20. 1911 Census of Ireland.

21. Costello, *A Most Delightful Station*, pp.196–7.

22. Muenger, *The British Military Dilemma in Ireland*, p.3–4.

23. Costello, *A Most Delightful Station*, pp.178–9.

24. *Leinster Leader*, 10 October 1914.

25. Costello, *A Most Delightful Station*, p.283.

26. Hastings, M., *Catastrophe: Europe Goes to War 1914* (London, 2013), p.107.

27. Durney, J., Corrigan, M., Roche, C and Holzgrawe, C., *The Co. Kildare Dead of the First World War* (Forthcoming, 2014.)

28. *Kildare Observer*, 22 July 1916.
29. Attestation paper of Arthur John Dowling, www.recordsearch.naa.gov.au (accessed 22 March 2013).
30. Durney, J., 'Maurice Alwyn Adams, Killed in Action', www.kildare.ie/ehistory (accessed 30 April 2014).

CHAPTER THREE

1. Horne, J. (ed.), *Our War: Ireland and the Great War* (Dublin, 2008), p.66.
2. Hastings, M., *Catastrophe: Europe goes to War 1914* (London, 2013), p.132.
3. Ferriter, D., *The Transformation of Ireland, 1900–2000* (London, 2005), p.127. What happened at the Curragh was not a 'mutiny' but resignations in anticipation of unwelcome orders, not refusal to obey such orders once issued.
4. Durney, J., *Far From the Short Grass: The Story of Kildaremen in Two World Wars* (Naas, 1999), p.11.
5. Hobsbawn, E., *The Age of Empire, 1875–1914* (London, 2006) pp.312, 320.
6. Hastings, *Catastrophe*, p.181.
7. Brewer, P., *The History of Modern Warfare: A Year-by-Year Illustrated Account From the Crimean War to the Present Day* (London, 2007), pp.98–100, 107.
8. Durney, J., Corrigan, M., Roche, C. and Holzgrawe, C., *The Co. Kildare Dead of the First World War* (Forthcoming, 2014).
9. Durney, J., *Far From the Short Grass*, p.13.
10. Ibid.
11. *Kildare Observer*, 12 September 1914.
12. Keegan, J., *The First World War* (London, 1998), pp.140, 146, 199; Hastings, *Catastrophe*, pp.442, 469.
13. Davies, N., *Europe: A History* (London, 1997), pp.902–3.
14. Fussell, P., *The Great War and Modern Memory* (Oxford, 2013), p.44.
15. Ibid., pp.45–6.
16. Ibid., p.51.

17. *Kildare Observer*, 8 May 1915.

18. Fussell, *The Great War and Modern Memory*, p.53.

19. *Kildare Observer*, 4 September 1915.

20. 'A war veteran looks back from battlefields of France to Gandhi's India', *Leinster Leader*, 3 August 1963.

21. Private papers of the Weldon family, Vol. I. Sourced Kildare Collections and Research Services, Newbridge Library.

22. Fussell, *The Great War and Modern Memory*, p.53.

23. Copping, J., 'Beef Tea, Potato Pie and Duff Pudding: How to Eat Like a WWI Tommy', *Daily Telegraph*, 19 May 2013; Food Safety Authority of Ireland, 2011.

24. Clarkson, L. A., Crawford, E. M., *Feast and Famine: A History of Food and Nutrition in Ireland, 1500–1920* (Oxford, 2001), pp.90–1.

25. Fussell, *The Great War and Modern Memory*, p.48.

26. Smith, Lt J. S., 'Trench warfare' (E. P. Dutton & Co., 1917).

27. Weld-Moore, J. and Newnham, L., 'Charles Weld: The Gentleman Soldier', in *Coiseanna: The Journal of Clane Local History Group*, 2012.

28. *Kildare Observer*, 7 November 1914.

29. Johnstone, T., *Orange, Green and Khaki: The Story of the Irish regiments in the Great War, 1914–18* (Dublin, 1992), p.79; 1901 Census of Ireland.

30. Fussell, *The Great War and Modern Memory*, p.50.

31. Johnstone, T., *Orange, Green and Khaki*, p.75.

32. *Kildare Observer*, 29 July & 5 August 1916; 1911 Census of Ireland.

33. Fussell, *The Great War and Modern Memory*, pp.71, 73.

34. *Leinster Leader*, 11 March 1916.

35. Ferguson, N., *The Pity of War* (London, 1998), p.253; Yeates, P., *A City in Wartime: Dublin, 1914–18* (Dublin, 2012), p.84.

36. *Kildare Observer*, 28 October 1916.

37. Fussell, P., *The Great War and Modern Memory*, p.51.

38. Weld-Moore and Newnham, 'Charles Weld: The Gentleman Soldier'.

39. *The Clongownian*, Vol. VII, No. 2, June 1915, pp.217-18.

40. Ibid., p.194; Vol. VIII, No. 1, June 1917, p.47.

41. Durney, Corrigan, Roche and Holzgrawe, *The Co. Kildare Dead of the First World War*.

CHAPTER FOUR

1. Horne, J. (ed.), *Our War: Ireland and the Great War* (Dublin, 2008), p.65.
2. Denman, T., *Ireland's Unknown Soldiers: The 16th (Irish) Division in the Great War* (Dublin, 1992, new edition 2014), p.31; 1911 Census of Ireland.
3. *Kildare Observer*, 17 October 1914 and 8 January 1916; Taylor, J.W., *The 2nd Royal Irish Rifles in the Great War* (Dublin, 2005), p.18; 1911 Census of Ireland.
4. Johnstone, T., *Orange, Green and Khaki: The Story of the Irish Regiments in the Great War, 1914–18* (Dublin, 1992), pp.6–7.
5. *Kildare Observer*, 15 August 1914.
6. Fitzpatrick, D., 'Militarism in Ireland, 1900–1922', in Bartlett, T. and Jeffery, K., *A Military History of Ireland* (Cambridge, 1996), p.388.
7. Fussell, P., *The Great War and Modern Memory* (Oxford, 2013), p.10.
8. Denman, *Ireland's Unknown Soldiers*, p.131.
9. *Kildare Observer*, 5 June 1915.
10. *Irish Times*, 24 April 1915.
11. *Kildare Observer*, 28 August 1915.
12. Fitzpatrick, 'Militarism in Ireland, 1900–1922', p.389.
13. *Kildare Observer*, October 1915.
14. Ibid., 30 October 1915.
15. Ibid., 25 December 1915.
16. *Nationalist and Leinster Times*, 28 November 1914.
17. Durney, Corrigan, et al., p.20; 1901 Census of Ireland; 1911 Census of Ireland.
18. *Kildare Observer*, 20 March 1915.
19. Ibid., 4 December 1915.
20. Ibid., 12 February 1916.
21. Ibid.
22. Ibid., 5 June 1915.

23. Ibid., 11 September 1915.

24. Ibid., 18 September 1915.

25. Dennehy, J., *In A Time of War: Tipperary, 1914–1918* (Sallins, 2013), pp.59–60.

26. Durney, J., *Far From the Short Grass: The Story of Kildaremen in Two World Wars* (Naas, 1999), p.68.

27. Walsh, F., 'The Impact of the First World War on Celbridge', in *The Journal of the County Kildare Archaeological Society*, 2012–2013, Vol. XX (Part III), p.290; Denman, *Ireland's Unknown Soldiers*, p.36.

28. Dennehy, *In A Time of War*, p.65; *Kildare Observer*, 23 October, 1915.

29. Hastings, M., *Catastrophe: Europe Goes to War 1914* (London, 2013), p.192.

30. *Kildare Observer*, 7 August 1915.

31. Durney, *Far From the Short Grass*, p.15.

32. *Kildare Observer*, 22 May 1915.

33. Eisenhower, J. S. D., *Yanks: The Epic Story of the American Army in World War I* (New York, 2001), p.5.

34. *Kildare Observer*, 29 May 1915.

35. Fitzpatrick, 'Militarism in Ireland, 1900–1922', p.388.

36. *Kildare Observer*, 28 August 1915.

37. Fitzpatrick, 'Militarism in Ireland, 1900–1922', p.388; Durney, *Far From the Short Grass*, p.68.

38. *Kildare Observer*, 5 February 1916.

39. Durney, Corrigan, Roche and Holzgrawe, *The Co. Kildare Dead of the First World War*.

40. Synnott, D., 'Diary of a recruiting drive for the British armed forces undertaken by Barbara Synnott, Co. Kildare (24 January to 2 February 1916)', in *The Journal of the County Kildare Archaeological Society*, 2005, Vol. XIX, pp.549–558.

41. *Kildare Observer*, 5 February 1916.

42. James, R. R., *Gallipoli* (London, 1999), p.348; Johnstone, *Orange, Green and Khaki*, p.152

43. *Kildare Observer*, 27 May 1916.

44. Ibid., 5 February 1916.
45. Ibid., 18 November 1916.
46. Foster, R. F., *Modern Ireland 1600–1972* (London, 1988), p.473.
47. Fitzpatrick, 'Militarism in Ireland, 1900–1922', p.397. The Military Service Act of 27 January 1916 brought conscription into effect in England, Scotland and Wales, for the first time in the war.

CHAPTER FIVE
1. Durney, J., *The War of Independence in Kildare* (Cork, 2013), pp.33–4.
2. Ibid., p.37.
3. Ibid.
4. Ibid., p.42.
5. Ibid., p.46.
6. Ibid., p.47.
7. Ibid., pp.47–8; Durney, J., Corrigan, M., Roche, C. and Holzgrawe, C., *The Co. Kildare Dead of the First World War* (Naas, 2014).
8. Ibid., p.48.
9. Ibid., p.49.
10. Durney et al., *The Co. Kildare Dead of the First World War*; Hourihane, A.M., 'Children of the revolution', *Irish Times*, 22 March 2014.
11. Durney et al., *The Co. Kildare Dead of the First World War*.
12. Durney, *The War of Independence in Kildare*, p.50.
13. Kildare Co. Council. Minutes of the County Council and its Committees. January–December 1916.
14. Yeates, P., *A City in Wartime: Dublin, 1914–18* (Dublin, 2012), p.115.
15. *Leinster Leader*, 13 May 1916.
16. Witness Statements 1155 and 850, Military Archives, Dublin; Yeates, P., *A City in Wartime*, p.116.
17. Durney et al., *The Co. Kildare Dead of the First World War*.
18. Denman, T., *Ireland's Unknown Soldiers: The 16th (Irish) Division in the Great War* (Dublin, 1992), p.69.
19. Ibid.
20. Ibid., p.70.

21. Ibid., pp.70–1.

22. Johnstone, T., *Orange, Green and Khaki: The Story of the Irish Regiments in the Great War, 1914–18* (Dublin, 1992), pp.212-13.

23. Denman, *Ireland's Unknown Soldiers*, p.143.

24. *Kildare Observer*, 20 May 1916.

25. Denman, *Ireland's Unknown Soldiers*, p.142.

26. Private papers of the Weldon family, Vol. I. Sourced Kildare Collections and Research Services, Newbridge Library.

27. 'A war veteran looks back from battlefields of France to Gandhi's India', *Leinster Leader*, 3 August 1963; Hourihane, A.M., 'Children of the revolution'.

28. *Kildare Observer*, 27 May 1916.

29. Lyons, F. S. L. *Ireland Since the Famine* (London, 1985), pp.379–80.

30. Durney, J., Corrigan, M., Roche, C., Holzgrawe, C., *The Co. Kildare Dead of the First World War* (Naas, 2014).

31. Denman, *Ireland's Unknown Soldiers. The 16th (Irish) Division in the Great War* (Dublin, 1992), pp. 138-9.

32. Durney, James. *The War of Independence in Kildare* (Cork, 2013), p. 59.

CHAPTER SIX

1. Foster, R. F., *Modern Ireland, 1600–1972* (London, 1988), p.471.

2. Hobsbawn, E., *The Age of Empire, 1875–1914* (London, 2006), pp.308, 317.

3. Horne, J. (ed.), *Our War: Ireland and the Great War* (Dublin, 2008), p.40.

4. Johnson, D., *The Interwar Economy* (Dublin, 1989), pp.3–4.

5. Gregory, A. and Pašeta, S. (eds), *Ireland and the Great War. 'A War to Unite Us All?'* (Manchester, 2002), p.76.

6. Fussell, P., *The Great War and Modern Memory* (Oxford, 2013), p.343.

7. Lyons, F.S.L., *Ireland Since the Famine* (London, 1985), p.359.

8. Ferriter, D., *The Transformation of Ireland, 1900–2000* (London, 2005), p.173.

9. *Leinster Leader*, 26 June 1916; *Kildare Observer*, 2 December 1916.

10. *Kildare Observer*, 17 July 1915.

11. Johnson, *The Interwar Economy*, pp.4–5.

12. Dennehy, J., *In A Time of War: Tipperary, 1914–1918* (Dublin, 2013), p.157.

13. *Nationalist and Leinster Times*, 28 November 1914.

14. *Leinster Leader*, 22 January 1916.

15. Dennehy, *In A Time of War: Tipperary, 1914–1918*, p.167.

16. *Leinster Leader*, 27 January 1917.

17. *Kildare Observer*, 13 March 1915, 3 February 1917, 3 March 1917.

18. Ibid., 24 March 1917, 30 March 1918.

19. Ibid., 10 November 1917.

20. Ibid., 28 August 1915.

21. Ferguson, N., *The Pity of War* (London, 1999), p.283.

22. Johnson, D., *The Interwar Economy* (Dublin, 1989), pp.3–4.

23. Dennehy, *In A Time of War: Tipperary, 1914–1918*, pp.166–7.

24. Johnson, *The Interwar Economy*, pp.4–5.

25. Dennehy, *In A Time of War: Tipperary, 1914–1918*, p.176.

26. *Irish Times*, 11 January 1917.

27. Naas Poor Law Union Minute Books, 10 January 1917–9 December 1917.

28. Ferguson, *The Pity of War*, p.276.

29. *Kildare Observer*, 10 March 1917.

30. Fitzpatrick, D., *Politics and Irish Life, 1913–1921: Provincial Experience of War and Revolution* (Dublin, 1998), p.140.

31. Michael O'Kelly, Witness Statement 1155, Military Archives, Cathal Brugha Barracks, Dublin.

32. *Kildare Observer*, 30 March 1918.

33. Michael O'Kelly, Witness Statement 1155, Military Archives, Cathal Brugha Barracks, Dublin.

34. Ferguson, *The Pity of War*, p.250.

35. *Kildare Observer*, 18 August 1917 and 25 May 1918.

36. Ibid., 6 April 1918.

37. Ibid., 20 July 1918.

CHAPTER SEVEN

1. Ferguson, N., *The Pity of War* (London, 1999), p.199.
2. Lynch, J. P., 'The Irish Soldiers in World War I.' *Irish Roots*, 2014, Number 1.
3. Australian War Memorial. See http://www.awm.gov.au/ (accessed 15 April 2014).
4. 1911 Census of Ireland.
5. Service record for William Wilmot, copy in family possession.
6. Johnstone, T., *Orange, Green and Khaki: The Story of the Irish Regiments in the Great War, 1914–18* (Dublin, 1992), pp.36, 84–5; Service record for William Wilmot.
7. Service record for William Wilmot.
8. Johnstone, *Orange, Green and Khaki*, pp.158–9.
9. *Kildare Observer*, 21 March 1931; Information from Deirdre Twomey, niece of William Wilmot.
10. Service record for Edward Reddy in family possession.
11. 1911 Census of Ireland.
12. *Kildare Observer*, 28 October 1911.
13. Ibid., 1 August 1914.
14. Service record for Edward Reddy.
15. Johnstone, T., *Orange, Green and Khaki*, pp.87–9.
16. Ibid., pp.97, 100.
17. Ibid., p.114.
18. Cooper, B., *The Tenth (Irish) Division in Gallipoli* (Dublin, 2003), p.24; Service record for Edward Reddy.
19. Johnstone, *Orange, Green and Khaki*, pp.134, 152.
20. Service record for Edward Reddy.
21. Johnstone, *Orange, Green and Khaki*, pp.179, 251, 265.
22. Ibid., p.319.
23. Service record for Edward Reddy.
24. Johnstone, *Orange, Green and Khaki*, pp.319, 323, 337.
25. Service record for Edward Reddy.

26. Brown, A., 'The Town of Naas and the Great War'; 1911 Census of Ireland.

27. Yeates, P., *A City in Wartime: Dublin, 1914–18* (Dublin, 2012), p.317.

28. Ibid., pp.41–2.

29. *Kildare Observer*, 10 July 1915; Johnstone, *Orange, Green and Khaki*, p.75.

30. *Kildare Observer*, 10 July 1915.

31. Brown, 'The Town of Naas and the Great War'.

32. *Kildare Observer*, 10 July 1915.

33. Brown, 'The Town of Naas and the Great War'.

34. 1911 Census of Ireland; *Leinster Leader*, 8 March 1975.

35. *Leinster Leader*, 8 March 1975.

36. *The Clongownian*, Vol. VII, No. 1, June 1917, p.48.

37. Whitton, Lt-Col F. E., *The History of the Prince of Wales's Leinster Regiment (Royal Canadians), 1914–1922*. Vol. II. (Cork, 1998) pp.309–10, 320.

38. Ibid., p.376.

39. *Kildare Observer*, 17 February 1917.

40. *Leinster Leader*, 8 March 1975.

CHAPTER EIGHT

1. *Kildare Observer*, 8 and 15 August 1914.

2. Ibid., 15 and 22 August 1914.

3. Ibid., 22 August 1914.

4. Ibid., 5 September 1914.

5. *Leinster Leader*, 12 September 1914; Athy UDC Minute Books, 4 April 1914–30 April 1920.

6. *Leinster Leader* project. *World War I. List of the Dead* (Naas, 1995), p.16.

7. Durney, J., *Far From the Short Grass: The Story of Kildaremen in the Two World Wars* (Naas, 1999), pp.88, 97–8.

8. *Leinster Leader* project. *World War I. List of the Dead* (Naas, 1995), p.16.

9. *Leinster Leader*, 1 April 1916, Durney, J., *Far From the Short Grass: The Story of Kildaremen in the Two World Wars* (Naas, 1999), p.87.

10. *Leinster Leader* project. *World War I. List of the Dead* (Naas, 1995), p.17; *Kildare Observer*, 25 December 1915.

11. Ibid.

12. *Kildare Observer*, 15 September 1914; 1911 Census of Ireland.

13. *Kildare Observer*, 31 October 1914, 4 September 1915.

14. Kenny, L., 'An austere Kildare house which sheltered the dying and wounded', Series no. 303, *Leinster Leader*, 30 October 2012; *Kildare Observer*, 8 June 1918.

15. Walsh, F., 'The Impact of the First World War on Celbridge', in *The Journal of the County Kildare Archaeological Society*, 2012–2013, Vol. XX, Part III, p.295.

16. 4457, Kildare County Council Minutes, 23 November 1914.

17. *Nationalist and Leinster Times*, 28 November 1914.

18. *Kildare Observer*, 24 October 1914.

19. Ibid., 14 November 1914.

20. Ibid., 21 November 1914.

21. Ibid., 6 March 1915.

22. Ibid., 9 January 1915.

23. Ibid., 3 April 1915.

24. Ibid., 15 April 1916.

25. Durney, J., *In the Shadow of Kings: Social Housing in Naas, 1898–1984* (Naas, 2007), pp.30, 33; *Kildare Observer*, 11 September 1915.

26. Athy UDC Minute Books, 4 April 1914–30 April 1920.

27. *Leinster Leader* Project. *World War I. List of the Dead* (Naas, 1995), p.62.

28. Durney, J., Corrigan, M. and Connelly, J., *Hearth and Home: A History of Social Housing in Kildare Town, 1889–2009* (Naas, 2012).

29. D'Arcy, F. A., *Horses, Lords and Racing Men: The Turf Club, 1790–1990* (Dublin, 1990) pp.243–53.

30. Smith, R. and Costello, C., *Peerless Punchestown: 150 Years of Glorious Tradition* (Dublin, 2000), pp.49–50.

31. *Kildare Observer*, 27 April 1918.

32. Ferguson, N., *The Pity of War* (London, 1999), pp.212, 221.

33. Durney, J., *The War of Independence in Kildare* (Cork, 2013), pp.27, 38.

34. *Kildare Observer*, 26 February 1916; Ferguson, *The Pity of War*, pp.244–5.

35. *The Clongownian*, Vol. VII, No. 2, June 1915, pp.191–208.

36. Ibid., Vol. VII, No. 3, June 1916, p.344.

37. Ibid., Vol. VII, No. 1, June 1917, p.47.

38. Ibid., Vol. VII, No. 2, June 1918, pp.145.

39. Ibid., p.148.

40. Costello, P., *Clongowes Wood: A History of Clongowes Wood College, 1814–1989* (Dublin, 1989), pp.196–7.

41. *The Clongownian*, Vol. VII, No. 2, June 1918, p.129.

42. Ibid., Vol. VIII, No. 3, June 1919, p.293.

CHAPTER NINE

1. Horne, J. (ed.), *Our War: Ireland and the Great War* (Dublin, 2008), p.161.

2. Mary Rose Everan, correspondence with author, 11 April 2013.

3. Mayhew, E., *From Battlefield to Blighty, 1914–1918* (London, 2013), p.243.

4. *Kildare Observer*, 18 August 1918.

5. Brown, A., 'The Town of Naas and the Great War'. Essay sourced at Kildare Collections and Resource Services, Newbridge Library.

6. Statistics from 'Women in the Great War', by Fionnuala Walsh, 8 March 2014.

7. *Kildare Observer*, 8 June 1916.

8. Costello, C., *A Most Delightful Station: The British Army on the Curragh of Kildare, Ireland, 1855–1922* (Cork, 1996), pp.275; 123–5.

9. National Archives of Ireland.

10. *The Times*, 11 November 1914.

11. See Imperial War Museum website: www.IWM.org.uk (accessed 15 April 2014).

12. *Kildare Observer*, 4 September 1915.

13. Ibid., 23 December 1916 and 24 March 1917.

14. Taaffe, F., 'Athy and the Great War', in Nolan, W. and McGrath, T. (eds), *Kildare. History and Society* (Dublin, 2006), p.604.

15. *Leinster Leader* Project. *World War I. List of the Dead* (Naas, 1995), p.90.

16. *Kildare Observer*, 4 September 1915.

17. *Leinster Leader*, 27 January 1917.

18. *Kildare Observer*, 22 April 1916.

19. *Leinster Leader*, 15 April 1916.

20. Durney, J., *Far From the Short Grass: The Story of Kildaremen in the Two World Wars* (Naas, 1999), p.10.

21. *Kildare Observer*, 10 December 1914.

22. *Leinster Leader*, 22 April 1916; Bence-Jones, M., *Twilight of the Ascendancy* (London, 1993), p.166.

23. *Kildare Observer*, 18 August 1917.

24. Durney, J., *The War of Independence in Kildare* (Cork, 2013), pp.142–3.

25. *Leinster Leader* Project. *World War I. List of the Dead* (Naas, 1995), p.92.

26. *Kildare Observer*, 8 June 1918.

CHAPTER TEN

1. Brown, M., *1918: Year of Victory* (London, 1998), pp.49.

2. *Nationalist and Leinster Times*, 6 April 1918.

3. *Nationalist and Leinster Times*, 13 April 1918; Commonwealth War Graves Commission.

4. Brown, *1918: Year of Victory*, pp.50, 83.

5. 'Thomas L. Cahill. 1897–1918' by John Malone. Illustrated talk by John Malone, copy given to author, 7 February 2014.

6. Durney, J., *The War of Independence in Kildare* (Cork, 2013), p.65.

7. *Kildare Observer*, 13 April 1918.

8. McDowell, R.B., *The Irish Convention 1917–18* (London, 1970), pp.186, 188.

9. Durney, *The War of Independence in Kildare*, p.66.

10. Copy of anti-conscription pledge, author's collection.

11. *Kildare Observer*, 20 April 1918.

12. Ferriter, D., *The Transformation of Ireland, 1900–2000* (London, 2005), p.182.

13. Witness statement 807, Patrick J. Doyle, Military Archives, Cathal Brugha Barracks, Dublin.

14. *Kildare Observer*, 20 April 1918.

15. Ibid., 27 April 1918.

16. Horne, J. (ed.), *Our War: Ireland and the Great War* (Dublin, 2008), pp.192–3.

17. *Kildare Observer*, 4 May 1918.

18. Witness Statement 1155, Michael O'Kelly. Military Archives, Cathal Brugha Barracks, Dublin.

19. Durney, J., *On the One Road. Political Unrest in Kildare, 1913–1994* (Naas, 2001), p.110.

20. Witness Statement 850, Patrick Colgan. Military Archives, Cathal Brugha Barracks, Dublin.

21. McDowell, *The Irish Convention 1917–18*, pp.188–9.

22. *Kildare Observer*, 11 May 1918.

23. Lyons, F. S. L., *Ireland Since the Famine* (London, 1985), p.395.

24. *Kildare Observer*, 25 May 1918.

25. Ibid., 1 June 1918.

26. McDowell, *The Irish Convention 1917–18*, p.190.

27. Lyons, F. S. L., *Ireland Since the Famine*, pp.395–6; *Kildare Observer*, 17 August 1918.

28. McDowell, *The Irish Convention 1917–18*, p.103.

29. Ibid., pp.218–227.

30. *Leinster Leader*, 3 August 1895.

31. *Leinster Leader*, 7 January 1928. The Earl of Mayo was nominated by President Cosgrave to the first Senate of the Irish Free State. During the Civil War Palmerstown House was burned down in January 1923. Lord Mayo died in London on 31 December 1927.

32. McDowell, *The Irish Convention 1917–18*, p.191.

33. Lyons, F.S.L., *Ireland Since the Famine* (London, 1985), p.393.

34. *Irish Times*, 12 November 1918.

CHAPTER ELEVEN

1. Brewer, P., *The History of Modern Warfare: A Year-by-Year Illustrated Account from the Crimean War to the Present Day* (London, 2007), pp.161–2.

2. Durney, J., Corrigan, M., Roche, C. and Holzgrawe, C., *The Co. Kildare Dead of the First World War* (Naas, 2014).

3. Brown, M., *1918: Year of Victory* (London, 1998), pp.168–70.

4. Durney, J., *In the Shadow of Kings: Social Housing in Naas, 1898–1984* (Naas, 2007), pp.35–6.

5. Foley, C., *The Last Irish Plague: The Great Flu Epidemic in Ireland, 1918–19* (Dublin, 2011), p.24.

6. Naas Poor Law Union Minute Book, 9 January 1918–11 December 1918.

7. Durney, *In the Shadow of Kings*, pp.35–6.

8. Foley, *The Last Irish Plague*, p.60.

9. *Kildare Observer*, 2 November 1918.

10. Ibid.

11. *Irish Times*, 9 October 1918.

12. *Leinster Leader*, 26 October 1918.

13. Ibid.

14. *Kildare Observer*, 2 November 1918.

15. *Leinster Leader*, 9 November 1918.

16. Durney, J., *A Bridge, A Town, A People: Social Housing in Newbridge, 1900–1996* (Naas, 2009), pp.31–2.

17. Athy Poor Law Union Minute Book, 23 March 1918–25 December 1918.

18. *Leinster Leader*, 16 November 1918; Durney et al., *The Co. Kildare Dead of the First World War*.

19. Athy Poor Law Union Minute Book, 4 January 1919–20 November 1919.

20. Ibid.

21. Naas Poor Law Union Minute Book, 9 January 1918–11 December 1918.

22. *Kildare Observer*, 1 March 1919.

23. Athy Poor Law Union Minute Book, 23 March 1918–25 December 1918.

24. Naas Poor Law Union Minute Book, 8 January 1919–10 December 1919.

25. *Kildare Observer*, 15 February 1919; *Leinster Leader*, 16 November 1918.

26. Durney, *A Bridge, A Town, A People*, pp.31–2.

27. Milne, I., 'The 1918–19 Influenza Pandemic: A Kildare Perspective of a Global Disaster', in *The Journal of the County Kildare Archaeological Society*, 2012–2013, Vol. XX, Part III, p.303.

28. Brewer, *The History of Modern Warfare*, p.166.

29. Brown, *1918: Year of Victory*, p.284.

30. *Nationalist and Leinster Times*, 18 and 23 November 1918.

31. Durney et al., *The Co. Kildare Dead of the First World War*.

32. *Irish Times*, 13 November 1918; *Kildare Observer*, 16 November 1918.

33. *Irish Times*, 14 November 1918.

34. *Leinster Leader*, 16 November 1918.

35. *Irish Times*, 12 November 1918.

36. *Kildare Observer*, 23 November 1918.

37. *Irish Times*, 18 November 1918; *Leinster Leader*, 23 November 1918.

38. *Irish Times*, 20 and 25 November 1918.

39. *Kildare Observer*, 15 February 1919.

CHAPTER TWELVE

1. Bourke, J., 'Shell-shock, psychiatry and the Irish soldier during the First World War', in Gregory, A. and Pašeta, S., *Ireland and the Great War: 'A War to Unite Us All?'* (Manchester, 2002), pp.156–7.

2. Ferguson, N., *The Pity of War* (London, 1999), p.437.

3. Bourke, 'Shell-shock, psychiatry and the Irish soldier during the First World War', pp.156–7.

4. Timmy Conway, oral interview with author, 23 December 2013, Naas; Conway, T., *Characters* (Naas, 2008), pp.46–8.

5. Mick Mulvey, oral interview with author, Newbridge Library, 2 January 2014.

6. 1911 Census of Ireland.

7. Durney, J., Corrigan, M., Roche, C. and Holzgrawe, C., *The Co. Kildare Dead of the First World War* (Naas, 2014).

8. Copy of last letter of Patrick Lewis, courtesy of Ger McCarthy, Naas.

9. Durney et al., *The Co. Kildare Dead of the First World War*.

10. Conway, *Characters*, pp.47–9.

11. *Leinster Leader*, 2 September 1916.

12. Eisenhower, J. S. D., *Yanks: The Epic Story of the American Army in World War I* (New York, 2001), p.313.

13. Jünger, E., *Storm of Steel*. Translated by Michael Hoffman (London, 2003), pp.80–1, 224–6.; Ferguson, N., *The Pity of War* (London, 1999), p.341.

14. *Kildare Observer*, 3 June 1916.

15. *Leinster Leader*, 18 March 1916.

16. *Kildare Observer*, 21 and 28 August; 18 December 1915.

17. Information supplied by Veronica Heavey, great-niece of John Geraghty, November 2013/March 2014.

18. *Kildare Observer*, 2 February 1918; Commonwealth War Graves Commission.

19. Corrigan, M., 'Cill Dara Historical Society: Kildare Town Heritage Series No. 187. World War I Graves St Brigid's Cathedral.'

20 *Kildare Observer*, 21 March 1926, 11 & 25 April 1925, 30 January 1926.

21. Durney, J., *The War of Independence in Kildare* (Cork, 2013), pp.69–70.

22. *Irish Times*, 25 November 1918.

23. Durney, *The War of Independence in Kildare*, pp.73–4.

24. *Irish Times*, 30 December 1918; Durney, *The War of Independence in Kildare*, pp.74–5.

EPILOGUE

1. *Forgotten Men*. Documentary by Sir John Hammerton, 1933.

2. *Leinster Leader*, 22 February 1919.

3. Service record for Denis Lawless, author's collection, courtesy of the Burke family, Naas.

4. Durney, J., *Far From the Short Grass: The Story of Kildaremen in the Two World Wars* (Naas, 1999), p.119.

5. Information provided by Kathleen Brophy, 8 March 2014.

6. Data gathered by author from *Leinster Leader* on various dates; Taaffe, F., *Eye on Athy's Past Volume 3* (Athy, 2007), p.124.

7. *Leinster Leader* Project, *World War I. List of the Dead* (Naas, 1995), p.68.

8. Durney, J., *The Civil War in Kildare* (Cork, 2012), pp.37, 82, 101.

9. Information supplied by Veronica Heavey, 26 March 2014.

10. Durney, J., Corrigan, M., Roche, C. and Holzgrawe, C., *The Co. Kildare Dead of the First World War* (Naas, 2014).

11. Taaffe, *Eye on Athy's past* (Athy, 2000), pp.124–5; Durney, Corrigan, et al. *The Co. Kildare Dead of the First World War.*

12. Taaffe, p.125; Durney, Corrigan, et al., *The Co. Kildare Dead of the First World War.*

13. Gregory, A. and Pašeta, S., *Ireland and the Great War: 'A war to unite us all?'* (Manchester, 2002), pp.39–41.

14. Dooley, T., *The Decline of the Big House in Ireland* (Dublin, 2001), pp.124–5.

15. Costello, C., *A Most Delightful Station: The British Army on the Curragh of Kildare, Ireland, 1855–1922* (Cork, 1996), p.308.

16. *The War Graves of the British Empire. Cemeteries and Churchyards in Leinster and Connaught and the Counties of Cavan, Monaghan and Donegal* (London, 1939), p.33.

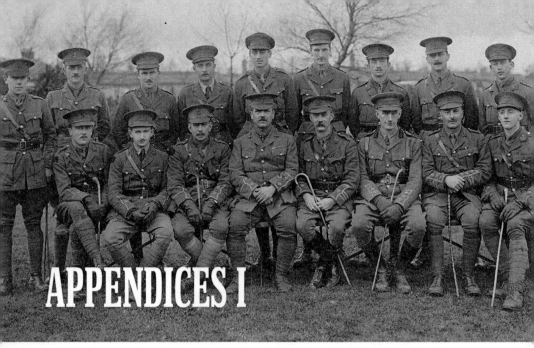

Captain A. E. Warmington, (sitting second from right), pictured in Cork some months before he was killed in action on Easter Monday 1916 during the fighting at the South Dublin Union. Photo: Brian Munnelly.

APPENDICES I

JOINING THE ARMY was not as simple as many would imagine, choices had to be made as the British Service was divided into several sections. The following was published in the *Kildare Observer*, 24 August 1914, detailing the sections:

INFANTRY. Every Irishman over 18 years, if accepted for service in the Infantry may join the particular regiment of his choice, whether Irish, English, Scottish or Welsh; the Irish Guards being especially offered, provided he attains the necessary physical standard.

CAVALRY. In this branch of the service there is opening for men over 40 years of age of grades 1 and 2. Choice of cavalry regiment is again given including North and South Irish Horse.

ROYAL ARTILLERY RH., HF. AND R.G.A. This regiment is open to all Irishmen between 18 years and 40 years, who are in Grade 1. A special opening is also offered in the R.C.A. for men over 40 years in Grade 2.

MACHINE GUN CORPS AND TANK CORPS. Owing to the particular training which recruits have to undergo for the above corps, they are posted to a special training reserve brigade, and are eligible provided they are between the ages of 18 years and 40 years and in Grade 1.

ROYAL ENGINEERS. This branch invites skilled and unskilled tradesmen, telegraphists, artificers, motorcyclists, railwaymen, stevedores, technical engineers, etc.

ARMY SERVICE CORPS. This branch's chief function is the transport of supplies. Men suitable as M.T. learner drivers will be examined. They must be in a grade other than Grade 1 and not below 25 years of age. H.T. 'remounts' require men accustomed to horses who are in a grade other than Grade 1 and not below the age of 30 years. 'Supply' accepts men as bakers, butchers and clerks, subject to a trade test, who are in Grade 3 and not below the age of 25 years.

ROYAL ARMY MEDICAL CORPS. As well as stretcher-bearers and hospital orderlies, this Corp needs men who are dental mechanics, pharmacists, masseurs or the like, proved they are of a Grade other than Grade 1 and not below the age of 30 years.

ARMY ORDNANCE CORPS. Men who are experienced in the receipt, storage and insuring of goods of all description and in accounting for them are useful for this corps, but must be a grade other than Grade 1 and not below the age of 30.

ARMY VETERINARY CORPS. All that is needed in this corps is that a man can handle a pickaxe and shovel or to do the ordinary work of a labourer in civil life. Recruits for this corps must be of Grade 3 and no man of this grade who is certified to be able to do a full day's work in the army will be rejected.

THE LABOUR CORPS. This is the Corps for the men whose age, health, ignorance of a trade unfit them for the frontline, or any of the special units mentioned above. Recruits for this job must be of Grade 3, and no man of this grade who is certified to be able to do a full day's work in the Army will be rejected.

PAY. The minimum rate of pay for all branches of the service is 1*s*. 6*d*. a day with free kit, rations and separation allowance. Engineer pay, corps pay, etc., will be issuable to certain men in the Royal Engineers, R.A.M.C., A.O.S. and A.V.C. The rates vary from 3*d*. to 2*s*. a day, according to the qualifications of the man and the corps he belongs to.

Leinster Leader, 15 August 1914

Soldiers required for the Royal Dublin Fusiliers

Ex-soldiers of Regular Army or Special Reserve, if from 19–42 years of age, can enlist for one year, or period of the war. Other men, from 19–30 years of age, can enlist for 3 years or period of the war.

APPENDICES II

Recruiting poster, Newbridge Barracks, c. 1910. Photo: Kildare Collections and Research Services.

Period	Naas
1st	9,718
2nd	5,675
3rd	5,450
4th	2,663
6th	1,238
TOTAL	26,611

These figures are based on returns received from Naas Depot from August 1914 to June 1917. After this date only totals for the entire county were given. So in the period from August 1914 to June 1917 26,611 soldiers were recruited into the army from Dublin, Kildare, Carlow and Wicklow. The Naas Depot recruited for the Royal Dublin Fusiliers from these four areas. It is obvious from the table that between the third and fourth quarter numbers began to drop. This marks the mid-1915 period – The Battle of Loos and the Dardanelles campaign.

APPENDICES III

The memorial 'death penny' for William Wilmot (Athgarvan), killed in action on the Western Front, March 1916. Photo: Deirdre Twomey.

County Kildare War Dead in Large Towns

Town	Number of Fatalities
Athy	122
Naas	103
Newbridge	75
Curragh	71
Kildare	55
Celbridge	25
Kilcullen	18
Castledermot	18
Monasterevan	17
Kilcock	15
Maynooth	12
Leixlip	9

County Kildare Deaths

Year	Number of Fatalities
1914	64
1915	220
1916	183
1917	187
1918	151

Bibliography

ARCHIVES

Athy Poor Law Union Minute Book, 23 March 1918–25 December 1918. Sourced at KCRS, Newbridge Library.

Athy Poor Law Union Minute Books, 4 January 1919–20 November 1919. Sourced at KCRS, Newbridge Library.

Naas Poor Law Union Minute Book 9 January 1918–11 December 1918. Sourced at KCRS, Newbridge Library.

Naas Poor Law Union Minute Book 8 January 1919–10 December 1919. Sourced at KCRS, Newbridge Library.

Athy UDC Minute Book, 4 April 1914–30 April 1920. Sourced at KCRS, Newbridge Library.

Kildare County Council. Minutes of the County Council and its Committees. January–December 1914. Sourced at KCRS, Newbridge Library.

Porter's Post Office Guide and Directory for the Counties Carlow and Kildare, Dublin, 1910.

Colgan, P., Witness statement 850, Military Archives, Cathal Brugha Barracks, Dublin.

O'Kelly, M., Witness statement 1155, Military Archives, Cathal Brugha Barracks, Dublin.

Service record for Edward Reddy, courtesy Tom Reddy.

Service record for William Wilmot, courtesy Deirdre Twomey.

Oral interview with Mick Mulvey, Newbridge Library, 2 January 2014.

Oral interview with Timmy Conway, Naas, 23 December 2013.

ESSAYS

Bourke, J., 'Shell-shock, psychiatry and the Irish soldier during the First World War', in Gregory, A. & Pašeta, S., *Ireland and the Great War: 'A War to Unite Us All?'* (Manchester, 2002).

Brown, A., 'The Town of Naas and the Great War'. Essay sourced at Kildare Collections and Resource Services, Newbridge Library.

Corry, E., 'The Orange Order in Kildare and Laois', *Kildare Voice*, July 7 2007.

Fitzpatrick, D., 'Militarism in Ireland, 1900–1922', in Bartlett, T. & Jeffery K. (eds), *A Military History of Ireland* (Cambridge, 1996).

Lynch, J.P., 'The Irish soldiers in World War 1', in *Irish Roots*, 2014, Number 1.

Martin, P., '*Dulce et Decorum*: Irish nobles and the Great War 1914–1919', in Gregory, A. & Pašeta, S., *Ireland and the Great War: 'A War to Unite Us All?'* (Manchester, 2002).

Milne, I., 'The 1918–19 influenza pandemic: a Kildare perspective of a global disaster', in *The Journal of the County Kildare Archaeological Society*, 2012–2013, Vol. XX, Part III.

Synnott, D., 'Diary of a recruiting drive for the British armed forces undertaken by Barbara Synnott, Co. Kildare (24 January to 2 February 1916)', in *The Journal of the County Kildare Archaeological Society*, 2005, Vol. XIX.

Taaffe, Frank., 'Athy and the Great War', in *Kildare. History and society.* (Eds) Nolan, William and McGrath, Thomas. Dublin, 2006.

Walsh, F., 'The impact of the First World War on Celbridge', in *The Journal of the County Kildare Archaeological Society*. 2012-2013, Vol. XX, Part III.

Weld-Moore, J. & Newnham, L., 'Charles Weld the gentleman soldier', in *Coiseanna: The Journal of Clane Local History Group*, 2012.

PERIODICALS

Daily Telegraph
Irish Times
Kildare Observer
Leinster Express
Leinster Leader
Nationalist and Leinster Times
The Clongownian
The Times

SECONDARY SOURCES

Bartlett, T. & Jeffery, K. (eds), *A Military History of Ireland* (Cambridge, 1996).

Bence-Jones, M., *Twilight of the Ascendancy* (London, 1993).

Brewer, P., *The History of Modern Warfare: A Year-by-Year Illustrated Account from the Crimean War to the Present Day* (London, 2007).

Brown, M., *1918: Year of Victory* (London, 1998).

Clarkson, L.A. & Crawford, E.M., *Feast and Famine: A History of Food and Nutrition in Ireland 1500–1920* (Oxford, 2001).

Connolly, S., *A Forlorn Hope: The Royal Dublin Fusiliers in the Kaiser's Battle March 1918* (Dublin, 2008).

Conway, T., *Characters* (Naas, 2008).

Cooper, B., *The Tenth (Irish) Division in Gallipoli* (Dublin, 2003).

Corrigan, M. (ed.), *Druim Craig – The Ridge of Clay* (Naas, 2009).

Costello, C., *A Most Delightful Station: The British Army on the Curragh of Kildare, Ireland, 1855–1922* (Cork, 1996).

Costello, P., *Clongowes Wood: A History of Clongowes Wood College 1814–1989* (Dublin, 1989).

Cullen, L.M., *An Economic History of Ireland since 1660* (London, 1993).

D'Arcy, F.A., *Horses, Lords and Racing Men: The Turf Club, 1790–1990* (Dublin, 1990).

Davies, N., *Europe: A History* (London, 1997).

Denman, T., *Ireland's Unknown Soldiers: The 16th (Irish) Division in the Great War* (Dublin, 1992).

Dennehy, J., *In A Time of War: Tipperary, 1914–1918* (Dublin, 2013).

Dooley, T., *The Decline of the Big House in Ireland* (Dublin, 2001).

Durney, J., *Far from the Short Grass: The Story of Kildaremen in the Two World Wars* (Naas, 1999).

—————————, *On the One Road: Political Unrest in Kildare, 1913–1994* (Naas, 2001).

—————————, *A Bridge, A Town, A People: Social Housing in Newbridge, 1900–1996* (Naas, 2009).

—————————, *In the Shadow of Kings: Social Housing in Naas, 1898–1984* (Naas, 2007).

—————————, *The Civil War in Kildare* (Cork, 2012).

—————————, *The War of Independence in Kildare* (Cork, 2013).

Durney, J., Corrigan, M., and Connelly, J., *Hearth and Home: A History of Social Housing in Kildare Town, 1889–2009* (Naas, 2012).

Durney, J., Corrigan, M., Roche, C. and Holzgrawe, C., *The Co. Kildare Dead of the First World War* (Naas, 2014).

Eisenhower, J.S.D., *Yanks: The Epic Story of the American Army in World War I* (New York, 2001).

Fenby, J., *The General: Charles de Gaulle and the France he Saved* (London, 2010).

Ferguson, N., *The Pity of War* (London, 1999).

Ferriter, D., *The Transformation of Ireland, 1900–2000* (London, 2005).

Fitzpatrick, D., *Politics and Irish Life, 1913–1921: Provincial Experience of War and Revolution* (Cork, 1998).

Foley, C., *The Last Irish Plague: The Great Flu Epidemic in Ireland, 1918–19* (Dublin, 2011).

Food Safety Authority of Ireland, 2011. *Healthy eating and active living for adults, teenagers and children over 5 years – a food guide for health professionals and catering services.*

Foster, R.F., *Modern Ireland, 1600–1972* (London, 1988).

Fussell, P., *The Great War and Modern Memory* (Oxford, 2013).

Gregory, A. & Pašeta, S., *Ireland and the Great War: 'A War to Unite Us All?'* (Manchester, 2002).

Hastings, M., *Catastrophe: Europe Goes to War 1914* (London, 2013).

Hobsbawn, E., *The Age of Empire, 1875–1914* (London, 2006).

Horne, J. (ed.), *Our War: Ireland and the Great War* (Dublin, 2008).

Imperial War Graves Commission, *The War Graves of the British Empire. Cemeteries and churchyards in Leinster and Connaught and the counties of Cavan, Monaghan and Donegal* (London, 1939).

James, R.R., *Gallipoli* (London, 1999).

Johnson, D., *The Interwar Economy* (Dublin, 1989).

Johnstone, T., *Orange, Green and Khaki: The Story of the Irish Regiments in the Great War, 1914–18* (Dublin, 1992).

Jünger, E., *Storm of Steel*, Translated by Michael Hofman (London, 2003).

Keegan, J., *The First World War* (London, 1998).

Keenan, D., *Ireland 1850–1920* (London, 2005).

Leinster Leader Project, *World War I: List of the Dead* (Naas, 1995).

Lyons, F.S.L., *Ireland Since the Famine* (London, 1985).

Mayhew, E., *From Battlefield to Blighty, 1914–1918* (London, 2013).

McCarthy, G., *The Forgotten History of Kildare* (Dublin, 2006).

McDowell, R.B., *The Irish Convention 1917–18* (London, 1970).

McGuire, J. & Quinn, J. (eds), *Dictionary of Irish Biography* (Cambridge, 2009).

Meleady, D., *John Redmond: The National Leader* (Sallins, 2013).

Muenger, E.A., *The British Military Dilemma in Ireland: Occupation Politics, 1886–1914* (Dublin, 1991).

Neillands, R., *The Great War Generals on the Western Front, 1914–18* (London, 1999).

O'Connor, E., *A Labour History of Ireland* (Dublin, 1992).

O'Donovan, F. (ed.), *Ní obair in aisce Í. Forty years of the Army Apprentice School. 1956–1996* (Naas, 1996).

Smith, R. & Costello, C., *Peerless Punchestown: 150 Years of Glorious Tradition* (Dublin, 2000).

Taaffe, F., *Eye on Athy's Past* (Athy, 2000).

Taylor, J.W., *The 1st Royal Irish Rifles in the Great War* (Dublin, 2001).

Taylor, J.W., *The 2nd Royal Irish Rifles in the Great War* (Dublin, 2005).

Whitton, Lt.-Col. F.E., *The History of the Prince of Wales's Leinster Regiment (Royal Canadians), 1914–1922*, Vol. II (Cork, 1998).

Yeates, P., *A City in Wartime: Dublin, 1914–18* (Dublin, 2012).

Index